*Deep listening is an art fo[...]
that can change the world[...]
this contemplative process[...]
about faith. In an age of [...]
a kaleidoscopic diversity of lives of faith.*

Ruth Harvey, Leader of The Iona Community

*If any of our 'faith traditions' are to survive into the future' then
surely the process of re-visioning will involve the types of honest
conversations we find in Jacci Bulman's Talking God. As she says,
"truly listening is itself a great teaching."*

**Dr Neil Douglas-Klotz, author of *The Hidden
Gospel* and *Prayers of the Cosmos***

*In a time when people increasingly want to find their own way, this
book offers a helpful and accessible means to finding one's own path
to God. Accessibly written, using the stories of others who have found
their way, we are given permission to pursue what is authentic for
us. A valuable offering rooted in both love and common sense.*

**Dr Justine Huxley, CEO, St Ethelburga's Centre
for Reconciliation and Peace**

*I'm not a religious person at all, but there's something about the way
Jacci writes that includes all.*

**Ronnie Goodyer, Co-Director of Indigo Dreams
Publishing**

We have two ears and one mouth so that we can listen twice
as much as we speak.
EPICTETUS

Whoever does not love does not know God,
for God is love.
1 JOHN 4:8

Talking
God

Daring to Listen

Jacci Bulman

LION

Text copyright © 2021 Jacci Bulman
This edition copyright © 2021 Lion Hudson IP Limited

The right of Jacci Bulman to be identified as the author of this work has been asserted by her
in accordance with the Copyright, Designs and Patents Act 1988.

All rights reserved. No part of this publication may be reproduced or transmitted in any
form or by any means, electronic or mechanical, including photocopy, recording, or any
information storage and retrieval system, without permission in writing from the publisher.

Published by
Lion Hudson Limited
Wilkinson House, Jordan Hill Business Park
Banbury Road, Oxford OX2 8DR, England
www.lionhudson.com

ISBN 978 0 7459 8101 7
e-ISBN 978 0 7459 8102 4

First edition 2021

Acknowledgments
Unless otherwise marked Scripture quotations taken from The New Revised Standard
Version of the Bible copyright © 1989 by the Division of Christian Education of the
National Council of Churches in the USA. Used by permission. All Rights Reserved.

Scripture quotations marked "NIV" are taken from the *Holy Bible, New International Version*,
copyright © 1973, 1978, 1984 International Bible Society. Used by permission of Hodder
& Stoughton, a member of the Hodder Headline Group. All rights reserved. "NIV" is a
trademark of International Bible Society. UK trademark number 1448790.

Scripture quotations marked "KJV" are taken from The Authorized (King James) Version.
Rights in the Authorized Version are vested in the Crown. Reproduced by permission of the
Crown's patentee, Cambridge University Press.

Extracts from The Book of Common Prayer, the rights in which are vested in the Crown, are
reproduced by permission of the Crown's patentee, Cambridge University Press.

p.48 lines taken from John Betjeman, "Before the Anaesthetic" in *Collected Poems* © The
Estate of John Betjeman 1955, 1958, 1960, 1962, 1964,1966, 1970, 1979, 1980, 1981, 2001.
Introduction Andrew Motion © 2006. Reproduced by permission of John Murray Press, an
imprint of Hodder and Stoughton Limited.

A catalogue record for this book is available from the British Library

Printed and bound in the United Kingdom, February 2021, LH26

For Annie and her brother, Joseph,
and for everyone who has an inkling
that there is a God…

Acknowledgments

With love and thanks to the many people and places who have helped me find my faith and inspired me with ideas on this book quest, including, as the eleven interviewed followers of Jesus: Margaret Ives, Bob Morley, Carol Purves, John, Martyn Halsall, Helen, Jyoti Saraswati, Father Richard Qunsworth, Brigid Rose, Revd Dr Andrew Gabriel Gosler, Revd Tim Cooke. You have all taught and challenged me when I listened.

In my links to Oxford: Dr Anthony Boyce and everyone connected to my studies of Human Sciences, particularly of anthropology; David; the Venerable Martin Gorick, Archdeacon of Oxford. Also, Anita and Professor Roger Bromley, with whom I re-connected in Edinburgh.

In my links to Iona: The Iona Community, who give me hope and roots; Amanda, Debbie and Neil; the people and land of the island, and the sea all around it, and (from the beginning of this book) Revd Susan Copley.

In my links to Penrith Methodist Church: local preachers Melville Harris and Irene McKay; Revd David Milner and Revd Keith Speck; and Pat, Olive, and Helen – whose warmth and friendliness encouraged me to come again to church services.

From my family: the late local preacher (my grandad) Frank Garside; cousin Hazel and aunt Renee; and my brother Stephen.

From my experiences of healing: spiritual healer John Fox, who first enabled me in 1993 to experience the presence of God; hypnotherapist Anna Cade, who taught me the power of symbols in visualization; healers Val Beardshaw and Deirdre Owen, who have helped me through some big transitions; and Christie Tonks and Jen Musgrave, whose reiki healing helps me stop for bliss.

For the workshop at the end of the book, thanks to Tracey Cooke and Revd Rachel Williams, who created the original workshop with me, and to Ruth Harvey, for connecting me to Place for Hope.

For her conversation with me about open boundaries, thanks to Revd Nicki Pennington.

Also, with thanks to Alan, Nicki, and my parents, who teach me love; Annie and Joseph, who teach me joy; Barbara, Joan, and Clifford, who teach me kindness and to have zest for life; Jackie who teaches me dedication; and Hilda, who teaches me to live lightly.

And to Blencathra mountain, always sacred to my heart.

Contents

PART ONE

Dare to Listen

Attention is the rarest and purest form of generosity.[1]
SIMONE WEIL

Dare to Listen

"Now that Christianity in Britain is dying out," said a lady on the radio, "perhaps football matches can take the place of religion, as a way of holding people together."

A week later, I went to a Huddersfield Town football match with my brother and my godson, Laurie. The atmosphere, for young and old, was fantastic! There was such a feeling of community among the crowd. We were all full of hope, of belief in what we were supporting and celebrating together – even in the hard patches we rallied round and held each other up.

"Wouldn't it be great," I thought, "if people were this enthusiastic about God?" A little naïve to say the least. But the hope was there. And so this book quest began.

There are many paths on the "mountain" of God. In truth there are approaching 8 billion pathways... because for every human being on earth there is a unique way to find God, a unique set of life events – things to see, to miss; things to question, to overcome. We are some of us busy searching for our next steps, while some of us have become disillusioned with the idea of God and given up, gone back down. Some of us are recovering or feeling weary. But we are all on a "journey" with our souls. Sorry to use this overused word, but that is what I believe our life is, a soul journey, and it cannot help being – because we are alive, and all our souls want nothing but to find peace. Finding God is peace.

Every one of us is travelling "home" to God, even if some of us are running in crazy and conflicting directions. We could each stay separated and follow our own narrow, individual pathway without ever linking up to anyone else. When we get confused, lonely, frightened, we could just keep going solo and not ask for help. But this appears to be leading a lot of us into lives that are bleak, poor in meaning, endlessly bumping into rocks in the dark. Or, we could come together on a common wider path, join a group, trust in a religion... yet many of us now are understandably wary of doing this.

The word "religion" itself, for some of us, represents hatred and conflict rather than love and harmony. Many of the people whose beliefs in God I find inspiring say things like "I am spiritual but not religious"; many people who follow closely the teachings of Jesus refuse to be called "Christian". Why? Because of what it represents to them, and because of its history involving prejudice, abuse, and war. But does it *have* to be this way?

Surely religions of all kinds are just a way of people trying to come together as we make our way to God. As we try to describe the ultimately indescribable. As we struggle to understand life. But we are best never to forget that *no* religion is the same as God. Religions are like guidebooks, helping us to find and even enjoy our way home, but they are not the mountain.

Many surveys today show that the percentage of people going to church or calling themselves "Christian" is falling dramatically. But this could partly be due to more people refusing to just "go along" with membership to a religion they know very little about or have little regard for. More people are now saying "but what about...?" and refusing to submissively accept weak answers from their church. So, a person who might once have said "yes" to the question "Are you a Christian?" is now much more likely to say "no" or "I'm not sure". People question. They no longer nod their heads without asking "why?" And this is potentially a good thing.

Could the religion of Christianity tempt such people again through its church doors? Re-involve the people like me (and possibly you) who seem to have "fallen out" with some of its traditions? And could it become vitalized, truer to God's hope for humanity, in the process? I decided to consider. To look around with fresh intention, avoiding old presumptions, because, as a great saying on my fridge door reminds me: "Don't look back, it's not where you're going!"

*

Something important was missing in my life – a *personal* connection to God. I believed very strongly in God as Love, in an "abstract" sense, but Jesus Christ felt like a "hand held out" that I couldn't quite grasp. I was brought up in Church of England schools but now the doctrines of the church had distanced me from Jesus. He seemed to be someone being "used" for teachings which did not ring true. I did not want to go to church and hear or repeat them. Many people around me seem to share this sense of disenchantment – a lost enthusiasm for the words in a church service – and with that loss comes a sense of mild confusion, of woolliness about where to "put ourselves" in terms of our spirituality. Just to say (as I had for many years) "I believe in Love" and leave it at that, began to feel like a flimsy excuse for not focusing deeper on my clear beliefs, and on putting them into action.

This "lacking" in me just would not settle. I think many people seem to be full of this itchy but hopeful question, which was stirring me up inside... "Who is Jesus, *to me*?" Not what are we told to believe, but what holds itself steady within us – what feels true? Perhaps you feel this too. A sense of "Could I have given up on Christianity a bit too soon?" or "Could an honest, supportive connection to Jesus as simply a great teacher, be just the link I am looking for?"

And what does it mean, to be "a Christian"? I needed to look at what this "label" for a faith means. Can I *not* believe that God is a judge, in the way we humans use this word? Can I not believe people get "sent to hell" as a punishment, or that Jesus' death was in any way a "ransom" to pay God, his Father, for human sins in some kind of "swop" of penalties or "sin debts", so that we might be forgiven? Can I struggle very much with the words of some hymns at a church service... but still be a Christian? These were my pressing questions, which will probably be different from your own, but the idea is this... *who* is a Christian? I hope you will find from this book that such a question can have a wide embrace of answers. In Part Two I will see how much the people I have listened to have all helped me find my way toward knowing what I honestly believe. Then I can answer with more confidence "Am *I* a Christian?... Do I *want* to be?" And I hope you will feel closer to answering this question too.

This book quest is not for the definite atheist – although if you are, and you read it, I hope it nudges you to think and feel again. Nor is it for the "absolutely-set-in-my-ways as right" – although again, if you are, and read it, I hope it nudges you to see there may be other angles and directions to at least acknowledge, even allow to stir you up. This is a book for people who are open (and curious) enough in their hearts and minds to be able to hear and learn from other people, as well as from their own soul.

In Part One we discover something which I think is to be admired: the number of denominations which can all be gathered under the "umbrella" of Christianity, as well as the many people beyond the edges of this faith, who do not wish to call themselves Christian, but whose lives are guided and inspired very much by Jesus. Perhaps a good collection of these varied kinds of Christians/Jesus-followers could help by telling us what their faith journey means to them... *what if I meet up with different kinds of pilgrim, stop a while to hear them each tell me of their ways to God... maybe this will help us "inkling-holders" find our own way*... that was my inspiration to set off.

I first began the practice of gathering people round for us all to discuss a question while I was staying at the Macleod Centre, which is a part of the Iona Community on Iona island, off the west coast of Scotland. "I don't believe hell is a place where God sends people to punish us, do you?" I nervously asked. And I was thrilled to discover I was not alone in my niggling "but, if…" curiosity. Several others around the fire that day also felt full of questions and enjoyed sharing different, even challenging, answers. I realized quickly that lots of people are forming new (and not so new) ideas about what Jesus and the Bible can teach us.

So, from my inspiring time around the fire on Iona came these eleven interviews which I set up for the book. They are, if you like, an "anthology of faith", the honest responses of people for whom a devoted spiritual pilgrimage is central to their lives. These are not "famous" people (neither am I), but so what? They are people whom I either knew to be on an active and interesting spiritual journey, or whom I came upon and was inspired to ask to join in with this adventure. I hope each chapter will help you to discover your own direction, within the context of who *you* are. None of these people are "right" or necessarily going the "best way" to God. But every one of them will, I hope, show you a little bit of light.

As I write each chapter and move along on this exploration of faith I have recorded honestly what the interviewee said to me, and sometimes what they challenged me to question and think about. As you set about reading this book, hopefully in the order of chapters as they are laid out, you will be following this quest very much "with me". It's true I had little conscious idea, when I began the book, what I would come to understand by the time I travelled back to Iona eighteen months later, to look at my own faith in Jesus, for my own "answers" in chapter twelve.

The interviews are with Anglicans and Catholics; with an Anglo-Catholic Franciscan, a contemplative, an evangelical, a Methodist, a Messianic, a mystic, a wise seeker… each with a strong love of Jesus, and of course all still seeking. Some may be certain theirs is the "only truth"; others are more willing to see there are lots of pathways to finding understanding. But they have each been open-minded enough to let me record their beliefs here, in a mixture among very different others. For that I hope we can respect them.

The metaphor of a mountain is used in this book to help us imagine taking our own pathway home to God. Pausing and choosing for now not to "go tell it" (as the popular Simon and Garfunkel song says) but instead to "go *listen* on the mountain", before we take our next steps. For the interviews, we did not cross paths and meet on real mountains (perhaps one day) but very often in the lovely George Hotel in my local Cumbrian town of Penrith, or in Oxford University study rooms or other various good places for lunch, lots of tea and coffee, and as I scribbled down their responses on reams of paper, we learned and felt God's presence. God's "mountain" was and is in every place we met and will meet in the future.

*

The more I interview people, the more it becomes clear that truly *listening* is itself a great teaching. I learn to know gratitude to people for opening up to me – not spending the time while they are talking thinking up my own responses and then, as soon as there is a chance, jumping in with "but I think this" or "but you cannot believe that". To give, as the quote from Simone Weil says at the beginning here, real *attention* to the person you are listening to. To simply receive what they say, not as a blank absorption but as a respectful acceptance of their words. For sure I learned that saying what someone had told me in one of these interviews was "bonkers" just does not sit right in my heart any longer. As soon as I said it, I knew that this was a defensive and self-righteous reaction. I hope you will find also that the less we try to impose ourselves, the more we can gain from others.

So, the idea as we follow these interviews is not to "agree" with each or any of them necessarily but to try to find where they are all coming from. We can think of standing on a bridge and watching a stream flow toward us, then going to the other side of the bridge to see how it flows away from there. Discover how opening ourselves up, even for a moment in our lives, to a "panoramic" vision, is a good way to learn. Imagine the horizontal part of the cross, stretching out wide with Jesus' arms, embracing a wide range of humanity and human beliefs, even wide-ranging *within* Christianity.

I hope for us to "embrace" as best we can these varied ideas, then to find what happily resonates with us personally, and what doesn't. To discover that the ideas that challenge us the most can clarify that no, we do not see God or Jesus like this... or perhaps they reveal that we have a "sore point", which could be explored, linked to our own life experiences. Difficult and very different ways of seeing to our own could teach us something important, if we can allow them this gift to us.

The gift is if we can stop ourselves giving in to the egotistical (insecure) urge to say, "I am right, and therefore you are wrong" and be willing to listen in a way that means we try to find what we can *relate* to in the words of the other person, rather than what we contest. So much of our western education system and way of thinking is focused on "criticism and analysis" of what we see, hear, and read. On "arguing our own point". Our "binary-thinking" brains want to label the in/out, good/bad, right/wrong, us/them. But the adventure of writing this book has taught me that there is *another* very beneficial way of learning – which is not always easy! This is by looking for where we agree and "connect" rather than disagree and "separate". This may seem to some people soft or unclear, but it is in truth a skill, an often dismissed but crucial and transforming way toward wisdom – aiming to come together and find our deep missing links, rather than reinforce superficial boundaries around our self and our own "correct" identity.

One thing we may learn from these interviews (and from our awareness of "them" and "us" viewpoints when it comes to religious or political troubles in the world), is that whenever we cling tightly to the idea that our way is the *only* way, the more we are perhaps clinging to a need to strengthen our identity. I hope this book will help suggest the question... do *any* of us really know the absolute Truth of God? And more importantly, perhaps, do we even *need* to be this certain of our complete "rightness"? Can we let go a bit, and just trust in One far greater than us knowing best? Let ourselves be held in safe arms?

Perhaps if we can understand the differences within one religion's way of seeing, we will then be better equipped to understand and connect with people from *all* different faiths, to learn from each of them? The more I remind myself that Jesus taught us by example to be humble, to not judge self-righteously or condescend, but to try to see the good in us all, the clearer the way feels. As we respect our individuality, meet up and celebrate our diversity, could we then discover a powerful unity? Could we not only come together with one group/religion whose way of moving forwards feels right for us, but also find a common bond with people of all faiths – a bond which underlies all our footsteps?

But why *dare* to listen? Because it takes some courage to be prepared to do this. To be flexible, open, not bound up in our own set values – to be willing to share rather than necessarily "own" the truth. In this book we dare to not need to be right.

This book contains real people's beliefs. The times when they are what some might call "mistaken" in their understandings of the Bible or Jesus' teaching, are not best seen as "mistakes". They are the understandings of unique souls, using their personal language, images, their own mind-sets. There would perhaps have been this same varied and personal understanding among Jesus' original followers and disciples.

None of us can read a word such as "kindness" or "journey" without these words meaning something different to every one of us, due to our own unique stacks of "recall" stored inside the brain. A vast collection of memories of people, events, scenes, and feelings we have experienced all link us to a single word by networks of images and sensations. We can learn from understanding how varied the interpretations of words in the Scriptures and of the words of Jesus can be. We each have our unique way of understanding every word we speak or think or read.

It is also helpful to understand that the vocabulary – the spiritual language – we prefer to use often determines the answers which feel best for us. You will see, I hope, that people from different spiritual groups often use different language styles to describe the same thing. And the language often alters the way the concept itself is understood. We can come to see that *context* – the context of our own culture, friends, family, education, our experiences in life, good and bad – these are all factors which influence what "language for God" best resonates with us, and so what we personally choose to believe to be true.

This book asks if language is what both limits us and gives us potential. Different ways of understanding Jesus or the Bible are often based in different ways of interpreting what the word "truth" means, in a spiritual context... Can poetry be truth? Can a story be "true" while not literally having happened exactly the way the story goes? Does truth have more to do with *meaning* than proof? Or is truth simply in the bare literal "facts" of the given evidence? But what are facts? Is anything spiritual ever a 100 per cent truth or fact? Does the dimension of God embrace such exact definition?

I hope you will join me to enjoy and explore all these ideas. And, just as I asked my eleven interviewed "disciples" of Jesus, please do not read the pieces with an aggressive or critical attitude, sorting out quickly what your mind does or does not rationally agree with. Please read them through first in a fresh and open way, not analyzing but aiming to understand in your heart how a fellow human being approaches the divine Truth. The beauty of these personal interviews is in their real humanity. These unique living faiths contain their individual vulnerability and strength. If you want to just read set denominational texts and doctrines, you need a different book!

Another important focus, as you will hear said in these interviews, is not just about clarifying our beliefs, but about putting them into *action*. I am reminded several times by people I talk to that action – working for bringing God's compassion, justice, and peace into the world, the sweat and tears of active service to God – is what really counts. To just "know" is nothing, if we do not then act, even if this is by silent prayer for others. A real relationship with the divine is one of active love – these are crucial words to take in.

However, being a compulsive thinker myself (!) I need to be honest that there are a lot of thinking things through moments in this book: plenty of listening and contemplating. The book of Job 12:11 says, "Does not the ear test words as the palate tastes food?" Books are of course made of words, not action, and the rolling around of ideas, challenges, questions, philosophies is important here. We are not so much testing as tasting a whole range of words and the beliefs they describe. We may cross pathways with others on the mountain, dare to listen, then feel better equipped to choose our next steps on our own "pilgrimage route" to connection with God... which may or may not be with the help of Jesus, and the companionship of Christianity.

To crystallize the purpose then of where we are going on this spiritual adventure, we are looking and listening for our own clarity in four key ways:

1) The "biggest" question: Do I want to be a Christian? To follow Jesus?
2) What is the "language" for understanding God that feels right for me?
3) What do I understand by the words "spiritual truth"?
4) Can I find unity, common fellowship, within all this diversity?

The first question is in the foreground of all the interviews, as people tell us what they believe and why. In the background, as the "setting" for the responses people give, the other three questions and their answers are to be found.

Practicalities

The interviews consisted (eventually) of fourteen "simple" questions such as "What does the word 'God' mean to you?" or "Do heaven and hell really exist?" We laughed at how "not-so-simple" many of my questions were. They all felt right to ask. People often felt that *voicing* their beliefs did help them to clarify their own faith inside. I suggest for you to try this in Part Two.

I gave everyone I interviewed a set of the questions before we met, plus some more detailed notes on what each question could lead to in their response. There is a set of these questions at the end of this chapter.

I also reassured the people I was listening to that they did not need to feel they must provide exact quotations from the Bible by book, chapter and verse, every time they wanted to tell me something which they remembered from Bible stories or teachings. The interviews were by spoken word and reliant on individuals' memories, so only if people chose to give me specific quotes/references at the time, or later upon consideration, have I then notated them as such in the main text. To aid the interested reader, however, I have added biblical references in the endnotes so you can look up the exact text, should you prefer. The Bible version I reference is then the New Revised Standard Version or NRSV, unless otherwise stated. I believe that the Bible in many ways belongs to our collective memory, and I very much wanted people to feel they could flow freely with their responses to my questions, without needing to search for exact citations.

For ease of flow of reading, I have not repeated the questions in every interview, but at times simply put a brief version of the question in, in bold. For example: **Who is Jesus, to you?**

These words in bold *always* represent when I am speaking to the interviewee. When I want to give clearer definitions of certain words/terms used or to briefly consider something coming up in the interview, then I put such text into brackets, to show you that these clarifications are my own, as we move along. When I want to record some of my own personal thoughts, stimulated by what we have been discussing, I use italicized, highlighted text.

There are times, I admit, when my thoughts seem more like a scene from my favourite old sitcom *Father Ted*, when the priests are trying to work something out. Fathers Ted, Jack, and Dougal dither on, confused and exasperated but ever hopeful of a solution, even that God may "leave us a note by the morning" of what the best answer may be! So please stay with me as I go over these thoughts and questions. My intention is that they may also help you think things through – to disagree or go along with me, ponder, philosophize, delve into your own sources of truth. By the time I come to chapter twelve, I am optimistically confident of more clarity. And, if this book works, the same will happen for you when you set pen to paper or talk your own way through the questions, in the thirteenth chapter.

Apart from these few personal thoughts in brackets or italicized, highlighted text, I do not judge, I hope, or comment very much during these eleven interviews. The person I interviewed is the focus. Just to "come together" with different ways from our own of describing God, really does seem to be a chance for a surprising gift – not of confusion, as you might expect – but of clarity. Almost ironically, it seems the less we judge, the more we know of certainty, and the wider we look, the sharper is our own focus. Bizarre, but beautiful to discover.

And of course, there is another kind of reader I hope this part of the book is for. It is for everyone who has a very secure set of beliefs, a church denomination or spiritual group which they comfortably belong to, or a clear mind-set about where they are going... for all the reasons laid out above I do invite you to read and enjoy listening to these interviews, to see other parts of the wide panorama, and to settle into your own faith more deeply (not less) by first watering it with some fresh questions, new perspectives, even some gritty challenges! The secure pilgrim can surely only know real security when they can look all about and still know which path they want to follow, in their heart.

Note. All the interviewees are introduced by Christian name only (just as most of the disciples of Jesus were). If they wanted me to do so, their full names are given in the Acknowledgments.

The fourteen questions

Below are the fourteen questions I asked each interviewee.

Looking at some questions about faith, in informal interviews with interesting people

To Everyone: Please note that these core questions are really to promote our discussion, and my own beliefs are not relevant here at all. As I interview more people I find it humbling and enlightening to discover how differently and yet with strong connections people relate to Jesus in our modern world. And I respect everyone's faith and beliefs as something I can learn from, with no judgment being involved. This is the genuine "listening to others" part of a journey to help myself and other people find our own faith.

The questions will be expanded upon and then the interviewee can answer them in WHATEVER WAY feels relevant or important to them. Please note, anyone who does not believe at all in the topics I am putting to them, can freely and confidently say so! The purpose of my talking to you is to gather a collection of good, challenging ideas and beliefs – linked to our understanding of Jesus, of Christianity, and of "spiritual truth" – in the modern world in which we live.

Below are fourteen points of focus to help us consider these "big questions":

1) *What or who is God, to you?*

2) *Who was Jesus of Nazareth, historically? (Do you think it matters to know the details of the "true life" of Jesus?)*

3) *Who wrote the Bible, as both Old and New Testaments, when was it written, and why?*

4) *What is the Bible? Can it be OK to see the Bible stories as often just that – collected human legends full of symbolic images, and so not necessarily literally true, even, for example, the nativity story? (Is all the Holy Bible literally the "Word of God", or is it more human-made… or can it be both?)*

5) *Why does the Bible (particularly perhaps the Old Testament) focus so much on human sin/guilt/punishment? (Why so much fear of God's wrath rather than hope in God's love?)*

6) *What are "heaven" and "hell" and even "purgatory"? (Does God judge us, punish us, and why?)*

7) *What was the crucial message of Jesus, his "song"? (Was it a new message, a rebel moral teaching?)*

8) *What is the meaning of the crucifixion, the cross? (Why would the Father want the bloody sacrifice of his Son – or is this not the point?) And what is the meaning to you of the Eucharist?*

9) *How can we connect to Jesus and Christianity in a more gender-balanced way? (Why is the Christian God a patriarch?)*

10) *What is the meaning of the Resurrection of Jesus, and his rising to heaven? (Do you believe Christ rose physically as well as symbolically from the dead? And why?)*

11) *What does the term the "devil" mean to you? (Does evil exist?)*

12) *What is the meaning and value of prayer? (Is trust enough?)*

13) *What does the term "Holy Spirit" mean to you? (What is the meaning and value of the Trinity?)*

14) *What is the possible future for an honest, balanced Christian faith? (Can Jesus help us, with or without the church, to find our way to God? Or can we get there without him?)*

CHAPTER ONE

Margaret

Margaret is a Reader, or Licensed Lay Minister, which means she can lead services and preach in an Anglican church (St Paul's, in Lancaster), but is not ordained to preside at the Eucharist. She calls herself gently a "cradle Anglican", who was born into this faith. Her grandmother was very "high church". She herself has been "into the wilderness" and come back from a period of doubt and questioning to a deeper understanding of God. Margaret feels she has, at times, experienced the presence of God physically, literally. At points of crisis, when almost overwhelmed, she has then become full of faith and a trust that all will be well. This support has very much guided her, and she has even at times felt the "light" of God uplifting her, such as once when sitting in the little church of Newlands Valley in the Lake District.

In 2016 Margaret went on a pilgrimage to Santiago de Compostela in Spain in memory of her friend Zara. She returned there a year later to walk the final 150 km from Sarria, staying in small farmhouses and praying in churches along the way. She found it a "truly wonderful experience, which does somehow change you". I know from reading her notes on this pilgrimage that in the journey's many surprises and gifts, frustrations, wrong turnings, supports, and challenges, Margaret could see a reflection of the similar journey we can make with Christ, when we choose to follow Him along "the Way".

Margaret has asked for me to follow her own practice of capitalization in this chapter, which includes using capitals for the personal pronouns "He" and "His", both when writing about God and about Jesus Christ after the Resurrection. She follows what she tells me is the Anglican tradition of using lower case "he" and "his" when writing about Jesus before Easter Sunday, as this helps us focus on the humanity of Jesus, while after the Resurrection we focus more on the divinity of Christ.

Who is God to you, Margaret?

God is the universal spirit of love and compassion. The spirit that is life-giving, sustaining, and directing all. The word "God" for her means "the first cause of everything that is". Margaret is now retired but was formerly a lecturer in the German Studies department of Lancaster University and tells me that the English word "God" is etymologically a Germanic word which comes from an ancient verb meaning "that to which we cry" (which I find quite beautiful, I tell her).

Why was Jesus more "famous" after he was crucified?

Margaret tells me that early followers of Christ began practising "the Way", later called Christianity, which then grew and spread into parts of India, Syria, and Egypt and then through St Paul into Europe, to Rome and onwards. Hence, as it spread geographically, its recognition and popularity as a faith, and the awareness of Jesus, also spread and grew.

I ask her to talk with me about the Bible.

She begins by saying that the Old Testament books are the Scriptures of the ancient Jewish people, which, in a sense, have been "appropriated" by Christians. These Scriptures were written over a very long period of time and we must never regard the Bible, as we have come to have it today, as a book written chronologically or by one author. The writing of texts, she tells me, probably began around 3000 BC, when ancient Jews felt the need to create a "theological framework" to their history as Jewish people. It contains their newly found insights, plus their evaluation and understanding of things that went wrong.

The New Testament began to be written from about AD 50, firstly it is thought by Paul with his epistles, then by the Gospel writers who were becoming aware that living witnesses of Jesus were now dying and they needed to get things written down before such crucial accounts were lost.

This risk is shown by the postulated "Q" text (some people call it the "Q" Gospel[1]), which may have contained many of Jesus' actual sayings, but which is now sadly only found by reference to apparent common sourcing in the Gospels of Matthew and Luke. So, it is best to regard the Bible as a collection of "passed down" texts, which are nevertheless sacred, since they record our growing understanding of the nature of God.

Determining who actually wrote the books of the New Testament is, Margaret tells me, a "scholarly minefield". There is agreement that the epistles were written by the "apostles", which includes those of Jesus' twelve disciples who are named, plus Luke, Paul, and some others. But care needs to be taken, Margaret later tells me, in being too firm on their exact authorship. Some scholars even dispute that Paul wrote all "his" epistles.

Most people do agree that the "canonical" Gospels of Matthew, Mark, Luke, and John were written by the people whose names they bear, after the epistles, and later than the events which they narrate. They would have used records of earlier oral traditions and eyewitness accounts extant among the first Christian communities. However, Margaret stresses to me here (and in later communications) we need to remember how much debate there is on this authorship issue, and it is really "best to be cautious".

Paul for sure "knew" Jesus in a spiritual sense, not physically. He had been a persecutor of the early Christians as heretics to Judaism, even witnessing the stoning of St Stephen, the first Christian martyr. But after a vision of Jesus on the road to Damascus, he became absolutely dedicated to Christ. So, "knowing" Jesus can be interpreted in different ways.

We must remember that the original texts of the Bible were written in Hebrew and Greek, then translated into Latin, before finally coming to us in English... a great change of languages which can become, in translation, rather like the game Chinese Whispers. Some idiomatic usages and euphemisms may be misunderstood when translated literally or divorced from their cultural context.

For example, some scholars believe that the name Abraham (the founding father of the Israelite nation) may stand for a whole tribal people. Margaret is unsure about this but says "Does it really matter?" What matters is not the exact factual truth but the deeper meaning on offer to us.

Within Judaeo-Christianity, she continues, it is only in relatively recent times that Christians have taken the Bible as literally the "Word of God". In the synagogues the sacred scrolls were seen as being given for the rabbis to *interpret*. Thus, there is room for variance when understanding the Old and New Testaments, and for discord! The word "Israel" itself means "he who struggles with God".

Margaret accepts that humans have evolved from apes and believes that, at some stage, we became aware of our difference. This perhaps links to our idea of the "fall of Man" – the beginning of our self-awareness. Millions of years ago, as the tribes spread out from Africa, we gradually evolved to question "what is Man?", "who are we?", and ancient religion was born, related to how we could placate the at times hostile forces of nature, ensure fertility, and succeed in our survival.

Then came the ancient Jewish people. Margaret sees Judaism as containing some very special, unique insights, and the ancient Jews as very gifted, very special people, advanced in some sense, given insight… but struggling with it.

From the nineteenth century onwards, biblical research by evangelical Christians has taken the Bible literally. But in earlier times, it was seen less strictly as the direct Word of God.

Why was this change? I ask.

Because, perhaps, of the restrictions of our new way of "standardization" – in technology, science, education, and much more. Importantly, Margaret says, we can call the Bible "holy" while not believing it to be literally so. "Holy" does not equal "the literal Word of God". No! It equals the "search and insight into God". Yes!

And yes again, the Bible does contain, in both Old and New Testaments, a lot about sin and guilt and the wrath of God. But it also contains throughout the text a promise of salvation. Indeed, some scholars see the Bible as a "salvation history", a record again of our search for God's saving of us by His love and forgiveness.

There are "primitive" aspects to the Bible, and so yes, it contains fear, because we were, and still are, very frail. Our ancestors were frail and primitive, they did not understand the science of nature like we do, or of sexuality, fertility, and so on. Therefore, when things went wrong, as they often did, they feared that they had offended God. If crops failed, or epidemics came, people feared they must have "done something wrong" in God's eyes.

When the nomadic Israelites became settled people in the "Promised Land" they needed rules to live by. They had reached a new stage in their/ our spiritual education. So they needed law enforcement; they needed to think about the consequences of their actions. An emphasis on sin and guilt was needed as "we" began to settle anew, regulate ourselves, and advance.

Margaret sees humans as the "crown" of God's creation, but we are not yet "fully human". Our animal side still prevails, with our self-concern, our need for food, shelter, safety, sex… Christianity is all about raising ourselves up, growing to a higher stage of living for others, not for self.

But, as we are not there yet, we still need rules! And we still need to be aware of our faults when we break them and say "sorry" to God for not being the people He wants us to be.

So, we certainly need to be aware of sin and our need for forgiveness and redemption, but Margaret would now like to see more emphasis within the Western churches on the need for *transformation*. Eastern Orthodox Christians, such as Greek Orthodox, have always, she believes, celebrated the transfiguration as a major festival. The transfiguration happened when people were asking "Who is Jesus?", "Is he the Messiah?", "Is he the prophet Elijah returned?"… and so, Jesus said to Peter, "Who do you think I am?" Peter replied, "You are the Messiah," and Jesus asked him to be quiet, then took Peter, James, and John up a mountain, where they suddenly could *see* Jesus in robes of light. He was the light! And he was talking miraculously with the long since passed away Moses and Elijah. This was their "transformation", one we can all aspire to: seeing the light of Christ. Entering into that light.

This is the way our own lives can be transformed. Jesus reveals to us a new way of life to which, by the grace of God, we can aspire. The ancient Christian church was much more focused on this. Paul said we should "live in the spirit, not the flesh", and reflect the light of Christ.

In an important sense this differs from the traditional focus of many Western churches, which is more on the incarnation of Jesus. This is by the celebration of Christmas as the birth of Jesus – 25 December being a date created by us, as it is not in the Bible. The focus is more on the *redemption* rather than transformation of Christians, through firstly the birth of Christ and then very much his "saving us" from our sins at his crucifixion: his redeeming us.

Why did this change in focus occur?

As the Christian religion became entangled in state power in the West, we have somehow moved away from this earlier focus, on being transformed by Christ's light. But note, says Margaret, there is change afoot! Groups such as the Iona Community are focusing again very much on transformation, which is so good, she tells me, happily.

And heaven and hell, what do these words mean to you?

Yes, there is another dimension, she tells me, which is "eternity". Within it, some people are closer to God's presence than others. So, they are in "heaven". Some are a long way away from God, in a state of denial of His love, so they are in "hell". Hell is not literally a fire, this is symbolic language, it is where people's souls, if not open to the love of God, find themselves, and they are therefore not in heaven. It is that simple.

And purgatory?

Yes, that exists, but it is not where God punishes us, it is where people's souls are being cleansed, taught, brought to a stage where they can accept God's love… and so be redeemed.

I ask Margaret if only Christians can go to heaven?

She replies that Jesus said, "No one comes to the Father except through me."[2] Such words, she agrees, are a stumbling block for many. But Margaret says that her "core belief" is that Jesus alone gives us a higher, true understanding of God. God as pure love and compassion, who wants us all to be "beautiful people". Who loves and extends forgiveness to all. And the only way we can ever come to even an inkling of the true nature of God is through the teachings of Jesus. Other religions can teach us similar insights into God. Buddhism, for example, teaches that "all life is sacred". So, it may be that people from other religions who are living with a Christ-like outlook of love and compassion will also be in heaven when they pass from time into eternity. Or even atheist "humanist" people who follow a Christian-values lifestyle.

I try to press Margaret now to clarify for me the difference between leading a Christian-values lifestyle and being a Christian by faith. What difference does this make when we die? Is the crucial point really how connected we are to God's love during our lifetime?

Margaret simply replies that our language for understanding this is inadequate. Human words are too limited to capture "God" as a truth. We use only a "shorthand", helped often by the language of poetry.

We leave the discussion of this point for now and move on.

Similarly, she says, we need to take care with language in understanding God's "wrath". In the Gospels Jesus does say that those who will not accept his teachings will have God's wrath come upon them. But his real song was that we are all children of God. That God loves us all. Therefore, he associated not only with the devout Jews, but also with the sinners, outcasts, and lepers, as well as with the Romans – outsiders to Judaism.

Such teaching was radically challenging in its day! And this teaching was not exclusively for Jews. Jesus wanted all people to hear and follow his teachings. He taught that it is not enough to obey God's laws – which we should – we need also to do much more, so much more it almost seems impossible! And we can only begin to aspire to living how God and Jesus want us to live through the grace of God.

After our third interview I ask Margaret what she herself means by the "grace" of God. She replies to me in the following way...

"Well, 'grace' is one of those words/concepts which are very difficult to explain. We have an intuitive idea of what we mean, but would struggle to describe it to, let us say, a puzzled Martian. One of the best explanations I have heard goes something like this... suppose a child has done something very wrong and needs to be reprimanded. 'Justice' would be when he/she gets what punishment they deserve (no pocket money for a week or their mobile phone confiscated). 'Mercy' would be when the parent says, 'I'm going to be lenient with you this time, but you really have been very naughty.' 'Grace' is when the parent says, 'You have been very naughty and deserve to be punished, but nevertheless I am going to be lenient and give you a chance to do better, because I love you and cherish you, and will always want the best for you, and will always be there for you, whatever you do.'

"Obviously, 'grace' and 'mercy' are both loosely related. Paul begins many of his epistles with the words 'Grace, mercy and peace from the Lord Jesus Christ be with you'. It is through the grace – the generosity, forbearance, patience, and loving-kindness – of God, that we obtain the peace and calmness of soul which inspires us to be the people God wants us to be. It is freely given. We cannot by our own merits do anything to deserve it but having received it we can try to show ourselves worthy, by being better people and giving thanks." (I found this a very helpful description of what the grace of Jesus Christ, of God, means to Margaret and to many Christians.)

Back to the original interview now, Margaret goes on to tell me that in all this, we must remember that Jesus, for Christians, is a revelation of divine love and is not only human, but also divine. People who see him simply as a great teacher – like Gandhi was – can be called Christian in outlook, but not in their distinct faith. In the Old Testament, Margaret tells me, and in the New Testament, those who accepted Judaic laws but were not Jewish were called "God-fearing" people. Likewise, people who follow the teachings of Jesus but do not have faith that he was divine, and so are not able to say the Creed and mean and believe it, could perhaps, she suggests, be called "para-Christians", just as we have "para-medics" – people who act alongside medics, but are not medics themselves. To be fully Christian you need to believe that Jesus was fully human and also fully divine. That is the truth for Margaret.

She tells me that the German philosopher Immanuel Kant spoke of truly "moral people" as being those who both act morally *and* know the moral law they are obeying, that is, know the difference between right and wrong. It is not the same, for example, not to steal chocolates just because you do not want to get caught, as to not steal them because you respect the law of not stealing. Only in this latter case can you be said to be truly moral. Likewise, if you follow the teachings of Christ, but do not accept that He is divine, you are Christian in your lifestyle, but not in your true faith.

I ask again, can we still go to heaven if we follow a Christian "lifestyle", but are not Christian by "true faith" in the divinity of Jesus?

Margaret confirms that she believes people are only true Christians if they believe in Jesus being the divine Son of God, who was crucified and rose again from the dead, who came to redeem us, but that people who live with Christian values, consciously or unconsciously, be they from other faiths or none, could yes go to heaven. However, she then asks, "but who am I to judge?"… as in, it is not for her to decide or speak on such things really, it is only for God to say.

We come to the question of the crucifixion.

Margaret points out something to me: I have not included, in my original questions, anything asking about the meaning and value of the Eucharist. I am shocked to realize this and agree of course for her to talk with me about her belief in this sacrament (and to include the Eucharist from now on in my set of questions!).

To Margaret, the cross has a very *positive* meaning. It is not about a holy Father *requiring* the bloody sacrifice of his Son. Indeed, she sees such a belief as verging on the sacrilegious. Paul himself said that Christ crucified was a "stumbling block to many".[3] And so it is, unless we see it in the context of the Eucharist.

And the Eucharist?

This is a thanksgiving for the sacrifice of Christ. We need, Margaret says, to go back in our mindset to the times of Jesus when people truly believed in sacrifice. It was their way of trying to say "sorry" for all the wrongs they had done, through ritual. To do this, they needed to give up something precious, for example a good "unblemished" animal, then offer it to God. To shed its blood, as a substitute for their own life, so that this blood could spill on and purify them of their sins. In a sense their old sinful life was being killed so that they could now try to do better. A new life. Purer. Higher.

Margaret sees the crucifixion very much in this light, as the offering by Jesus to cleanse the sins of all the world by offering and sacrificing the ultimate gift… Himself!

Through sacrificing his own pure life, Jesus reconciles us to God. He takes our sins *upon himself*, as for example a slaughtered lamb would have done in the popular rituals of the time.

She stresses here to me how important it is to understand that Jesus *is* God. So, God is sacrificing *Himself*. If we see it in this way we can understand better how He did this to show us how great His love for us really is.

In the "blood of Christ" as the wine of the Eucharist we take this blood "spilled for us" into us so that we can become cleansed and try to do better. To become purer, better people.

Margaret now wonders if God perhaps had a "plan A" for Jesus to come as the divine in human form to create a new kingdom on earth, but that when his mission was rejected, "plan B" (the crucifixion) had to be activated. She then asks me "Am I being heretical here?" and we talk light-heartedly about how easily Christians can fear being guilty of "heresy" (a belief or opinion contrary to orthodox Christian doctrine) and of being punished for heresy. Then we assure each other that God knows how much we love Him and that our questioning and curious searching is all a *part of*, not in conflict with, that strong faith.

The crucifixion shows us, she says, just how much God will do for us out of His love for us. And through the Eucharist we are shown how Jesus' sacrifice can renew and purify us. It is crucial to see that it was in truth God on the cross. We very much need not to see the cross as a symbol of God's wrathful need for revenge, a punishment for humanity through the sacrificial substitution of Christ his Son. No. The cross, for Margaret, is a symbol of His great love for us, His willingness to take all our sins upon Himself.

But perhaps, she wonders, we need a new language now? We are a long way from the mindset of people who understood the regular practice of sacrifice. It could be that a new focus, a re-balancing is required. She now adds, in a lovely manner "Am I being heretical again, Jacci?" then we laugh, and she continues to question… do we perhaps need a new way of talking about the Eucharist, for example, rather than about us "drinking the blood of Christ"? Such words can offend and confuse some modern people, so perhaps we do need to think about this.

Another confusion, Margaret feels, is the Western "gender-obsessed" idea that the Bible and the Church are too patriarchal. God has no gender, but then again is definitely not an "it", an impersonal force. The Judaeo-Christian tradition has always been to develop a *personal* relationship with God who, in both Old and New Testaments, has both masculine and feminine attributes. When Jesus spoke of the Father, he meant not a "tyrannical" but a "protective" force. It is more we, in the modern world, who see "Father" as emphasizing wrath and tyranny. And we overplay the gender issue, Margaret believes.[4]

She notes how evidence of the authenticity of truth in the Gospels can be found in their relation to women. In a society where women were not so respected as witnesses, why then do women fare so highly in the stories of Jesus? For example, the "woman at the well", and of course Mary Magdalene being the first person to see Jesus after his Resurrection. Jesus could have found "stronger" witnesses to his mission if he was at all insecure. But he knew his truth. So, he often happily chose women to be his prime witnesses and allies. And the writers of the Gospels also chose to relate these stories with honesty and with passion, which surely emphasizes their authenticity. A woman being the first one to see the risen Christ is not, Margaret says, "something you would make up!"

In later Christian times, in the West, the theme of God's "might" became more relevant to both Roman and feudal rule, but way back, in the Old Testament times, Margaret believes Jewish women had a powerful role in their religion and within the household. This was also, to some extent, true for women in early Christian times.

And the Resurrection?

Yes, for certain Margaret believes in this. There is evidence! Peter said, "we are the witnesses". And this was such an overwhelming experience that it totally convinced them of the divinity of Christ and enabled them to proclaim the Gospel, despite ridicule and persecution. Where would they have found the strength to do that if they had not truly seen the risen Christ? The Resurrection is the most important event in human history. It points us up to the dimension of the divine. And reassures us of this.

Margaret tells me that at some stage, in time or eternity, she believes we shall "resurrect" in the physical form of the best we ever were in our mortal lives, into a new eternal world where creation will be restored. It is of course very hard to speculate how! But God has a design and purpose for the universe, and divine power is shaping it toward that end – the "new creation" that we can read about in the book of Revelation.

For now, Jesus is the aspect of God which communicates to us in human form. He is the way by which we can approach the Godhead. "In a crude analogy," she tells me, "Jesus is like a smart phone to God!" In the Eucharist, she believes Jesus is truly present; that we can there truly experience "communion" with the divine.

Yes, the second coming will happen. It is spoken of clearly in the book of Revelation when the "four horsemen of the Apocalypse" – famine, pestilence, war, and death, bring the world as we know it to an end. And then there will be a "new heaven and a new earth". But when? How? That is beyond our knowing. Margaret simply has trust in God. God wants the best for us and His purposes for us are good. That is her faith.

What about human sin?

Margaret tells me that Genesis reveals a "true story" of the six stages of creation: chaos-light-water-vegetation-animals-humans. It puts forward the idea of God being "in charge" and seeing that all is good. But then how to account for so much that seemed to have gone wrong for the Israelites? For wars, disease, death? The writers of Genesis needed someone to blame and that could not be God. So, the idea of the "Fall" came about, beginning with the "original sin" of Adam and Eve and their banishment from the Garden of Eden.

Now beliefs have changed in the wake of the theories of Darwin about evolution. Margaret believes in a continuously evolving creation. We are all in a "divine experiment". God watches. Steers occasionally. And we have not yet reached our true humanity, not yet fulfilled our best potential. We have moved forward from being mere animals, but we have free will, which sometimes leads us to make wrong decisions and act selfishly to the detriment of others, and so evil comes into the world.

Yes, evil does exist, you say. It is a force, almost like electricity. It can get hold of people. But, I ask, where does it come from?

This is difficult to understand, Margaret now tells me. Other religions teach that there is a dualism of good and evil to help them comprehend the negative forces at work in the world, but Christianity asserts that God really is "in charge". So how do we explain the bad energies? Is it something that has come about from all the times when we have misused our free will? A force that we ourselves generate? This would be the traditional Christian view, she tells me. Because we haven't yet learned how to use the gift of free will correctly. One way of reading the Gospels is to say that Jesus came into the world to show us clearly how to do this.

And prayer. What is prayer?

Margaret says that questions about prayer often reveal our confusion about what it is. It has been over-simplified over time. Lots of people take a very "please this... please that" approach, but this is not really the best way. Because God knows what is best! No "bargaining" with God is needed. Prayer, she says, is the bringing of the self into the *presence* of God. Being aware. And then aiming to direct God's love toward those for whom we pray, so that they may also be aware of this loving. If we pray in awareness of the presence of God, those for whom we pray can be *held up* to God's love and mercy, and also held up to His generosity – for God to then choose what is best for them (what a brilliant description of prayer this is, I tell her).

So, it is in a sense a two-part process:

1) We *ask*, hold up people and situations, to channel God's love toward those for whom we are praying.
2) We *submit*, we surrender to God's love and wisdom and will.

In the passion narrative, Jesus did pray and ask, "Please Father, do I have to suffer being crucified?" But then he said, "Not my will be done but yours."[5] He surrendered to the one who knows best, which is the highest form of prayer.

When we pray "Lord. Please have mercy on X", we could see it as asking for X to be more able to feel this surrender, this trust in God's mercy. It is a different way of understanding how and why we pray.

Margaret now digresses (in an interesting way!) to tell me about the Lutheran theologian named Dietrich Bonhoeffer (1906–1945). He was a founder member of the "Confessing Church", which was opposed to the policies of the Nazi regime during the Third Reich (1933–45). He returned to Germany from a safe place, to try to defeat the evil being done there, and rebuild good. To do this, he knew that he would have to put himself right in among the badness, working for change. He was involved in 1944 in a plot to try to assassinate Hitler and was executed two to three weeks before the end of the war. Before his death, he wrote several works, including *The Cost of Discipleship*, which examines the role of Christianity in a modern secular world.[6] The compromises we must make. The challenges facing our ethics.

Bonhoeffer wrestled, Margaret tells me, with the concept of "religion-less Christianity", advocating a return to the radical Gospels of the New Testament, without all the accumulated liturgies and rituals of the more recent past.

We are now, Margaret says, living in a very secular society in the West, so we need to know what is *authentic* about our Christian faith, how we can promote and communicate that to others, and encourage them to consider Christianity. It may even be we need to re-examine the language and imagery that we use.

And we need to find our common link with other faiths. To connect to the "universal religion of love", which for Margaret is through Christ, but can, yes, be by other ways for other people.

And we need to come together in our faith. The word "church", she says, means people gathered together to worship. We now so very much need a new "witnessing community" to form. A new authenticity, with perhaps less focus on ritual, but still a gathering together in God's presence. "A church cannot be a party of one!" she tells me wisely.

We need new groups to form, not of extreme sects which pervert and misuse the Holy Spirit, which has always happened – as St Paul warned us when suspicious people of his time were "speaking in tongues". Even if we do not all agree that Jesus was and is divine, we can agree on his teachings, and this would be a great step forwards in human development.

Remember, says Margaret, how in its day the early church was so incredibly radical. We now have a very different culture and popular images, and different languages, so we may need to reinterpret the Scriptures. But the basic message of Jesus (his "song") is still crucial: the *inclusivity* of God's love. For the rich, poor, black, white, sick, healthy, Jew, gentile… the "excluded" are included!

In the past, societal exclusion may have had survival reasons behind it – such as the exclusion of lepers from common places – but Jesus came and said, radically, "No one should be written off!" This has always been the core message of true Christianity.

Margaret is positive about the future. Yes, we do need control guidelines, which are always evolving. She trusts in the Holy Spirit to guide us in a good direction. "Ultimately what is important is *love,*" she says. "Do emphasize that in your book, Jacci. We can all agree on this." "I do, and I will," I reply.

After this wonderful and very informative interview with Margaret – which took three in-depth sessions, as she told me so much I wanted to record – I became sure that these meetings with Christian or Jesus-connected people would be a great way to learn about the living faith.

From now on, with the next ten interviews I have recorded, I shall try not to repeat things said in the same way twice but shall show things seen in different ways – even the same text, teaching, or way of seeing, from different angles – and I shall make sure to always show you the inspiring, challenging, curious, and revealing things said by each person. To help us find our own best journey to God. To come a little closer to "consciously comprehending" the almost unknowable, as it fits just right in our own hearts.

CHAPTER TWO

Bob

Bob tells me he really has no "denomination". "I am who I am," he says. He is not a "Christian" in the commonly used sense, and believes all religions are worthy. A good way to describe himself is as a "contemplative". In the past he has been an Associate (like me) of the Iona Community, and in the more distant past a part of the Church of England. Currently, Bob attends Quaker meetings and is part of the World Community for Christian Meditation. He arranges a "Living with Mystics" group which meets every three months after spending time reading and contemplating upon a specific "mystic" teacher – such as Jesus himself, or Julian of Norwich, Eckhart Tolle, Thich Nhat Hanh. Bob is also a bereavement counsellor.

To Bob, God is Love. That's it! God is Love and those who love live in God and God lives in them.

When we do not love, we *veil* God, and our ego takes over. But God is there 100 per cent of the time always anyway. If we can refer to God as Love, this really helps – helps us stop "humanizing" what God is.

God is not a "he". God is in everything. And that means God is also in the suffering.

There is plenty of independent evidence that Jesus existed. As a human. He was probably born in Nazareth, Bob says. Lots of stories are "added" to his real life, perhaps to create deeper meaning, deeper messages. But Jesus was indeed a hugely intuitive person, who literally did "live with God" as part of himself. He was "enlightened".

Was he born this way? Bob does not know, but he was more enlightened than we are, and was killed for being so radical.

When any child is born, he tells me, we each have an awesome "knowing" inside of us. This is our communion with God, before the ego gets in our way, gets hold of us. This obstacle comes partly from what we teach our children, but they, we, are all born pure. And Jesus somehow retained this purity. This knowing of God.

He was a human person who had great extra insight, like some other great mystics, but probably more so. "He *epitomized love*," says Bob. He goes on to describe to me how for him Jesus epitomizes "kenosis" – which means "self-emptying love". There are two forms of love "eros" and "agape". To Bob the former, eros, means romantic, sexual love of another, in a personal ego sense. The latter, agape, is a universal love for all. Jesus gave himself up so much with his agape love for others that he challenged the status quo, even the "communal ego".

The Old Testament was written by Jewish leaders to keep their religion and people on a Godly path. The focus of it was more religious and spiritual than as a way of "keeping control" of a socio-political kind. They did see themselves as God's chosen people, which was an important responsibility.

The New Testament is more interesting to Bob. There were many more than the four standard biblical Gospels, but they were ordered to be destroyed by certain religious people such as Irenaeus, around AD 200 , and later under the order of the Roman emperor Constantine, who wanted to unify his empire and its religion, and didn't like the diverse views of early Christianity. He decided what was "orthodox" and what wasn't, around 300 years after Jesus lived.

The earliest known writing is Paul's letter to the Thessalonians, around CE 50 , which was about twenty years after Jesus had died, in around CE 30. (Bob now explains to ignorant me that "BCE" means "Before the Common Era" and "CE" means "Common Era"; such signs are interchangeable in timescale to the terms with which I am familiar, BC and AD, but as these mean "before Christ" and "Anno Domini" or "after Christ", they are not often used now in many texts, to avoid a "Christian slant"… we learn, we learn!)

To Bob, the earliest known, and the most meaningful Gospel, is the Gospel of Thomas, which some historical scholars believe was written about AD 60–65 (other scholars believe this text was written later, in the second century). Bob regards this as the Gospel nearest to the truth of Jesus' sayings as it has no narrative and has only relatively recently been re-discovered in its entirety (1945), thus is less likely to have been altered by the church. Mark's Gospel is from a similar time, with Luke and Matthew coming after, around AD 80, both having been influenced by the "lost Gospel" of "Q". Then followed John's Gospel, in around AD 90–100 . All the Gospels have probably been edited and added to (there is also still much debate on when they were written, in which order and by whom!).

The Gospels were not necessarily written, for example, "by Matthew", Bob believes, but by unknown people trying to put forward a point of view. Around the time of the "fall of Jerusalem" in AD 70, a lot of the Gospel writing occurred. Is this a coincidence? Or is it because of fear by the early Jewish-Christians that the Temple would be destroyed (it was), and that their recollection of Jesus' sayings and wisdom, and an emerging belief that he was the promised Messiah of the Old Testament, would be forgotten?

There is no arguing that Jesus' popularity became strong and most apparent *after* he died. It is very possible to Bob that events in Jesus' life were looked for in the prophesies of the Old Testament by the Gospel writers, to try to fit and find places where they could say "he did this to fulfil that prophecy", in order to make him more popular to the new church of Christian believers.

> We spend a little time talking about our curiosity regarding why Jesus was not written about more during his lifetime, or even in the years just after his death, rather than a delay of perhaps twenty to thirty years – we wonder on...

Certainly, the Bible is not all literal truth. Neither is it all the "Word of God", as is suggested in Paul's "Charge to Timothy" in 2 Timothy 3:16 "All scripture is inspired by God and is useful for teaching, for reproof, for correction, and for training in righteousness"... no, because God is Love, remember, and we cannot ever humanize this. God *has* no words. The language of God, very importantly to Bob, is silence. This is one of the biggest truths to him.

Yes, some stories are true. Some others are embellished. Lots were written for their deeper meaning, embedded within them. We now live, unfortunately, in a very "literal" rational/fact-seeking age, as we have for the past 300 years, in the West. In the East this is less so, and religions are more "mystical" therefore in their approach to God. In fact, Bob jokes, the Age of Enlightenment in the 1700s, was really an age of "Endarkenment"!

This was a time of negating spiritual intuition, when the West could not seem to accept anything to be true that was not "science". However, we seem now to be discovering that people like the Romans and Egyptians could invent things with great wisdom, even though they kept a "spiritual" aspect central to their lives. This shows us there are other ways of moving forwards.

Bob stresses that he would never use the phrase "Word of God", for the Bible or other Scriptures, as he so disagrees with the way this phrase is often used today. He tells me it was not meant, when used by the ancient church, to be taken literally.

We are in a society, he says, which is patriarchal and "androcentric" (male-centred) rather than "gynocentric" (female-centred), or neutral (person-centred). This was also very prevalent in biblical times. The "Constantinian" church, for the past 1,700 years since Roman emperor Constantine made Christianity the state religion, needs to keep us in control, and does so by doctrines – such as the Nicene Creed. It is to keep us in place. Society is therefore upheld by the "will of God", which was really the will of a man, or men.

And sin?

"*God does not know sin,*" Bob emphasizes to me. God does not even recognize it. "God is *un*conditional love. Stress the '*un*'!" Only humans, the church, has created the concept of sin. We can, if we like, interpret it as a "turning away from God", a lack of awareness of the God within us. Within all of us. A turning away from God toward our ego. But God does not know sin. How can God turn away from God?

> *I reflect upon what this might mean – that love cannot know non-love because wherever there is love there is love! Just as light cannot know darkness, because when light is there, even from a weak small candle, darkness is perforce gone. The absence of one being nullified by the presence… interesting.*

The word "Emmanuel" means "God with us". Sin is the turning away from Emmanuel, toward our ego. But the church uses "sin" as a concept to make people come to them, the church powers, for forgiveness. We are encouraged to go to the church priest and so on for confession and forgiveness, rather than going within.

Bob even questions why we should always feel we need to go through Jesus to commune with God. Can we not go directly to God, in our hearts? It is wrong, he says, to make out that things are "necessary" in order to get God's love – that makes it conditional, which is totally not what God is! Saying "*If* you confess your sins, *if* you turn to Jesus, then and only then will God love you" – no!

Because this implies that if you do not do these required things, believe these required things, then God will not love or forgive you. To Bob, this is wrong. (I ask him, did Jesus himself not say that the only way to the Father was through him? Yes, Bob says, but not in the way we often think. We interpret too literally. He may not have been saying to go "only through him", in an almost egotistical sense, but through the way Jesus himself was going. To follow his way, of the heart. To use the self-emptying, self-giving "kenosis" of love.)

We all have to ask ourselves – and we often do this only in times of despair – "Who am I? Why am I here?" And the simple answer is "to love". It involves suffering, yes, and rejection, yes. But we are each here to *express* God through whom we are.

And hell is another "human creation". It is a non-physical place, where God is not. It is the place of our ego, our selfish self. This is not the *true* self, the real us. It can certainly be here and now because, Bob says, there is only the here and now! The future and past are illusions of the human mind. Heaven and hell are states of being that belong outside of time. They are concepts that belong in "kairos" which means, in Greek, "outside of time", as opposed to "chronos" which is time-based.

Heaven and hell do not exist literally, as places. They are states of mind. Now Bob tells me something which will shake me in a way that truly shocks me, because I did not expect it to be a concern – he says that when we die, every last one of us, we are *all* "in heaven". Because we are with God, as our true selves. The true self is the spirit of love. The physical body is of the earth and so goes back to the earth "ashes to ashes".

Our spirit, the Emmanuel, of God expressing Godself through us, is in all things. And "heaven" is our complete being in God again, after we have left our bodies. So, we *all* go to heaven, and, as time does not exist in such a dimension-less state, we are all in heaven, *now*!

Heaven is "kairos", eternal, outside of time, so we do not "go" where we already are. We are there now, outside of time, our whole true self is there, without any earthly hindrances of the physical.

Furthermore (and this is what truly shakes my conscience) Bob believes there is no gradation in this universal "being-in-heaven-ness". There is no difference between souls, as in some being fully there and some not quite, some closer or further from God's love. Because we are *all* God's love. The "I" of different persons is not there, because it is ego, from another dimension of humans on earth. This is not our true centre. It is, Bob tells me, the "periphery". As souls we are all together with God, in God.

There are no "bad souls", and no "evil" exists in the reality of the spirit. Again, evil is linked to ego, which stays on earth. Moreover the "kingdom of heaven" told of in the Bible, is here, now, because there is no other, in the dimension of divinity. We need to realize that we are each a part of God, loved eternally and unconditionally, and that God does not recognize sin – that is all human ego. It has nothing to do with our souls.

As there is no time in "kairos", this means when we die we are in heaven, and that we are therefore in heaven *now*! Because kairos is eternity. Timeless.

> *I almost need at this point in the interview to take a spiritual as well as physical breathing space, some time out from this timeless and space-less dimension talk, to comprehend even a glimpse of what Bob is telling me. I also realize how much it is shocking, unnerving me even, to consider the possibility of, no matter how much we might try in this life to be a "good soul" or a "good Christian", whether it be by doing compassionate works or by having true faith in Jesus, could none of this really matter, none of it count a jot when we die, because every one of us goes completely to heaven? I am not sure I feel steady with this idea. How egotistically selfish I realize I am!*
>
> *For so long I have been wanting to get "closer" to God when I die. Closer than whom? Whom do I want to be left further out? I realize how much I want to be "rewarded" for all my spiritual seeking, as if I'm in some homo sapiens "school for the soul". The idea that God loves every one of us equally and completely, is preached by so many Christian churches, but to believe this to our core, I realize now, could mean something which perhaps very few people find comfortable to accept. I know I am finding it hard. That we are all God's children could, according to Bob – and I dare say according to Jesus – mean that we are all equally a part of the embracing love of God. And to that we shall all return, not eventually, after a spiritual cleansing or justice punishment or time for forgiveness, he says, not even after we die, but right now, as we are now, eternal loving souls, every one of us. Wow! I struggle to take this in. But I do want to.*

Bob also does not believe that Jesus said, "I am the *only Son* of God." He may have said "I am a son." But then he would have added "and so are you all!" Because we are all God's sons and daughters. Much loved. It is just that Jesus fully realized what we do not, yet. Jesus even said, "even greater things than this you will do."[1] So, Bob believes he must surely not have wanted to be put on a "pedestal". He wanted us to truly know that we are all One. Any teachings contrary to this are the work of the human church, not Jesus.

The message of Jesus was love. It was the "be all and end all" of his message. By loving one another, we are loving God who is in everyone and everything. In all creation. And within that love is all forgiveness.

Bob prefers, he tells me, to see God as love rather than as "light". Because love is the key.

When I tell Bob of my love of the painting in Oxford's Keble College Chapel, "The Light of the World" by Holman Hunt (1853), he replies that to him –

Jesus was and is *a* light, not *the* light. In his time, Jesus was talking about his own people and religion. He was born a Jew, circumcised, but then baptized by John the Baptist in the River Jordan, into the freedom of no traditional religion, but with a direct relationship with God.

I ask Bob if this is a correct interpretation of baptism at this time, by John, and he thinks so.

Indeed, part of Jesus' message was to *free* others from their religion into the freedom of Oneness with God. According to many stories in the Bible, Jesus did reject some Jewish laws because he did not want people subjected to rules. He wanted to give us a "freedom invitation"! This is the teaching that struck a chord with Bob.

I ask further: what religion was John baptizing people into? A new one? Christianity did not then exist.

Bob simply believes it was the freedom of movement toward a new way, with no religion, rules, regulations, doctrines, dogmas, and so on – just into Oneness with God.

> *I look into this and come to understand that baptism is related to a Jewish purification ritual for the "washing away" of the old life and sins. John was baptizing many people in the River Jordan in a "baptism of repentance for the forgiveness of sins". This was a part of his "messianic movement" because he believed, he prophesied, that a new Messiah was coming soon. John predicted, "I have baptised you with water; but he will baptise you with the Holy Spirit" (Mark 1:8). Paul distinguished this baptism by John as a "baptism of repentance", in comparison to baptism "in the name of Jesus", which is seen as a sacrament by Christians, an admission and adoption of the Christian faith.*

And the crucifixion?

Bob says this was what it was. It was what happened to many trouble-stirrers at this time. Thousands of them! Execution of those who were a threat either to the Pharisees or the Romans. The rulers. The killing of Jesus was almost inevitable and was not "remarkable" in the sense of being unexpected or unusual. And was not the "fulfilment of a prophecy". But still to Bob it was very meaningful, because of how much it showed Jesus' *innocence* as well as his *knowing* that although humans can destroy the body, they cannot destroy what is eternal, that is, they could not destroy Jesus' true self.

Jesus, the man who was perhaps a "good Jew" for most of his life but then, even though the evidence is scant, was certainly a rebel for what is right and just, rather than the "religious" rules. For example, he healed people on the sabbath rest day. He may have also said, regarding purity eating laws that "it is not what goes into the mouth that is sinful, but what comes out of it".[2] This is an important saying for Bob. It shows that God cares about our hearts, our love, not our rule-keeping.

What about the meaning of the cross?

This is largely a construct of the church. To give it power the church focuses heavily on the "sacrifice of Jesus" for us all, and all that goes with this teaching. To Bob, Jesus was simply but of course tragically killed, for his rebelliously loving teachings. Yes, it was a willing sacrifice by Jesus, because he wanted to show people "you can kill my body but not my soul". So, he chose not to resist arrest or being beaten or even the crucifixion.

The emphasis on Christ as our "Saviour" is predominantly a church focus. The Gospels were written when people were desperate to be saved – the Temple being destroyed and so on – and so people were asking "who can save us now?" People thought of Jesus and the great things he had taught in an "after-response" to this need. Remember, Jesus did not create Christianity as a religion: it was done by people after his death, even by Constantine making it an "exclusive" religion 300 years later.

I am beginning in some ways to wonder how and why, then, Jesus is important to Bob. And he reminds me:

It is because of his message of love. The Eucharist is a moment to savour this love of Jesus. But Bob does not care who gives it to him. It does not need a priest to make it holy. It is an invitation to remember God's love for us, through Jesus' demonstration of his own unconditional perfect love.

When we talk about gender issues in the church, Bob tells me of his own poem, sourced from Aramaic (the language of Jesus' people of Galilee) and then translated into English, as the Lord's Prayer. Interestingly, he tells me that the poem comes "originally" from Neil Douglas-Klotz in his book *Prayers of the Cosmos*.[3] The thing to understand and learn is that Aramaic words and phrases often had *several choices* of meanings. From one of the earliest versions of the Gospels, which is an Aramaic manuscript, the words of the Lord's Prayer can therefore be interpreted/translated with several possible meanings per line. As we have moved through many languages and translated this prayer into and between them, the biblical scholars have repeatedly chosen which meanings to lay down as "correct". But Bob has taken the several options which Douglas-Klotz offered for each *possible* line translation from the Aramaic into English, then created the Prayer for himself, in the way which best resonates with his own understanding of what Jesus was praying.

In Bob's translation version, therefore, the first line reads "Creator God, your name is One, the Universe." How different this is to "Our Father, who art in heaven". Bob invites us in this poem to ask ourselves if this translation feels more inclusive – by including *everything* – than the prayer we are used to reciting. The implications of all biblical (mis)translations, from Jesus' original words in Aramaic, into other languages via Greek/Latin/English, over many centuries and cultures, could be huge.

Aramaic is a language hardly used in the Bible. One example of an Aramaic word is "maranatha" – which Bob later tells me is in 1 Corinthians 16:22 and means "Come Lord" or "The Lord is here". The spoken word of Jesus was probably passed on orally, but the written words about him, several decades later, were passed on and translated into the languages fitting with other cultures – and agendas – over time. Cultures which were, and are, like our own, androcentric. Patriarchal. How easy it was for the culture of these languages to affect what we read today. And what we believe. I ask him whether Jesus' own culture was not also patriarchal? Probably, he replies, but this was the culture Jesus lived in as his "ego-self".

This Aramaic/English version of the Lord's Prayer was a wonderful gift from Bob. It is included at the end of this book, for you to enjoy.

And the Resurrection?

To Bob, the Resurrection of Jesus is not to be taken literally but symbolically. Without being physical, it still meant a lot in the wondrous experience of those who felt him spiritually, alive in spirit, after he died. And still now, as he is still with us. It is a spiritual awareness of his presence.

This is how Bob understands why, when he met disciples on the road to Emmaus, and indeed when he met Mary Magdalene in the garden where his tomb lay open, they recognized Jesus not physically as a person, but spiritually, when he spoke from his soul to them. This great Resurrection, or as it is "never dying", of the soul of Jesus, the love of God, was not just then but is *now*, continuously happening. The realization that Jesus is alive is an event happening all the time, because it is in the soul, and the soul is timeless.

"What dies?" This teaches us. Only the body and the ego-mind. The soul never dies. Jesus was not his body but his soul, his love. Inside we are all eternal beings, Jesus and all of us. This was the teaching of the Resurrection.

How do you understand the "second coming"?

This is a revelation which we all have when we die. The "veil" is drawn back, and we see God "face to face", as Paul said. The second coming is our own dying, not the return of Jesus to this earth. It is a symbolic event, again, of knowing our Oneness with God, without any earthly attachments.

The "devil" is purely a religious construct. Totally human-made. The popular idea of the devil fits with the laws and culture of the time. He/it is the one who "breaks all the rules". For Bob it is definitely not a "being", as there are no evil forces. It is a construct to keep people in place and society in order, to maintain state/church power and control.

Yes, many of us humans are "deranged" in having unhealthy minds, but this problem is a human-made phenomenon. Evil, the devil, are not made by, or even recognized by, God.

But what about when Jesus himself talked about judgment and hell?

Yes, Jesus may have talked about these things, but this shows his humanness, in the context of the culture of his time, not his divine insight. However, the church has projected these human teachings as being divine teachings, which is wrong. Jesus was an enlightened teacher, but he was also human.

And what about prayer, Bob?

Bob says his favourite form of prayer is silence. He tells me that many churches do not like too much silence in a service. They may say "it gives the devil a chance to come in". It is like a deep fear of silence, prevalent except among groups like the Quakers, and very different from Eastern religions.

But to the ancient mystics, silence was the language of God. To pray silently is to be in God's presence, to accept what is here, now, and *trust* that what will be is in accordance with who God is. To trust that God is Love. When we pray "please get my wife better..." etc, we are treating God in a mistaken way, as if God is a human being.

But no, God is *in* the death, the wars, diseases, suffering, as the love that God is, within these things. (This takes me a moment to take in, but I do hear what he says.)

Prayer can be a humbling. If we call upon God to help with things, this is a human, understandable habit. Bob says, "I do this!" If we feel helpless with a problem, we appeal to God our creator. "But," he continues, "I know deep down that this appeal is not needed, if I trust in God."

He tells me that Paul said, we do not know how to pray, but the Holy Spirit "intercedes for us in groans that words cannot express". In other words, God does the praying. We just need to keep quiet and "be open" to God's love. It is why mystics recognize meditation as "pure prayer". We could stop asking for things, because God of course knows what we want, before we ask for it. But we are human, so we keep asking!

People ask, "Why does God let this bad thing happen?" But this is understanding God in a human sense, with a human image of God, which is just not true. It is we that are created in God's image, as the spirit of love, within our souls. This love of God is in all situations, even disasters, which is a hard truth for us to fully understand.

Some troubles such as wars we humans create. Others are a part of nature. **I say to him that I do not understand the hope and belief people have that in some great future time "sheep will lie down with wolves"... surely God made sheep and wolves just as God wanted them to be, right now?**

Bob tells me this lesson is symbolic, and means that as spiritual, not physical beings, we will all one day "lie together" because we are all One. This is how we are when we die. We all go back to the Oneness.

This idea still shakes me – the total loss of my hard-working individual self-hood. No benefits to be "earned"... this acceptance of a "non-ego-oneness" is going to take time for me to grasp. It goes perhaps to the very roots of our "tribal" human desire for a "them" and "us", a competitive "fail" and "succeed" structure to life. This is shamefully worrying me: do I not simply want the bliss of heaven, do I actually want it to just be for "us" (if I make it) more deserving ones, which means of course that "them", the less deserving, are in a less blissful, even unpleasant place? Do we humans often desire not only to be rewarded for being "good", but also (sub-consciously) for some less fortunate others to have it tough? Just to make our own reward somehow "mean" more, to our fragile egos?

The very fact that someone "does well" with God, has to mean, within its own structure as a concept, that someone else "does worse". The bliss of heaven requiring as a comparison state the horridness of hell – but does it have to be that way? If we all fare brilliantly, and God loves us all equally when we die, does this somehow, to the insecure human ego, create less of a sense of "success" for some of us? Or can we rise above such primitive human hopes, to welcoming a higher state for all of us? I have a lot to think about and question in myself from this interview!

The Holy Spirit is to Bob just another word for God, but he prefers always the word Love. We cannot say what God truly is, only what God is not. (Bob explains to me at a later meeting that this is an "apophatic" way of describing God, as in by what God *is not*, rather than a "cataphatic" way, which is trying to actually define what God *is*. A new and interesting concept!) However, "God is Love" is the closest we humans can get. The Trinity is simply a concept made up by the church, but you can use this term if it works for you! The name "Creator" is better than the word "Father" or even "Mother", because it avoids humanizing God. It is much more inclusive.

And the future?

We are all human, not fully loving all the time. Sometimes we, and the Bible, just don't "get there". Bob tells me of a time he heard a preacher talking about Jesus throwing over the tables of the moneylenders at the Temple. She said he was acting out of "compassion". But Bob says no, of course not! Jesus was violently angry. Because as a human he did get angry. We should be more honest. Not try to make Jesus and the Bible what they are not or refuse them to be what they are. This denies their truth.

All religions probably come down to one – worshipping our creator. With the help of Jesus or the Buddha or Mohammed… they all lead us to one place. And the future for Christianity is to accept other religions, accept that other people may find a different path to God.

And Christianity needs to accept our human nature more. It needs to lose the hierarchical power structure, which includes losing such reliance on not just priests and bishops and the Pope but even Jesus himself. That is, in terms of the Christian institution teaching that the only way to God is through Jesus, which is just not true. It is *a* way, it is the way Bob has chosen, but it is not *the* way.

He goes on to confirm that he accepts and follows the teachings of Jesus of Nazareth, but does not adhere to the idea of Jesus Christ, which he believes is purely a church construct, putting words into Jesus' mouth, and "miracles" into his life-story, for centuries now. Aspects of his story are now not taken for their original meaning.

For example, the story of the "virgin birth". This was a popular story image around the time of Jesus. For example, the emperor Augustus Caesar was held by the Romans to be a great leader. So, they gave him a "virgin birth", the status of which meant "born of god", as he was seen to be so great the people needed to elevate him above humanity. In the same way that Jesus was said to have a "virgin birth", the Romans also held this story of their brilliant emperor to be "true", but in a sense which we struggle to grasp now. The word "true" can mean so many different things to people over time and across cultures and ways of communicating.

Bob follows with love the teachings of Jesus of Nazareth, some of which may have originated elsewhere, such as the teaching "do unto others as you would have them do unto you",[4] which comes from the Old Testament. Some of "his" teachings may have been handed down sayings or proverbs, but no matter, they are great teachings and Bob follows them from his heart. But the idea of Christ, the focus of the Christian religion by the church which has created it, is one he contends with, because it teaches *conditional*, instead of unconditional, love. It teaches "if you are good, then you will be saved... if you believe this... if you feel that..." which is in discord with all Bob's awareness of God. There are too many "ifs"!

He does not believe Jesus of Nazareth actually said such conditional things, but they have been put in the Bible, by the church, by an institution wanting to retain power. Jesus said God's love was unconditional, and that is all we need to know. We cannot be certain what Jesus specifically said, but his whole message and life stands for this one lesson, which is central to Bob's faith.

There is a Buddhist saying, he tells me, which is "the finger pointing to the moon is not the moon". So, Jesus pointed a wise finger for us, to God. But he was not God. When Jesus said, "I am the way, the truth, and the life"[5] he meant "follow me, my ways, for I am pointing you to God, I am the finger pointing to the moon".

Moreover, he meant, if you follow my ways, you will have eternal life which you *already constantly* have, but I will help reveal it to you, in this lifetime, here and now – that which deep down you already know.

Jesus was a great teacher. But was Jesus God? Bob believes he was only ("only" is the wrong word here, it being such a great thing) God in the way we are *all* God. You and I, in our true being, are God. There is nothing else we are. We are God's children. Jesus was trying to help us see that.

It is ultimately a circle. Our end is our beginning and our beginning our end. A circle of One Love.

Perhaps this final stanza from one of Bob's poems "Identity and Images" puts it best when it comes to who we each and all are:

To see me through your own eyes
You will see but a reflection
Of your own love,
Made in my image.[6]

Inclusion and heaven

As I finish typing up the first draft of this powerful interview, I realize slowly that what has shaken me is not actually the idea we all go to heaven, no matter how much we may "deserve" it. It goes deeper, into the core of all identity. Identity which places the division not just between "them" and "us" – affording the individual person potential membership of a secure group of the "rewarded", which has a definite boundary – but also between "you" and "me".

What I begin to see is that my greatest fear may be of losing my "self" completely. Of becoming part of a great "Oneness", which could be bliss, but… when I consider losing the individual "me" who has strived so hard not only to develop as a person but even just to stay alive, I see how challenging this concept truly is.

What if the ego of the self does not like the idea of being gone? I begin to understand how much of our life is to do with defining and securing our identity because without it, do we all disappear, dissolved into an eternal "mixture"? Or… are we crucially something very different from this, and free?

All this now presents the chance to consider the following great question for the soul: could such universal Oneness in love bring us not a sense of being "lost" without self-identity, but be a heavenly "homecoming", after all…?

So, I choose to take an interlude from my interviews and go on a bit of an adventure with this challenge, to see where it takes me.

I am, at the time of writing, staying as a guest at my old college, St John's, in Oxford. I meet there another graduate, David, who tells me about the Oxford mathematician, Sir Roger Penrose. In 1974 Penrose designed something which is described as "a pattern of beauty and intrigue" which "confronts you". I decide to go and see an example of this. It is a work of art and mathematical design, displayed on the ground outside the main entrance of the new Mathematics Institute building, which was once the Radcliffe Infirmary. I know the Radcliffe well as it was the place where I had life-saving surgery for a brain-tumour, back in 1992–93. As I approach the entrance area, my memory recalls the dread fear I began to have back then of death. In a poem, I wrote "this mortal smack has shaken every perspective."[7]

I go to stand on the "Penrose Pavings" – this "non-periodic" design consists of diamond shapes and circular arcs in a non-repeating pattern of exact copies, shown here in flat stone, which could potentially go on into infinity. I stare down at the "infinity" before and all around me. Is this how it would feel? I try to "lose" myself in the eternal (while not looking too odd to students coming out from lectures), and it feels not at all uncomfortable... a tiny sense of freedom is lurking!

Then (after a wonderful experience of peace sitting quietly in St Aloysius Chapel, nearby), I return to my room and listen to a recital just sent to me online by David, of Sir John Betjeman reading his poem "Before the Anaesthetic, or A Real Fright" which is (ironically?) about his time before an operation in the same Radcliffe Infirmary. There are some lines in the poem which reflect upon the repetitively chiming bells of St Giles Church nearby, and his own fear of death... "Oh better far those echoing hells / Half-threaten'd in the pealing bells / Than that this 'I' should cease to be...".[8]

I know that fear. The night before my second brain tumour operation in this hospital, I panicked so much about possibly losing my life – my "I" – that I literally could not stop shaking.

That evening (it is a busy day) I go to a lecture at Regent's Park College, run by the Centre for Religion & Culture. The lecture is on "Inclusion"(!). Afterwards I walk along with a lady and tell her of Bob's interview, the challenges it has put to me with the idea that we all in our soul essence return to God in heaven. That we are all of us now "in God", and become One again when we die, with no differentiation between "good" and "bad" or "them" and "us" or even "you" and "me" as separate egos, or even separate souls.

She replies that no, she doesn't like such an idea of "giving up my personhood". And I go to my room to cook dinner. The idea of the "person", of some sort of individual differentiation... what if we know deep down, our ego knows, that we ourselves are not a "person", as in a separate soul, but a part of One universal loving soul? And what if our fear, as our core fear inside us, is a deep knowing that ultimately, when we die, we do lose all our "separateness" as person, even as soul, and become One, in God? Perhaps this is the truth which our ego knows and so terribly fears, because it senses that one day itself, and our individuality, will be gone from us?

If this is true (and I know not!), then it would go a long way to explain our desperate need while alive to forge a clear, secure "identity" with definite boundaries around ourselves. It would explain why we fight and strive continuously to have a social structure based on "them" and "us" even to the extent of needing to believe that only some of us go to heaven. Because this (falsely?) reassures us that boundaries, those precious things which our egos cannot live without, are real.

But if they are not? Is our deepest fear that when we die, we will lose all our precious singularity? I think this is for sure a deep fear within me. To be a soul in heaven (or hell) would be strange unknown, if it meant not being the created identity which I call "me". And that is the crux – to be a soul is an unknown dimension to us! For sure a lot of Christians do strive to assure that a soul is still a "person", with a boundary around him or herself, but what if...?

Perhaps we strive in our Christianity (and other religions) to satisfy more than our longing to be connected to God's love. Does our ego, in its dread of being lost, strive to protect us from its own fear that when we die, it goes? And most of all, is this the fear that, when we see it for its lack of truth, even its foolishness, we can let go of and become free – not lost but free?

All worth pondering. The concept that as a soul we truly, in this case literally, are "One" in and with God. As Love. This possible truth is something that shakes me and also very much whispers of bliss.

Furthermore...

Furthermore, I realize as I am having my next-morning cuppa, is this the greatest inkling we can have that there really is a "More" after/beyond this life? If we simply die and are gone, then our ego only needs to make the best of being here on earth while it can. But our core craving for an "identity", which requires not one but often multiple "them" and "us" or "me" and "you" boundaries to be created around ourselves, is a powerful indication that our ego, or something sub-conscious within us, knows that we truly belong to a "we", which it selfishly – but naturally – resists.

It knows this, and fears it, because we are born as human individuals, with separate egos and flesh. But perhaps the greatest challenge, the greatest opportunity we have in this life, is to realize our Oneness, our "we" belonging, even while living in separate bodies? So, we can be free to love one another as each being a part of the One, the God, to which we all belong. To be individual but not. To be "in the world" as a separate person, but "not of it" because we realize that essentially, we are a "we", a Love which is without any boundaries, physical or spiritual. And without boundaries of time?

This possible truth is a great one. It means that deep inside us we know that there is an eternal life (which I like the sound of), a "more than this" which is God. All we need to do is allow our self-protecting head to let go of the fear that in this very eternity, we lose our "me-ness", to become an "us".

*

I get a real experience of this in a hard and immediate way now when I go outside college to do some shopping. There is a young man begging as he sits outside the college wall. His face is gaunt. I feel, as a part of that to which I know I belong, as a part of God, this man's pain is also somehow mine. I don't feel it very powerfully – the selfish "me" cannot suddenly feel enough compassion to be put into great turmoil – but I get a distressing taste of it. That while he is in pain, I am in pain, in God. Instead of giving him money, I go buy him a coffee, as a small attempt to help him, and we both say, "God bless". But as I walk away, with my own identity boundaries a little shaken up, I begin to sense that such connection is not a "danger" to my own inner peace as a separate soul. Perhaps keeping ourselves tightly protected as individual beings with clear boundaries to ourselves, is not how God intends us to be, or how Jesus showed us the way to be?

When this book is about to be completed, I talk with my friend Nicki, an Anglican vicar in West Cumbria, about this lesson of connection – how the traditional advice to "protect your own boundaries" may not be the only way to live well. She tells me one of her favourite stories in the Gospels (in Mark 5:25–34), of Jesus feeling energy go out from him when a woman who has been haemorrhaging blood for many years touches his cloak, without him seeing her, and is healed. How Jesus was so open to the needs of other souls, so unfixed in his own boundaries, that he was able to do this. Such connection is a teaching for how we all could begin to live. It questions our ideas about "self-protection" and asks us to become aware of our common belonging.

CHAPTER THREE

Carol

Carol attends a Hebron Evangelical church. She also runs a local Christian writers' group for people of all denominations, and is a volunteer visitor on three wards at her local infirmary, where she talks and listens to people and prays with them.

She believes in God as a "Tri" divinity – Father, Son, and Holy Spirit, who sent the Son to redeem us. He is a God of love but also very much of justice. Her relationship with God is a deeply personal one.

Yes, Carol sees that there is symbolism in the Bible, but still she believes every word of it to be true. As she says, "You cannot pick and choose!" The Bible was guided by God as it was being written, and of course God is strong enough to be sure that what *He* wants to be there, is in the Bible.

She is confident that events recorded in both Old and New Testaments actually in reality happened – for example the great flood and Noah's ark, God making rainbows as a future promise to humankind, the story of Adam and Eve. "Why," she asks, "would this not be possible for God?" If it is not true, then why would it be in the Bible? It is only that our own limited minds cannot fully understand these miracles.

What about the "seven days" of creation?
Carols says that this can be taken to mean the "seven stages". When I respond that this story is therefore being taken symbolically, not literally, Carol agrees. At several points during our meeting, when I suggest that an interpretation/understanding she has of the Bible is not actually literal, she agrees, and says that my questions are perhaps helping her question and come to understand her own faith a little more.

For example, we now talk about Eve listening to the devil in the Garden of Eden. She believes here that the devil is/was not literally a serpent, as

51

in not all snakes are evil. The meaning of this story is that Eve disobeyed God because of giving in to temptations from the devil. The main impact of Carol's faith is that she has no difficulty in believing that God *could* create Eve from Adam's rib, or any of the miracles in the Bible – such as the parting of the Red Sea for Moses and the Jewish people during their exodus from Egypt – because this is totally possible. It is just that we fail to comprehend how.

Carol's faith places a big emphasis on sin. Because we do sin! We are, since Adam and Eve made their wicked choice, wicked ourselves. As God is all-knowing, he knew this would happen, knew the devil would come to try and claim us, but God wants us back! Hence, we are a struggling mix of good and bad. The New Testament says, "the good that I would I do not".[1]

Humans are not, however, originally wicked. We have no "original sin" because God made us. We became wicked through making our choice to disobey God, in the Garden of Eden. Hence, life is hard, we are pulled in two directions all our lives, until we die. So, there is a huge need for us to fear God's wrath, because of the great struggle going on within us all.

"Heaven is where God is. Hell is where God is not," Carol says. It is impossible for us to imagine this, in time and space. But heaven is a place for those who accept that Jesus died for our sins. We do not go to heaven for doing good deeds. If you believe in Jesus' message, even on your death bed, then you can go to heaven. For example, the thief who was on the cross beside Jesus. Jesus said to him "today you will be with me in Paradise."[2]

What we need, all of us, is to be born again. When Nicodemus asked Jesus "What must I do to inherit eternal life?", Jesus replied "You must be born again." Nicodemus was unsure if this meant being born from his mother's womb again, but Jesus said, "no, be born again *in spirit*".[3]

What we need to do is *believe*. That very believing will make you want to be a good person. But be clear, being good is a result, it is not a cause and will not be the key for you to "get into heaven". So, we need not hide behind good works! We believe, therefore we want to be good people, to love others more. But Jesus himself told us we need to believe in him as our Saviour if we want to go to heaven.

Yes, God is our judge. And there will be a day of judgment. God will then see perfection in Christians because, no matter what they have done wickedly in their lives, their sins have been paid for by Jesus' blood. Jesus needed to be punished by God, and suffer, because all wrongs need justice. The Bible says Jesus came to earth to "die for our sins", and Carol believes this was even more his purpose than his other one, which was to teach us about love. Justice, Carol says, is crucial to life.

Heaven needs to be a perfect place, so to be there we need to be cleansed of our sins. Hence, we need to believe that Jesus Christ took *our place* and died for our sins.

Why would the Father do this to his Son?, I ask.

Because, Carol says, he loves us so much.

Sin, punishment, and justice are not human constructs. They are in the Bible as God's idea, not ours. If there is love, there must be non-love, which is sin. But if we are born again, then God will tell us how to live lovingly. Carol says how she cares for people in the hospital *because* of her faith. God's love for us helps us feel real love for him, and for others.

Be clear, Jesus *had* to die on the cross as the sacrifice for our sins. It was an important part of God's justice which needed to be carried out. Because sin has consequence. Jesus' dying meant that God would no longer see Christians as sinners, on Judgment Day. As Jesus was punished *for* us, there is no need for God to punish twice.

But who does go to heaven, and who to hell?

Carol is clear in saying "Who am I to judge?" It is not for her to say. All we must do is look to ourselves. We can think who could go to heaven, but never claim surety on this, God's decision. We need to "let it be". However, she adds, Jesus did say we must be born again to go to heaven... it must be true. "I believe what I read in the Bible!" she reminds me.

The Bible is God's Word. Literally. He can and did make sure of this, and woe unto anyone who tries to alter God's words.

> *I tell Carol here that I do respect her belief that whatever God wants to do, of course God can. But what God wants, what God's actual intention is – for example did God intend to literally put Noah and his paired animals into an ark – that is the understanding we many of us differ upon. We seem to both be nervously enjoying this! But I now keep silent and continue to listen...*

Carol now talks about God being neither male nor female, as there is no such thing in heaven. Our culture is patriarchal, hence calling God a "He" is a human construct. But she does not truly see God like this. God is much bigger than such ideas.

And yes of course the Resurrection did happen. Then, when Jesus Christ rose to heaven, the Holy Spirit came to his disciples so that scared, weak people could then become strong, brave workers for Jesus.

One day there will be a "second coming", as Jesus said, when life as we know it will cease, and the physical shall end. Then there will be the day of judgment when we will all be before God and judged to be his or not. We shall all be asked, "What think you of Jesus?" and, as she said before, it will not matter how much good we have or have not done before this day.

This will also be a time of great suffering, so we shall all want to be dead rather than alive. And what will truly matter will be if we see Jesus as our Redeemer.

What about those who have not even heard of Jesus?

Carol says God will sort this out; it's not up to her. All we do know is that we need to spread the word! And we need to teach that God is love but then move on to teach that judgment happens.

Because of her strong belief in the devil, Carol continues to stress the need to fear punishment for sin. Not to shy away from this truth. When I suggest that I am not sure the devil even exists, she tells me that he will delight in hearing it, because he loves to hear when people do not believe in him, as this makes them vulnerable to his powers. (This does make me feel a little anxious!)

What is the devil?

A force that God has allowed to be. "Why this is," Carol says, "is beyond me." But the devil knows he will ultimately be defeated, so is trying hard to convert us while he can! He comes from a group of angels in the Bible who wanted to be all-powerful, and so were thrown out of heaven. So, Lucifer was originally created by God, and then expelled.

Yet God said, "I am a jealous God." And "you will have no other gods but me."[4] He did not want any imposter to have power.

> *I struggle with the idea that there can even be any other gods to be jealous of, and ask is "jealous" not just a human emotion?*

Carol reaffirms that what is in the Bible is the Truth. I respect her faith, and we move on. She tells me again that we do not *fear* God enough these days. The Bible is not simply a book "inspired" by God. Remember, it is God's literal Word. There can be no "half measures" on what we believe from it.

And prayer?

Carol tells me we are asking for things too often. Yes, it is fine to make requests to God, but there is also much need for thanksgiving and praise. God wants us to talk to him as our "best friend". It is a personal relationship for us to develop between ourselves and God, and this is very important to Carol. God alone is the decider but asking "please God…" is an understandable way for us to communicate with him and hold people in his love.

Carol believes that more people now are conscious of God. But we need to think about him more. Christianity will never die out, because it is ultimately controlled by God. It is growing in some ways, shrinking in others. Some people in all churches, including hers, the evangelicals, are blinkered, and our churches suffer. In parts of the world such as China, Christianity is indeed flourishing. In others, such as Africa, much mission work is needed.

Carol repeats her belief that hers is a "jealous God", who does not want to share his power with others such as Allah.

I again question how there can possibly be a rival to our one God of all?

Still Carol holds to her belief that the Bible says our God is jealous of a "rival" god, rather than another "interpretation" of God. And I again remind myself to openly respect her belief.

"Any faith without Jesus I am not happy about," she says. And I listen.

In an interesting and inspiring image, she asks me to think of us all "pulling ourselves up to God by our shoelaces". In fact, she invites me to try this very act (and I do), of pulling myself up in this way! We are so often all too weak, too vain, too full of pride, thinking "I am good, I am kind in God's eyes". But we do need Jesus! And we also need not to think too much of how bad we are, but how good God is. That is the way.

After we part, I go over my time spent with Carol, my notes and scribbles, and see more clearly my own need to simply listen. I have learned so much from someone with quite a different way of relating to God and Jesus from my own. I have particularly enjoyed her reminder that, of course, God can do anything. There is much inspiration as well as plenty of challenges in her words.

But, surprisingly, it was during my interview with Bob, whose beliefs are much closer to my own, that I felt more stirred up! All of this is teaching me an increasingly crucial lesson: if we are to learn anything from "others" – either from within our own spiritual "mindset", from within Christianity, or from other world religions, we need to make a conscious effort to be open to the new, not narrowly pre-certain and self-righteous. This is what feels to be our big human challenge. To "only connect", as the great E. M. Forster put it so aptly.[5]

Chapter Four

John

John and I first met as students. He was at "Plater" (the Catholic Workers' College) at Oxford, which is now closed. He is now a teacher of religious education in a school near Glasgow. John is married to Margaret and has a son called Sean. When we meet, he is about to take forty-four students on a pilgrimage to Poland "in the footsteps of St John Paul II", where they plan to visit Auschwitz to lay a wreath and pray for God to encourage people to stop being racist and violent.

John intends to use the "Ravensbruck Prayer", which was a Jewish woman's prayer to God to help her forgive those who had murdered her family and race. This he hopes will help the students reflect on their own faith, and the conflict in our modern world.

He also wants the students to connect to the example of St Maximilian Kolbe, who mirrored himself on Jesus and gave his own life so that another in Auschwitz concentration camp would survive.

John is a very good-humoured person, and I reflect on how this will help the children still enjoy their trip, while taking in such difficult world history. He takes children on these pilgrimages regularly, and when he was growing up, he used to help his family and others in taking disabled children to Lourdes, to pray for healing.

Today we meet at a Jesuit presbytery called the Ignatian Spirituality Centre in Glasgow. It is a study centre where Gerard Manley Hopkins (1844–89), a great poet and spiritual thinker, lived and worked for a while – the same Hopkins who was priest for a time at the Oxford Oratory, the Chapel of St Aloysius Gonzaga, where in Oxford I found such peace.

So, what is God, to John?

God is our loving Father and creator, giving us all unique souls and identities, so that we each have a vocation in this life, which we need to discern. And we need to help build the kingdom of God now, in this world.

John has grown up immersed in the Roman Catholic Church, and he laughs about how he was born prematurely, requiring an emergency baptism by a nurse. He jokes, "That's why I grew up so full of faith!" The church rituals and sacraments are very important to John's life as a Christian, and he believes that God reveals himself through the church, the sacraments, and through the inspiring people John meets within the church family. "Through them I experience Jesus, I experience God," he tells me.

"I have a sacramental faith," he continues, "held in common with others in my tradition, and trusting God to intervene, to send graces to help with life's joys and sorrows, to help bring about the kingdom of God." By "sacramental" John means not only the rituals of baptism, confirmation, and penance but also very much the ritual of the Eucharist.

(It may be helpful to note that the Oxford Dictionary defines "sacrament" as "a ceremony regarded as imparting spiritual grace". There are seven of these ritual ceremonies for Catholic and Orthodox Christians, including the four mentioned above plus "anointing of the sick, ordination and matrimony". The "Holy Sacrament" is the consecrated bread and wine of the Eucharist. The definition goes on to say that a sacrament can be "a thing of mysterious and sacred significance; a religious symbol". It comes originally from the Greek word *musterion*, meaning "mystery".)

Jesus was/is the Messiah, says John. I ask if he believes in the virgin birth and yes he does, because, as he often tells me during our interview, that is the "mystery of faith". Such a mystery he trusts in, and truly believes.

Jesus is the "incarnate Word of God". He knew his purpose on earth, to be God revealed as Man. To teach compassion and mercy. He tells me of the Bible words where Jesus says, in the Gospel of John, "I am the way, and the truth, and the life. No one comes to the Father except through me".[1]

When I wonder during our interview if Bible teachings are at times just being "quoted" (here John 14:6), he tells me –

Yes, *but* he is not "just" quoting the Bible, he *believes* the Bible. That makes the difference. Jesus knew he was the Messiah. He said, in the Garden of Gethsemane, about his suffering "Father, if you are willing, remove this cup from me".[2] He knew he had to suffer for us. He also knew he was a man. Both fully human and fully divine. When Jesus got angry in the Temple, this was not a sin, John says, because anger itself is not a sin. It was a justifiable reaction to the wrongs being done there.

Was he a social and political rebel?

John agrees that Jesus sought social justice, yes, but he says that liberation theology is not like Marxism, or political ideologies. Jesus' focus was in teaching us to overcome sin, in a spiritual and religious sense. He connected to the marginalized in his society because he was responding against sin in his land at that time.

As with so many people I interview, the actual dating in time of the writing of the Old Testament of the Bible, and who it was written by, is not crucially important to John. For John, the Bible was written by "people of faith".

When?

Perhaps "thousands of years ago". By gifted writers inspired by God. These are sacred Scriptures, whereby God speaks to us through the literature, but, unlike Islam and the Qur'an, they are not purely literal recitations. They are a way of God showing his relationship with his people. How God built this relationship, through Israelites and then Christians, and all this is illuminated in the Bible.

Parts of the Bible have different genres – historical story, law, a writer's personal relationship to God, and so on, but the only way any book in the Bible can be interpreted, is by faith. The Bible could be regarded as "an anthropology of life". It is God's relationship with his people, which is a mystery understood by faith, and as we grow in our faith, we understand more.

An important part of John's Catholic faith is that the books of the Scriptures are *without error*. They teach us the Truth, inspired by the Holy Spirit, and God is their true author. We draw our strength of life and faith through the sacred Scriptures and the sacraments. You cannot separate these two things.

(I try to understand how God can be the *author* of the Bible when also the Bible is to be seen as being *inspired* by God, with human interpretations of events and stories being written down by people in the context of their time. But I cannot.)

John tells me again this is a question of faith – faith in the mystery. Whatever the genre or the language used, the Bible is there to teach us, and we need to discern and interpret what it is teaching – how we can cope with life and interpret our own society, to then live our lives through it.

John points out that we are sitting in a huge Jesuit library, literally full of words! In one room are millions of words, all of which, like the Bible, people can interpret differently. We are all on individual pilgrimages, just like the people of the Old and New Testaments, and we all have the chance to learn from the teachings of the Bible. The different genres help us understand the *nature* of God, through historical events and more. But the Bible always holds the Truth. It is we who might make mistakes in how we interpret it.

For the New Testament, as with the Old, it is what we are being *taught* that matters more than who wrote it, when, and why. Each Gospel is unique, with its own interpretation of events. But by varying in their details, the Gospels give us a wider view of who Jesus was as God and man. They are not meant to be a "biography". They are more about who he was, the Messiah, in teachings often handed down orally, by perhaps illiterate people, before they could be written down by scribes.

And symbolism in the Bible?

John now tells me what he believes and emphasizes that this is his *personal* belief. He is cautious not ever to disagree with or make assumptions about Catholic Church teachings…

He says that yes, symbolism does matter in the Bible. Jesus was, after all, the "light of the world"[3]! And of course, books like Genesis contain a human understanding of creation. It is an analogy, *but* it is still the Word of God. And the nativity story? John tells me that the Gospels offer him an interpretation of his faith, and that he, in his intellectual capacity to do so, believes this nativity story to be, yes, absolutely literally true. By believing this, it then *allows* him to be able to see Jesus as the Son of God and of man, as a divine human.

The Old Testament prophesized this birth of the Messiah. And it is easier for him to grasp the New Testament if he can have faith in these miracles being true. Which he does. The teachings of the miracles allow John to *envisage* God, in Christ.

"It is through the miraculous nature of Jesus' life," says John, "that I find it easier to envisage God. These intertwined miracles and events help me do that. Through believing in sacred Scripture, and through prayer and through grace, I can see Jesus, and so see who God is."

Bearing in mind our human nature, which limits any full interpretation of God, the miracles do help him to believe and understand the teachings of the Scriptures, but it is *faith* which is central to all this for John. It is the gift which enables us to illumine the Scriptures. It is the key.

The church teaches without error. This is the reality of John's Catholic faith. (I note to myself that this interview is teaching me some differences between my Protestant upbringing, and the very "respectful to authority of church" way John has been brought up, in his Catholicism.) To him the church is the "magisterium", a body of authority succeeding from St Peter. He was the first apostle to whom Jesus gave authority to spread his teachings. The Catholic Church therefore hands on this "deposit of the faith" and has "a grave responsibility to do so". But it is our individual human pilgrimage to interpret those teachings and live out our own life of faith. We will each be judged individually for how we live, and what we believe, John tells me.

And the matter of sin?

The Old Testament illuminates that we as humans often sin and turn away from God, through greed and error. Through Exodus and the Ten Commandments we can see the will of God in a "rule book" – how we should live a life of obligation and responsibility to the Lord. This then allows us to have a more fulfilled life.

Yes, humans are naturally sinful. We are born with original sin. Only baptism can bring us into a new relationship with God, because the sacraments help us to have hope, grace, and salvation.

But what do you really mean by "sinful"?

Sin is in human nature, not God's nature. It is destructive and negative. John tells me he is confined here by the limits of human language, but certainly sin causes emotional, physical, and spiritual human suffering. There is both personal and structural sin in society. For example, the ideologies of materialism and communism, Nazism – they all move us away from God with erroneous human ideologies.

Such ideologies can attract us because we are greedy. Materialism can encourage us to want more, to be tempted to sin. In our short lives, in our haste to "have it all", we all make both good and bad decisions.

And heaven?

Heaven is an eternal place, but yes, a place. God is present there as absolute Love. There is no negative capacity in heaven. No pain, no suffering of any kind. As well as a place, heaven is a spiritual reality, which human language again limits our ability to describe or understand. We prefer to call it a "place" rather than an "entity", but it is both.

I say, we could choose to call it only an entity, a state of being, could we not?

John confirms that for him, as in the Bible, Jesus calls the kingdom of God *both* a place and a state of peace, joy, and requited love, with saints and angels all at peace, and where God is fully praised.

John believes he will be reunited with loved ones when he dies, and he will experience a communion of saints. He will see God as God really is, in God's absolute nature. "My end goal in life," says John, "is honestly to get to heaven. My pilgrimage here on earth, is to get there."

I ask if God's kingdom is not meant to be here, now?

John says on earth we can get only a glimpse of it. Jesus asks us to build this kingdom on earth now, urgently, but we battle and struggle to do this because of our human nature holding us back. It is not possible to create God's kingdom ourselves fully on earth. Only through Jesus and only in heaven is it fully possible.

We can glimpse it when we believe and worship and fulfil God's will, but Jesus did talk about Judgment Day, and about heaven being somewhere else. He told the good thief "you will be with me in my Father's mansions"[4], thus this must be a place, and it must be somewhere we can hope to go, when we die.

"The only way to heaven is through Jesus Christ. As Catholics we do believe this," John confirms. And yes, for sure hell is a reality. It is an absolute separation from God.

Who goes there? I ask.

People who have deliberately and consciously chosen to go against the nature and will of God. Those who are in a state of mortal sin – that is, those who, in full knowledge, go against the Commandments

But no, we cannot interpret how God will judge us. God has divine mercy.

So how can some be sent to hell? I ask.

We do not know the will or judgment of God. But if, in our last moments of life, we ask for God's forgiveness, then God is all merciful.

This is the reason why Catholic people take the "sacraments of the sick". A priest anoints them to afford them God's mercy as they are offered the graces, and God's forgiveness. Some cannot ask for this themselves, verbally, but people who are Catholic can still be given it. It is presumed they will want forgiveness by God's loving benevolent nature, so the sacraments are given freely, out of love, as a vehicle for God's grace.

But still, who goes to hell? I persist.

John says that in his personal interpretation, people who refuse God's love and separate themselves deliberately from God through mortal sin are in severe danger of going to hell.

I later decide to ask John how he personally would define "mortal sin" and he replies...

"The concept of 'mortal sin' has always been a constant source of debate within the Catholic Church. As a cradle Catholic I am obviously aware of the Church teaching regarding the individual's conscious decision to try to avoid sin. I believe that prayer and regular attendance at Mass and receiving the sacraments gives me the opportunity to examine my conscience and accept sacramental grace to live a life more befitting of a Christian.

"Mortal sin is when a person freely and with full knowledge commits an action which is destructive and intentionally evil. Mortal sin separates us from the love of God because of our actions. I fully realize as a Catholic, however, that during the sacrament of reconciliation we are given the privilege and grace to fully acknowledge our sins and be penitent. Through faith I am fully convinced of God's loving compassion and his ocean of mercy. God, through an unconditional love, will forgive us our sins both mortal and venial if we are truly repentant. All humans are by nature open to sin and this is part of our human condition. It is only God who can provide us with the grace and fortitude to avoid sin."

I thank John for this elucidation of his beliefs about sin, mercy, and God's grace. People whom he calls "anonymous Christians", who did not/do not know of Christ, either in times past before Jesus was born, or places with no knowledge of Christ now – if these persons live with values mirroring those of the Roman Catholic Church, then John tells me that, as a Catholic, "we understand they will be at the mercy and compassion of God".

So, what of people with good lives from other faiths?, I ask.

John wants to be honest (which I do respect) that he believes the "only way to heaven is through Jesus Christ". People must live their life through Christ, and they must be baptized, in order to go to heaven. Baptism is our "vehicle to salvation".

And yet who goes to hell?

This is a "double-edged sword" he says, as how do we, as individuals, have the right to make the judgment of who specifically will go to either heaven or hell? We are not God! "I am human, and it is not my place to judge," he says.

John

(I have heard several people say this now, and it is challenging me to understand how we can say there are definitely "rules" to obey and follow in order to get into heaven, but then also say we cannot as humans judge on those rules. I decide to let it go, and trust that, again, this is a question of a person's faith. It is also an example, I think, of the limits of human language to articulate something so big, and so important.)

Indeed, John goes on to confirm this with "My faith leads me to an understanding". Yes. John believes there are rules, and that he/we cannot judge on them, but that the sacraments, Scriptures, prayer, and deep respect for the church's authority, help him to live with that mystery. To live his faith.

And purgatory? I dare to ask.

"Hard to grasp," says John, and we smile. We all have unique souls which are not in a state of grace. So, we pray for the souls in purgatory – which is the way for *most* of us into heaven – for God to purify their souls and, in his own time and through his holy will, they will yes eventually be accepted into heaven.

People who have sinned but are aware of God's grace and mercy, aware they need help and forgiveness – they go to purgatory. People who have consciously and utterly turned from God's loving mercy – they go to hell. It is possible even to commit a "mortal sin" (such as murder) and, if we still ask God for forgiveness, ask to make reparation, acknowledge and turn away from our sin, back to God, then we can still find a way, through purgatory, into heaven.

John quotes here God "desires everyone to be saved and to come to the knowledge of truth" (1 Timothy 2:4).

Very, very few of us, only the saints for example, go straight to heaven. The rest of us, as sinning mortals, go to purgatory first, for however long it takes to purify and forgive us. Souls can also be helped to be forgiven by us praying for them on earth, such as for our passed-away loved ones. They are also helped by the saints in heaven, to whom we pray that they might "intercede" for the faithfully departed.

I mention that I hear this was the root of a lot of the troubles of the Reformation, was it not? The dislike by Martin Luther and future Protestants of perhaps corrupt paying of "indulgences" to Catholic priests to help get their loved ones out of purgatory? But John and I have much more interesting current things to talk about just now, rather than troubles from the past.

John tells me it is interesting how one of my questions is about the "song" of Jesus. He likes this, because Jesus himself was very knowledgeable of the psalms, which were like "songs" of the soul.

The message of Jesus was that God is the God of Love, who has intervened in human history, given us precious unique lives to live through all the challenges and joys, until we are judged by God's holy will. We must make the conscious decision to accept God's love and mercy, but many of us walk away, or are not even aware of it.

Jesus brought us the chance of a new relationship with God through the Trinity, of Father, *Son*, and Holy Spirit, and he ultimately came to be our Saviour.

And the meaning of the crucifixion?

It was that through his bloody sacrifice he would save us as humans, make up for our sinful nature, and allow through this a new relationship with the God of love and salvation. He freely, as a divine human, chose to suffer on our behalf, and this itself is a great teaching.

The Holy Eucharist is a great sacrament. It helps us celebrate and remember the death of Jesus. It also unites us with the person of Christ. Yes, John believes that the bread and wine of the Eucharist, when consecrated by the priest, are literally the body and blood of Christ. They become so. The Eucharist actually *is* God revealed to us. It is Christ.

Of course, this makes little rational sense in "human" terms! But Jesus gives us the gift of faith and so allows us into that new reality. "Transubstantiation" is indeed the substance of wheat becoming the body, the flesh of Christ, and the wine his blood. It is a supernatural gift of grace, an energy, a zeal, which allows us to interpret our faith.

He says, "I believe in an umbrella of thought. If we limit people by language, tell them what exactly to believe, then we are limiting God. We learn through our senses, through symbolism as well as Scripture and the sacraments. God has given us imaginative and creative natures, to see, hear, and 'touch upon' him."

But why did Jesus save us by being sacrificed?

Because God gave us the gift of his precious Son. Through his death, Jesus atones for our sins, because his life and death were given freely by choice.

(I struggle again to understand why this is an "atonement", which the Oxford Dictionary defines as "reparation or expiation for sin", and expiation as "making

amends for guilt or wrongdoing". The Atonement it defines as "the reconciliation of God and mankind through Jesus Christ".)

John also struggles to define his belief in words now, saying only it is "very hard to define or limit" the atonement of Christ's sacrifice.

And yet for me, to my appreciation, he tries...

By our human nature we can be selfish or reciprocal. God gave us the eternal gift of Jesus as an absolute gift, a gift of absolute Love, so revealing his own nature. Jesus as both God and human gave his life in absolute Love for us, a sacrifice with no limits or conditions. It was for the ultimate goal of a new relationship for us, with God.

But still how does sacrifice atone?

John relents, "It is a mystery of faith for me," he says. "How does God fully reveal himself through a sacrifice? I can only tell you this is a mystery of faith, but when I tell you this, I mean it sincerely, honestly, not as a brushing off but as a real, powerful truth to me."

And I can see this is true. Faith is John's answer.

He is kind enough to try again!

Jesus, out of love, respect, and solidarity, freely gave his ultimate love to us, for us. Jesus was on the cross, with his arms outstretched, saying, "This is how much I (God) love you!" It was a symbol of love and hope. And when Jesus cried out "Father, forgive them!" his whole being was geared toward forgiveness and mercy. After the Resurrection, we understood that this was his gift of salvation to us. As the Gospel of John says, Jesus' whole reason for incarnation was his death and Resurrection, for *our* salvation. John in the room with me now stresses the word *our* here. It was for the salvation of the individual and for us as the common people of God.

Life is an individual pilgrimage, but it is also a common pilgrimage, as we have the responsibility to tell others about the good news of Christ, our Saviour.

Christ defeated death on the cross, by rising from the dead, on Easter Sunday. He was aware of the prophecies, and of his mission to die for our salvation, as a person both human and divine. This rising was the most important event in human history. John says Christ was the first to die for immortal life. He quotes for me "If Christ be not risen, then is our preaching vain, and your faith is also vain" (1 Corinthians 15:14, KJV).

Through the Eucharist sacraments, we have the chance to share in this, to encounter the rising as well as the sacrifice of Jesus – to approach understanding the deep mystery, which we can never fully appreciate within our human vision. We can begin to see that Christ humbled himself to be our Messiah.

We meet the risen Christ in our daily prayer, in the Eucharist, and in our quiet contemplation. Also, we meet him in the communal life of the church. Christ is with us in our hopes, joys, and despair.

And will Jesus return?

We are taught, as Catholics, that we are in the final age of the world. Jesus taught of the second coming where war and suffering will have no place. We do not know when this is. We are preparing the kingdom of God on earth now, as best we can, as Jesus taught, but we need to be ready for the time when the second coming, the new kingdom, fully happens. Then Christ will destroy all evil in an instant. Until that day, the Christian life needs to be one of prayer, thanksgiving, and a building of the kingdom by works of what John calls "corporal" and "spiritual" acts of mercy (I take that to be love).

But does the devil exist?

He does, and he is a fallen angel, who wants to turn us away from God toward sin. We need to be aware of Satan as a reality of temptation. It is only through the gifts of the Holy Spirit and grace that we can truly refuse to participate in a life of sin. We need God's mercy to keep us awake, so we can know our vocation and his will for us in this lifetime.

To avoid this reality of the devil and temptation we really do need to be alert and turn from sin by praying and receiving the sacraments.

Prayer, what is that?

It is our conversation with God. Our opportunity to spend time with him and realize that we are not alone in our pilgrimage on this earth. Through our singular initiative of praying alone, we may struggle to focus and be directed toward the sacred. Prayer is, by John's experience, easier and more conversant in church, with others in our community, and especially so during Mass.

It is an act of trust. Of worship which links our minds and souls to Christ and God the Father, by acknowledging them. When we realize God is present in our lives, prayer becomes both natural and a source of grace, allowing us to deal with real challenges. We can say "Jesus, I trust in you" in both the joyous and the despairing moments of our life.

The routine and structure of prayer can strengthen us and give us dignity among any difficulties – help us to not ignore or refuse to acknowledge God's presence. We can also ask God to help us overcome temptation. Jesus, the Scriptures say, often prayed – in the temple, the desert, the garden, by the lake, and when he cried at the death of his friend. So we also can pray, during every kind of occasion in our lives.

Prayer for John is a deliberate act of trust and one of praise. And devotional prayer helps us to be more aware, especially in the adoration of the sacraments such as the Eucharist. It is a blessing to be "spending time with God" in prayer.

He has visited many pilgrimage sites in his life so far where there is a real sense of prayer, both communally and in a tangible experience of walking, sharing, talking, seeing. He calls it an "extraordinary privilege" to encounter and assist people at Lourdes who are sick and asking God for strength to deal with real difficulties.

Prayer in the Catholic Church consists of petition, thanksgiving, intercession, and praise. Of giving thanks on all occasions. John believes that God listens, to both informal and formal prayers. It is also very important to him to pray to the saints to intercede on our behalf. Prayer is a "rich treasury within the mystery of the life of the church".

It can be both rewarding and challenging. The deeper our relationship becomes with God, the more we begin to accept that in our prayers we can turn to God. Just as Christ did, we can ask the God of all mercies for help, comfort, inspiration – and we can also discern his will for us, on our life's journey.

What of the future, John?

We are all called to live a devotional life of faith in God's service. Christ is the model for our faith and our icon of a person who truly serves God. This faith "dialogue" has been initiated by God. It is a supernatural power, which cannot be interpreted by the limits of human science. (I am humbly reminded again how strong John's faith really is.) We are on a pilgrimage here on earth, he tells me, of a faith to be lived, explored, questioned, in order to truly understand what "living faith" means. Faith tempered and shaped by a genuine love of God, family, and neighbour. He goes on to say, "We find love of God in our family and in all of the opportunities of life and serving, even when it is difficult. As a Catholic I was brought up in a devotional family who taught me Christian values and how to overcome difficulties through prayer and being realistic."

"On an experiential level," he tells me, "my faith is illuminated when

I witness fellow Christians living out the Gospels, in charity and service of their neighbour. It is often in small acts of Christian charity that I find real inspiration that Christ is present. We can also read about the lives of saints, to help deepen our appreciation of who Christ is."

It is certainly clear to John that Jesus came as incarnate God to share with us in our experience of being human. We too, as the Gospels say, will need to carry our own crosses in life, to share in the passion of Christ, with Christ.

John goes on pilgrimages as they are a good way for him to encounter God. To listen, pray, observe, and to be at peace with Christ. To meditate on the image of who Christ is, and to really listen to the words of Scripture.

He has confidence that the future of the Catholic Church is assured by Christ. The society we live in perpetually attacks Christ's church, and human ideologies have always tried to defeat religion. People will always stray from God's message and turn to sin. But of course Christ can, and will, prevail against all human counter-ideologies.

The church remains alive and active in secular society, as people still clearly search for God, and for a stable belief system with which to underpin and secure their lives, in an increasingly challenging world. John has faith.

After a long and rewarding interview we ran out of the earthly dimensions of time and space to talk any further, so John wrote out for me his responses to my last few questions, and we discussed them online. So much has been revealed! I feel very grateful to him for giving me an insight into his life-long and actively dedicated belonging to the Catholic Church. His trust in the "mystery of his faith" seems to me to indeed be a gift from God.

CHAPTER FIVE

Martyn

Martyn is an Anglican, married to Isobel, a retired vicar. His career in journalism included reporting for local and regional newspapers before joining *The Guardian* to specialize first in religious affairs, and later in industrial reporting. After retiring from subsequent work as a communications advisor in the Church of England he became the first Poet in Residence at Carlisle Cathedral, which led to the publication of his poetry collection *Sanctuary.*[1] He continues to write about poets and poetry for the *Church Times*.

For Martyn, God is the source of all life, the "starter" and "re-newer" of everything. The Holy Trinity is important to him as he sees God, the Creator, as *part* of the three elements, which also includes Jesus, the human interpreter, and the Holy Spirit, the continuing influence of God in the world.

Jesus was a pivot point in human history. He brought with him a radically new engagement of God in human affairs.

The Bible is not at all a "biography" of Jesus in terms of his life-story. It is more a spiritual biography. Yes, there was an expectation among the Jewish people that God would reveal himself in a new way at some important point. A prophecy – which most Jews are still waiting to happen. But there is always a danger of trying to "fit" events to "reverse readings", fit prophesies to real life occurring afterwards. Perhaps the Gospel writers did too much of this. But what really matters is that yes, an expectation was strong around the time of Jesus' birth, that someone crucial to God's will, the "Messiah", the one who would reveal God on earth, was coming.

We see this even in the nativity story, where the three Magi, the "three wise men", were already looking for a special person to come to earth. They saw a star and followed it – but they must have been looking for a star!

The Bible is not one book! It is more a library. A collection of books, some of which contain ideas, others poetry, others history, hymns and songs, rules, laws... and the Old Testament was certainly not written in the order that we see it now. For example, Genesis was perhaps written by the exiled Jews, in Babylon (after Exodus). What is important to see is that in the ancient world, "historical record" in the Bible was not seen in the same way as many of us do now. The motive was more spiritual – as in considering "what was God's involvement with his people?" To look at the Bible literally, in the sense of seeing it as "literal truth" is to limit and undermine God; limit God to a human level of understanding. One example is of Archbishop James Ussher (1581–1656) painstakingly working out the exact day of creation by counting backwards from Bible text to "the entrance of the night preceding the 23rd October, year before Christ 4004", that is, about 6 p.m., 22 October 4004 BC!

We need to extract from each Bible story what enables us to learn more about God. The Bible is inspired by God and written by humans. Therefore, yes, there is room for humans to have "misunderstood" or "misinterpreted" God, but still the Bible is a holy book. It is both holy and human. Because of this, the reader needs to take personal responsibility for how they read it, with their given minds and intellect. It is not a "blueprint" directly from God.

The term "heretic" in the past could have been applied to people who were "outside" of the beliefs of the power system of the time – such as the fierce accusations between Protestants and Catholics, as the people of Britain battled over their state religion and monarchy. But such loyalties would not be denigrated now in this way.

The change from Old to New Testament does involve a move from a more judgmental to a more loving approach. This is because human perceptions changed with the coming of Jesus – by his revelation of who God is.

There is an understandable sense of fear in the Old Testament. People were more overwhelmed by a feeling of being "judged" – society was even more hierarchical than now, and the mass of the lower classes very much feared the few high above. The Bible text was written by men who very likely came from the higher levels of society, and so would reflect that sense of a hierarchy that was "right".

The idea of "sin" comes again from this sense of inadequacy for the masses. During Old Testament times of writing, the power structure was very definite, with clear rules for behaviour. Jewish worship itself was accurately "prescribed". Therefore, we have such books as Deuteronomy, which is full of clear divine laws and codes.

We need to see that religion and legal systems were, and still are, intertwined.

But if now we focus too much on "judgment" by God, we could deny God's *re*-creative nature – unbalance our picture of the whole truth.

Basically, Martyn tells me, there is much more to our reading of the Bible than the book itself.

In the book of John (John 3:16), we are told that God's intention for the world is individual and societal forgiveness. So, Jesus came not just to save individuals from sin but also to influence all of society: how we live together. To help us re-create our society into one closer to, or even into, the kingdom of God.

Martyn notes to me that my original questions missed out this important concept of the "kingdom of God"… I see my error and ask him what he believes this to be?

It is human society living completely according to the will of God. To be *fully human*. To realize our full potential. It is an aspect of heaven, but can be made here, while we are still alive.

And heaven?

Heaven is where God's priorities dominate. The fulfilment of God's purposes for each of us. Martyn does see it as having a "geography", as in being a place where we feel truly "at home". Because, he says, of being the person that he is, "place" is something that matters a lot in his life. And so, for him, heaven is a place. (And I respect his truth.)

But hell?

Hell could be in this life. Your life could be "hellish". It is being alien to God, separated from God's good intentions for humanity. Martyn does not wish to focus on "afterlife hell". No need for geography here! It serves him no purpose. The word "punishment" is just a human word. Perhaps it is in an "opting out" of God's intentions. Perhaps it is a self-inflicted punishment… he is not clear and does not focus on it as something he needs to be totally clear on… how can we be?

Martyn prefers to leave the working out of punishment or not, all to God. Is hell self-inflicted or inflicted by God? He does not know. It is a "grey area" in Christian faith, within which our human definitions are too limited. We cannot fully comprehend heaven or hell. And these things are not vital to Martyn's focus, which is on faith in the immediate world of here and now. How he actively lives that out. He understands how some people, for example when suffering deeply, may choose to focus on heaven and the afterlife – for the suffering poor in the past, it was a big hope of future relief – but for Martyn, *now* is what matters.

Jesus did not fiercely proclaim he was the Messiah, no. But he did not deny it. He agreed with Peter, when his disciple called him this. And he showed us he was the Messiah more by deeds than words. He proclaimed the Truth by his actions. He also brought us the new outlook and idea of the kingdom of God coming to earth, being built here, which is so important to Martyn.

When Jesus said he would rise from the dead on the third day, this was the first time anyone had said they would do this, and such a proposal caused the priests to call him a heretic. Here, yes, he was proclaiming his divinity.

I mention that to say this, at the time, would perhaps have seemed quite strange?

Martyn tells me that Jesus was "adventurously pointing to a new way of being, a new promise by God."

To be fully a Christian we do, yes, need to see this divinity in Jesus. If you see him as simply a unique figure in history, then you miss out on the glory of who he was. You miss the full potential of his message.

However, Martyn tells me he would be reluctant to say whether anyone else was, or was not, a Christian... for "who are we to judge?". Labels get us nowhere. However again (!), to see Jesus as just a human, even a very special, wise human is, to him, an inadequate understanding of Christ. We "miss out" if we cannot think for ourselves and realize this divinity is possible.

What does the crucifixion mean to you?

To Martyn this was not a negative punishment of Jesus, no. He mentions the poem by R. S. Thomas, "The Coming", which talks of Jesus *opting into* humanity on earth, being incarnated, as opposed to the idea of him being sent by God in order to be punished for our sins. In a sense Jesus was seeing the needs in the world and asking his Father to let him go there, let him help. The crucifixion does need to be at the heart of Christian belief, and yes, sin is in the background, as the separation of what God had intended for us from how we were – and still are – living.

The cross was – and is – the *bridge* over that sin, which was – and is – a "failure" by us to follow God. The cross links the "gap between" symbolically, by the vertical part representing what God wants us to be, in a connecting line between the divine and ourselves, and the horizontal part representing what we are in danger of becoming – not connected to God at all.

By Christ's death *and* Resurrection, we are given a key to an eternal perspective. But we need crucially to see the two events *together,* connected. It was not just a death, but a Rising afterwards!

The Resurrection shows us that God can renew us all.

He tells me of the teaching by Paul, that if *anyone* is in Christ, there is a new creation, which could be interpreted as a new world. That is, if just one person comes to the Christian faith, they in effect bring the kingdom of God closer to earth. And yes, even non-Christian people, who live by Christ's values, are part of this bringing of the kingdom. Because yes, God uses other ways to bring his own intentions to earth. By the *effect* of others' good loving ways, rather than their beliefs, non-Christian people can bring God's kingdom closer.

And the Eucharist?

That is our opportunity to re-focus, to gather in God's love for us, to remind and enable us to stop, and celebrate our Christian community. It both literally and symbolically "feeds us".

And the issue of gender in Christianity?

Jesus, Martyn says, was very radical in his view of women. In the story of the woman Jesus met at the well, he broke every rule! She was a Samaritan, so a non-Jew; she was someone who had been married many times, and she was living "in sin". Yet still he asked her for a gift of water! This was a living message.

The first person to see the resurrected Jesus was Mary Magdalene, again a woman, and a woman with whom he was very close. Many women were supporters and a part of the living, mixed community of Jesus and his disciples. Martyn points out how, in a similar form of teaching, the first people Jesus was revealed to were wandering shepherds, who would be regarded as not very clean or acceptable, as outsiders to society. Again, the word of such witnesses would not be completely trusted, and yet these were his chosen witnesses, for his birth and his Resurrection – outsider, lowly, less respected people.

At the key points in his life then, Jesus showed his message of non-judgmental love and inclusion. And, Martyn says to me (as Margaret did) it is amazingly relevant that the Scriptures were not altered, that the Gospel writers also saw the importance of what their Messiah had shown to the world.

The Resurrection of Jesus is yes, vital to our faith. We too can be "resurrected" in part, within our human potential, by this belief. We can be more fully alive. The renewal can begin for us during our human life.

Martyn talks now about the charismatic "renewal movement" of the 1970s/80s, which did bring fresh life to Christianity, and was only spoiled by becoming too extreme in some areas. It would be great however, to re-kindle the good aspects of faith that were found in this movement, such as people from all denominations worshipping together, discerning the word of God together, which led to social action, and was perhaps more like the very early church, in the way Christian communities physically lived together.

Martyn is unsure what happened physically when Jesus himself "ascended" into heaven. All that matters is that he left a commission with his followers to spread the "good news" *everywhere*. This work began on the day of the "Pentecost", when the disciples could suddenly speak in "all tongues", so that they could spread the word to all people, across all boundaries.

Paul and Peter then saw that the Christian message was for all of us, so they broke the mould of the Old Testament, which was geared toward a Jewish community, and the New Testament became a Scripture for a *universal* community.

What of the "second coming"?

Yes, Martyn replies, there will be one. But even though Jesus did speak of a physical return, this is not a focus for Martyn. He continues to focus his faith actively in the now. To him the second coming is more of an abstract idea that was made into a picture, an image, in revelations in the Bible, as a teaching aid to help people understand its messages. It was written of in a "code" which people could read in the context of their time. Nowadays, we perhaps should not waste time wondering about when it will happen?

He repeats this focus of his to me – which does in fact teach me a great deal – when I ask him about evil powers/the devil, does he believe they exist, and if so, are they created by or outside of God?

Martyn replies that too much battling in our minds to intensely analyse life, the spiritual, can be in itself a risk – a risk of being "side-tracked" from living out our faith in God. Sometimes we need to just let it be that we do not, cannot, ever know, while we are humans, all the deepest Truth of why and how God has the world the way it is! But we can live a Christian life.

We can better focus on alleviating the *effects* of negative forces in the world, which achieves more, he feels, than theorizing about why the negative exists.

And what is the value of prayer?

Martyn likes the communicative power of prayer to acknowledge, worship, and ask God for things, as a child may speak to their parent. There is a value in communal as well as in repeated prayers. And prayer is both a duty and a joy.

Martyn wants the church to be more *prophetic* – that is to speak out against injustice, for the sake of creation. He feels institutions are needed that can bring God's presence right into difficult situations, with more engagement by the church in world affairs. Indeed, we need to renew! To bring the church closer again to God. To "radicalize" it, like Jesus did. "What we need," says Martyn, "is a new helping of Jesus!"

We need the church to return more to how it was in its infancy, with small communities of devoted people, committed to Jesus' desire for positive change.

I tell him that sounds good.

The church, he says, is indeed "exploding" in some parts of the world, such as parts of Africa and South America. Martyn went to Namibia, to a church service in the "bush" there. People filling a packed-out church were seated on tree trunks or chairs that they had carried a long way with them. Some had walked for two days to get there. Everyone sang and prayed vibrantly for a five-hour-long confirmation service. This was inspiring.

We finish now, and Martyn has indeed inspired me, with the important reminder that theory alone is not the way to God. Action is also crucial. Acting out our faith, living God's love.

*

During our first meeting for this interview, I listened to Martyn talk about his doctoral thesis related to "exile and truth".[2] He agrees to meet with me again, as this sounds fascinating. "Poetic truth in times of exile" and the "poetic expression of faith"... what does he mean by all this?

We sit together over lunch, and I am again inspired, as well as humbled, by what he teaches me about his study of three different "concepts of truth":

1) *Absolute* truth – as represented by the writings in the Bible of the prophet Isaiah, whom Martyn views as a poet of the exile of the Hebrew people, in Babylon.

It is the idea that there is one universal Truth, the Word of God. A Truth to be known and respected in an exact, literal way. Many Christians believe the Creed to be absolute in its truth, as a literal statement of faith. Some "conservative" Christians see all biblical truth as being absolute, and inerrant.

2) *Conditional* truth – as represented by the poet Samuel Taylor Coleridge, who was a troubled "exilic figure" of the Romantic period in literature.

The focus here is on the symbolic meaning of stories and text, where the person needs to choose for themselves if a specific story is literally true or is indeed a "picture story", with its meaning found in the symbolic imagery of its words. For example, the story in the Bible about the Garden of Eden or the parting of the Red Sea by Moses.

3) *Relative* truth – as represented in Martyn's thesis by some writings of Carol Ann Duffy and Ted Hughes.

Duffy takes a spiritual poem about prayer by George Herbert (1593–1633) and makes it into a secular poem, also entitled "Prayer".[3] Hughes writes a story "What is the truth?" in which an unnamed son of God comes to earth to try to understand humanity and the planet – rather than coming to teach humanity about God.[4]

The concept of relative truth is that one person's idea of what is true is *equally* valid to all others, as they are all subjective and individual, not objective and universal. There is no "hierarchy" on who knows the actual or "best" truth.

The sense is that all of humanity, each person has their own idea on who God is – if we have an idea of God existing at all – and if we do, we seek to define God from the "bottom up", in contrast to the sense that God reveals Godself to us, through divine events and inspirations, from the "top down".

A post-modernist/relativism-based approach would declare a true equality of all spiritual and non-spiritual ideas. God is one "option", of equal validity with all others.

("Postmodernism" is a broad movement developed in the late twentieth century, after "modernism". It covers such things as art, philosophy, architecture, criticism, and involves a sense of self-conscious freedom. It is characteristically self-referential, sceptical, subjective, relativist, distrusting of "theories" and "anti-rational".)

This is a way of thinking which, Martyn affirms to me, holds dangers from a Christian perspective, because it can lead to a liberal but potentially vague widening of acceptance, where "anything goes" implies a risk that if all our ideas about God's truth are relative and equally valid, then we could lose our grasp of the universal absolute Truth which God wants us to know. We could lose our awareness of Truth ultimately coming from a divine rather than a human source. We could lose our awareness of the divine "revelation" that we seek.

Martyn then goes on to talk to me about exile itself, and how, just as with the exile of the Jews in Babylon, our Christian church could be seen at present to be "in exile". It is no longer "at home" or grounded in our secularized Western world. It is not strongly connected to the people, as shown by drastically falling attendance figures both in the UK, and even in the US, where church attendance has always been stronger.

This post-modern era has "bought into" so much individualism, to the extent that there are no longer any "absolutes", no "collective mutuality", which he sees as essential for bringing God's kingdom to earth. To be connected and compassionate is replaced by selfishness, where there is a desperate lack of "big stories" or "grand narratives" to hold us all together. We are in too many little selfish pieces – lost in exile.

The church, Martyn tells me, needs to recognize more urgently this state of "philosophical exile" which we are in, where religion has become a "lifestyle choice", like choosing to play golf, and is no longer therefore "imperative, energetic, and electric!"

However, I suggest to Martyn, are many people now seeming to very much be looking for a "home" for their lost or "exiled" souls, a universal spiritual Truth which gives a meaning and purpose to our lives?

He agrees, and we now discuss how perhaps, now this post-modern era of "relativism" has gone too far, with individualism becoming self-pre-occupation, it is losing hold of people as it fails to fulfil us, and so a new possibility for communal faith is again emerging. A possibility for re-engagement with God with radical and relevant spirituality, which the church so much needs to grasp and activate.

Martyn then defines for me the concept of "poetic truth" as containing all three elements of absolute, conditional, and relative truth... *and then some!* Something indefinable. Poetic truth is very much present in the Bible. Psalm 137, he tells me, is a great example of this, where the exiled Jewish poets and singers, their lyres and harps left hanging in the willow trees by the river, are tormented by the Babylonians to "sing us a song of Zion". They reply, broken-hearted in their exile, "How shall we sing the Lord's song, in a strange land?" (verse 4, KJV).

Yet it seems the exiled Hebrew poets did formulate a response. Some theologians believe the drafting of Genesis – which ascribes to an absolute God the creation of all life – was carried out by the exiles as a foundation document of hope and purpose, for a people devoid of both.

I learn so much from Martyn in all this discussion. To consider whether, just as we can be wary of complete literal "absolutism", we need also to not be naïve about the opposite end of the spectrum of truth, where "relativism" accepts all individualistic approaches as being equally valid, and so "casts out" the universal which is the Oneness of God.

And yet, whenever we say we definitely "know the Truth of God" in any absolute but complicated way, are we not more likely to be searching for our own individual security in this life, rather than our simple "homecoming"?

I see the need for balance. To be ever conscious that we are human, therefore inevitably subjective as well as potentially wise. To try to stay humble and as closely connected to simple truth as possible, in that God is Oneness, and God is Love. But then wait… is our individual understanding of love not also "relative" and subjective?

Perhaps not. I do believe that there is an "absolute" understanding of what love is, God's Love as one universal Truth… but ask me (or anyone) to define it, and we stumble!

Love is an experience of the heart, not a belief of the mind. And perhaps, as my talk with Martyn says to me, love is only truly known in action. Does a good church, a Christian, or a person following Jesus' teachings do so fundamentally in their loving actions, here and now?

This was an enlightening meeting.

CHAPTER SIX

Helen

Helen tells me she belongs mainly to a Messianic church, a mix of Jewish and gentile Christians ("Messianic" means relating to the "messianic role" of Jesus as our Messiah). She was brought up as Church of England, and went to church regularly until she was about eighteen. At the age of thirty-six she felt the need to go back to church and joined a modern evangelical church, where she became a "born-again" Christian. Over time, however, she felt the need for a stronger biblical-based teaching and felt moved to attend the Messianic Church, although she still visits her previous church on occasions. Helen has asked that I reference the Bible in relation to her comments throughout this interview.

She is born-again, Helen tells me, because she is now born anew in the spirit of God (John 3:1–8). This makes her very demonstrably joyful! She laughs that when she first became born again, she was almost "bouncing off the ceiling" with happiness! Helen says she has spent a lot of her life searching, through relationships, promiscuity, drink, drugs, and so on (she is still a lovely young woman) and has now found what she always felt was the missing piece within her.

She is honest to me (as she is right through our interview) that she now prefers the company of fellow Christians and that bad habits which she used to have, such as swearing, have just "dropped off me". God is changing her from the inside out.

Helen tells me God is the spiritual Father, so great that we cannot describe him (Revelation 1:8). "My starting point in faith was in God, the Father of Jesus, as this was how I was brought up. Now I see that many people have their own *idea* of who God is, but my relationship with God has only grown through becoming a born-again Christian, being guided by the Holy Spirit, prayer, and study of his Word in the Bible.

"God meets me where I'm at in my walk with him, and the closer you get to him in everyday life, the more you get to know him. If you draw close to him he will draw close to you," she smiles (James 4:8).

"People *think* they know who God is, but God is who he is, and we need to learn from the Bible, who he truly says he is. We need to accept what he says there, and not try to make him "fit" how we might want him to be. So, yes, he is good and loving, of course, but yes, there will be Judgment Day when he will judge all of us.

"Too many Christians don't even get off the starting block in their relationship and knowledge of God," she tells me. "And I am amazed now, shocked even, by how few Christians read the Bible, or pray every day… I'm not judging, as I myself was naïve and ignorant to how important this is at first, but we grow spiritually in our faith and understanding by reading his Word, praying, and being around other Christians."

Helen jokes that brain surgeons of course study brains. "You don't say you 'are' something and then not do anything to study or learn about it, about what it is you say you are, what you believe in!" (I laugh with her and see what she says.)

Helen believes the entire Bible to be literally true and that it is the inspired Word of God. She believes the Gospels were written by apostles who knew Jesus and were witnesses to him. Jesus was God in the flesh, the Emmanuel (John 1:1–14, Matthew 1:22–23).

She tells me that sometimes people seem uncomfortable when she talks to them about Jesus, because he is the only Truth, and "the Truth is the Truth is the Truth" she says, happily. "You cannot dress up the Truth, you cannot alter it, and this is what makes people uncomfortable, because deep down they know there really is only one God, and people do not like being told 'there is only one way' to do anything. But the truth is, there *is* only one way to be spiritually born again. And there is only one way to heaven" (John 8:31–32, John 14:6).

Helen is shocked that when people of other Christian denominations are asked, "How much of the Bible do you think is literally true?" some say "50/50." "That's appalling!" she says. "*All* Scripture is God-inspired. And all the Bible is written in a certain way for a reason. The Truth is *not* relative. The Bible Truth is all literally and absolutely true."

I suggest that the phrase "inspired by God" and even the word "true" can perhaps mean different things to different people. Does "true" need to mean literally true?

Helen continues that every bit of the Bible is inspired by God and not present by mistake. For example, Lazarus was raised from the dead by Jesus after *four* days, and this was significant because Jewish people believe that the spirit of a person stays around for three days after they die, but still Jesus could raise Lazarus on the fourth day, because he was the Messiah. Every word or phrase is placed significantly in the Bible. Everything is there for a purpose, and the exact way it is written is to teach or reveal something to us. And, without question, it all happened just as the Bible says it did.

She tells me that her own spiritual walk mirrors exactly the way the apostles describe and teach in the Bible – the spiritual battles, lessons, and growth – how it will happen as a person walks in faith, with God's guidance.

"My truth is God's truth," she says. "These are not my personal opinions. They are God's." (And as I listen to Helen I feel not discord or disturbance, but an unexpected kind of humbleness, which I think comes from trying my best to listen to someone and not judge them. To learn from them, however that learning comes about.)

Of the Old Testament, Helen is unclear when this was written, but, she says, trying to pin down dates misses the point. That it was written "over a large span of time", is enough for her. (I hear this response most often when I ask this question, which is very interesting.) She does believe, yes, that Noah was in the ark in a flood and, she excitedly tells me, it has now been discovered that the biblical description of the structure for the ark is the absolutely ideal way to build such a boat. How's that for perfect truth? God gave Noah the best exact dimensions that the ark must be built to! (I enjoy the way Helen is so passionate about her faith.)

"The Bible was written mostly before Christ and just after. Done. No need for more detail than that," she says. The truth and meaning of the Bible and that it comes from God is what matters.

"It is written by humans but inspired by God, and every story is literally true. The parables are told to make a point, so, OK, they are symbolic stories, but why would we ever think stories such as the nativity story are anything but true? My brain just doesn't get that!" says Helen.

When I suggest that some people think symbolic elements and images have been put into the stories, to teach us something, Helen replies that it is "just like God to do this!" As in, he puts the symbols into the stories to help us learn things, but the stories themselves still literally happened, as God intended. God can easily do both!

"The Bible is fascinating; you have accounts of people, prophecies, teachings – there can be so much depth to just one paragraph. Even the wording of one verse of Scripture can have profound significance, but it's important that you always read the Scripture in its context."

Helen jokes in a funny voice that her friend describes the Bible as if the Old Testament seems to be full of God saying, "I kill you!" and the New, "I love you!"

But it is all one Bible, and on your journey of faith you keep learning all the time what it all means. The Old Testament leads us to the New; it was showing us what was to come. The whole of the Old Testament is pointing to Jesus throughout. "What is crucial," she says, "is not to rely on your own understanding of the Bible, but to rely on God's (Proverbs 3:5). His ways are higher, and if you feel you don't like or understand something that is in the Bible, then you should ask, 'Who am I to judge, or to know best?' If you ask God to help you understand, he will (James 1:5)."

"It is like ants and an ant farmer," she continues. "People are like the ants, who are questioning the farmer. But how tiny we are, while how almighty is God."

We must accept the Bible as the inspired Word of God.

The Jewish people were so much a focus of all the biblical events. They were a tiny area of people, yet so distinctive. "Israel could be seen," she says, "as the centre of the world map. They were God's chosen people, and we have been 'grafted on' to these people. All God's chosen ones are the Messianic Jews and the gentile Christians, all those who believe in Christ as their Saviour" (Hebrews 11:11–24).

This is a short summary, Helen records, of how things happened: "God made us. He saw we couldn't obey him. So, he wiped out humanity with the flood – except Noah and his family. He starts again. Moses comes. God gives us commandments on how to live. The Jews are in exodus to a new land. But even while Moses is up the mountain talking to God, the Jews mess up again. God keeps trying to show us we must not sin and simply be obedient to and trust in him. But since the Fall in the Garden of Eden we all have the sinful nature of Adam. We cannot enter the presence of God in the state we are in. So God sends us Jesus. Jesus is the sacrifice to pay the due penalty, so we can all start again. God offered us the ultimate gift of his Son. Jesus is the Saviour who paid our debt by dying, so there will be no condemnation now for those who 'clothe themselves'] with Jesus, in God's eyes".

Helen quotes me John 3:16 "God so loved the world that he gave his one and only Son, that whoever believes in him shall not perish but have eternal life" (NIV). God is Love, and he loves everyone, and wants everyone to trust in his Son. But we must realize, she tells me, that it is not ever by good works that we may enter God's heaven; it is by faith alone that we can be justified with God.

(It may be useful to know here that the term "to justify" means, in traditional theological terms, to "declare or make righteous in the eyes of God". Therefore, "justification by faith alone" means to be held righteous of salvation in God's eyes, and therefore of going to heaven when you die, singularly by your faith.)

Faith in Jesus as our Saviour saves us from God's coming judgment and wrath. We may struggle with this idea, but it's in the Bible and so they are God's true words of his love for us. Pride in our own intelligence, of how good we think we are, can sometimes blind us to this (Romans 3:22–23, Ephesians 2:8–9).

I ask Helen about heaven, hell, and purgatory.

Purgatory, she tells me, is a man-made idea, a false teaching. It is loosely based on Scripture which has either been misinterpreted, at best, or manipulated for humankind's gain, at worst. Heaven and hell are real and yes, are literally places. Jesus tells us about hell about fifty-five times, in his teachings. "We need to 'man up'," says Helen, "and stop pretending to ourselves Jesus is just a 'gentle, nice, good moral teacher'. We need to read what he really says. How we will be judged. Jesus said he was going to heaven to 'prepare a place for us'. So, it's a real place" (John 14:2). And we will every one of us be judged, on the day of judgment (Hebrews 9:27–28).

We try to talk about what judgment day will be like.

"This is when Jesus returns in the second coming, and the rapture happens, where the 'dead in Christ' rise first – meaning already dead Christians – followed by the rest of the living believers. We will be 'caught in the air' with Jesus in this rapture," she tells me (1 Thessalonians 4:16–17). She suggests reading Luke 17:34–36 or Matthew 24:38–41, as all the answers to questions on this subject can be found in the Bible, as they should be.

She is not certain, however, if the dead are judged before this, or if they just stay "spiritually asleep" until this judgment day.

And what of people born before Jesus came?

Helen says Adam did go up to heaven, but she is not certain if there is any difference in what happens to the "pre-Christ" people of God.

One thing is certain, Helen is not bothered about when she dies because, she tells me, "my hope is in Him" (Psalm 33:20–22). She has been waiting and yearning for something for much of her life, something she could not put her finger on… was it in a circumstance, a job, a man, personal satisfaction within herself? Now she is born-again, that "need for something missing" is gone. She was once spoken to directly by Jesus, and it overwhelmed her. "I was driving home late one night, thinking about a story I'd just been told about a little boy and Jesus, then I heard him. Jesus spoke to me. His words were so very clear, they seemed to penetrate into my very core. I felt overwhelmed by a presence, a love, it was as if my heart exploded in my chest and I was so overcome, I started weeping and crying in a way I'd only experienced slightly in the recent months at church, only in a much, much, more dramatic way. I knew I had encountered the living God in a way I didn't even know was possible."

How she wishes she could have that moment back. For the memory to stay crystal clear. "In hindsight, and significantly, that was the first night I truly 'trusted' in Jesus, in a specific circumstance. I was still very much struggling with alcohol at that point, and just wanted to go to bed that night, for one night, sober. Before I started the drive home, I told him I was trusting in him to help me do that. He did."

Helen now tells me a story… she's heard that apparently some states in the USA won't allow two Christians to pilot an aeroplane together. This is because the Bible says, when Jesus returns for the second coming, "Two men will be in the field; one will be taken and the other left. Two women will be grinding with a hand mill; one will be taken, the other left" (Matthew 24:40–41, NIV). That is, the true Christian will be taken to join Christ, suddenly disappearing out of their clothes and shoes, and the non-Christian left behind – to fly the plane! Helen makes reference to the 2014 film *Left Behind* starring Nicholas Cage, which is based on this "biblical rapture" story.

She does strongly believe that we are living in the last days, and we are far closer to the Lord's return than people realize. This is because wickedness is increasing so rapidly and many of Jesus' warnings and biblical prophecies are coming to fruition (Matthew 24:36–39, 2 Timothy 3:1–5).

The media suggests to us that Christianity is dying out. But there are many "new" non-denominational churches emerging which are hugely popular and growing fast. Many people are coming to faith in Jesus, especially among the younger generation. However, Jesus said in Revelation that in the last days there will be a great "falling away" from true doctrine. Helen believes that unfortunately some of these new churches are like this. They have man-made philosophies which are not Bible-based. They fit Bible Scriptures to back up their own ways of thinking. Jesus warned us so much about this. Helen is adamant I put down her belief that these are "ear ticklers" (as mentioned in 2 Timothy 4:3–4) who lack true fear or reverence of God, and are misusing Scripture in their teachings. They are all signs that the last days are coming closer.

What is the "song" of Jesus?

Jesus helps you reconcile with God. He is saying, "I am here, you can trust in me. Repent, turn back to God." His teachings may be moral, yes, but their main purpose is that they are God's teachings, to love God and others, and the warning of what will happen to you if you do not repent. We can repent, reconcile, and be saved only by accepting Jesus as our Saviour. He is the gift of God.

The two greatest commandments of Jesus are in Matthew 22:37–39. Helen tells me she has this Bible reference tattooed onto her foot and laughs that she had this done even before she became a born-again Christian – a strange coincidence looking back. But at the time she wanted a tattoo with a message that would withstand time, and for her, this is basically to love God and love other people. It is very clear that Helen's faith is in the foreground of her life. Jesus' primary teaching is to "Love the Lord your God with all your heart, and with all your soul, and with all your mind".[2] His secondary teaching, and commandment, is to "love your neighbour as yourself".

I begin to mention to Helen that this second teaching is known as the "Golden Rule" of all major religions, as it is a common thread in the basis of most faiths, but this is not something she wants to go further with, as she feels it would be diverting from the point of this interview.

And the sacrifice of Jesus?

God instructed Moses, Helen tells me, to tell his people to put lambs' blood on the lintels of their doorways during the Passover. (The book of Exodus explains that this occurred so that during God's tenth and final plague, he would know who the Israelites were and wouldn't enter their houses in order to slaughter their firstborn sons. Instead, he would "pass over" them. This means their exodus and freedom from slavery in ancient Egypt, thought to be between 1580 and 1200 BC, would be enabled.) This, Helen says, was a "mirroring" of the sacrificial slaughter of Jesus that was to come, as the "innocent lamb", crucified to atone for our sins.

Those people who accept Jesus are protected, just as the Israelites were protected. Likewise, Christians are "clothed" in Jesus' blood, and so not judged. "It is finished" Jesus said on the cross (John 19:28–30). His was the ultimate, needed sacrifice.

Due to sin we deserve God's judgment and wrath, and ultimately death. But Christ's death pays our debt, therefore he is our Saviour. If you believe in him, then he saves you from that debt of punishment and you will have eternal life. The Bible helps us to be clear – if you do not follow what God tells us to do, there are consequences to this.

So, if you don't?

Then yes, Helen says honestly, if you are an atheist, and you had the chance to choose Jesus, but refused, then you will go to hell and be separated from God forever. You will not be saved.

I ask Helen to clarify: did Jesus not die to save us all?

Yes, she tells me earnestly, but if you deny God and Jesus, then you will not be saved by Jesus' sacrifice on the cross. But, she adds, "At the end of the day, God allows us to make a choice. He's made his existence known to all. But only God truly knows the heart and mind of an individual."

Did Jesus actually say he came to be our Saviour?

Helen tells me he said he would save the world through himself (John 3:17–18). Another of Jesus' teachings, she says, is "I am the way, and the truth, and the life. No one comes to the Father, except through me" (John 14:6). This is incredibly important to her. No other way is open, she says. Reject Jesus, and you reject God's offer of a relationship with him – his love, forgiveness, salvation, and eternal life. People find this hard to accept, but it is the truth.

What is the Eucharist?

Helen sees no need for a church hierarchy to be involved in the receiving of the Eucharist. This is a man-made instruction and is not in the Bible. She has no problem with taking Communion in a small group, with no priest or vicar involved.

The Eucharist is a way of remembering Jesus' sacrifice, and Helen sees it not as literally the body and blood of Jesus, but as a symbolic remembrance of his body and blood (Luke 22:19–20).

And what about the issue of gender in the church?

Helen feels that worldly influences are wrongly creeping in if we start to see God as also female. He is not. God is our spiritual Father. God is Love, nurturing and caring. Man was made in God's image (Genesis 1:26). Woman was taken from man's rib, to be by man's side, a companion.

We are equally valued, but we are made male and female for different roles. Men are always best as the head of a household, and Helen is happy with this: God has ordered all things to work best in a given way, and the Bible teaches this in all aspects of life.

I ask Helen to clarify whether she actually believes woman, Eve, came from Adam's rib.

"Yes," she says. "Why not? I have a childlike faith. If God can throw stars into the sky, why is it such a big deal if he made Eve out of Adam's rib? If our blood vessels, stretched out, could go around the whole world, it is no big feat at all for God to do this!"

Even though these are not my beliefs, and Helen knows this, I do feel and tell her that her absolute faith in what God can easily do, is a lesson for me.

She digresses to talk about evolution. Who would ever say of Shakespeare's sonnets, "a typewriter must have exploded"? Likewise, "evolution" is far too weak a theory to explain the amazingness of creation! No "big bang" could possibly create such wonders: the senses of right and wrong; the inbuilt compasses of morals within us all. The idea of "survival of the fittest" just doesn't work to explain enough; Helen suggests we'd all be a super-species by now if this was behind everything! "There is so much scientific evidence that points to and backs up a 'Creator' or God. But people tend to accept what they are told rather than digging deeper for themselves."

"It is as it is in the Bible," she emphasizes. She gets frustrated when people don't believe the Bible as God's Word. So, no she does not agree with women being heads of households or of churches. It is dangerous, to her, to be sucked into a worldly point of view on gender, rather than God's instructions on this. If the Bible tells us how to live, act, believe, pray, behave with others etc... then we need to stay loyal to Scripture (and this is what Helen believes is written in the Bible). "You cannot pick and choose what Scriptures suit you. *All* Scripture is of value," she tells me. And it is good to get an understanding of both the Old and New Testament (2 Timothy 3:16).

The meaning of the Resurrection?
Helen says Jesus was the only person to ever conquer death.

When I try to debate this point, saying that for example, Lazarus in the New Testament rose from the dead, as did "many saints" at the time of Jesus' death, she agrees with me, and later gives me the Bible reference for this (Matthew 27:51–53). We are enjoying a lively discussion now, with me mostly just listening, but sometimes being moved to put another perspective, and then being quiet to listen again to Helen's response.

For Helen, the physical rising of Christ on Easter Sunday is the greatest event; it is *through him* that we all can rise again and have new life after death.

"This matters a lot to me," says Helen, "that this little life is not the end. There is hope." OK, Jesus raised Lazarus from the dead, but who raised Jesus? God did.

And the "second coming"?

Helen is humbly honest that she is still on a learning journey and is not sure if we stay "asleep" spiritually until this time, after we die, or if we can go to heaven before the judgment day. We are definitely not judged the way many religions claim, on our "merits" of good works; no, we are judged on our faith. This alone decides if we enter the kingdom of heaven. But then of course, with faith inside your heart, you will want to do good deeds! Goodness is the "fruit" of our faith.

Helen becomes emphatic now that we really need to urgently realize the "season" we are in, as Jesus warned us of the "birth pains" before his second coming. The end times are approaching, she believes, because the signs of what will be happening in the world before Christ's return have never been so clear. There is much more wickedness, spread wide across the world. And many of the countries which the Bible says will be involved in the last days (she lists Syria, China, Israel, Russia, Iran, America...) are all front players on the world stage. There is a great increase in travel and the media is full of violence and sexual perversion. People are also being more self-indulgent, moving away from God (Daniel 12:4; 2 Timothy 3:1–5).

The Bible warns of an "army of 200 million" coming from the East across the Euphrates river. What is correct, she tells me, is that China now has almost enough soldiers to call up to make this happen (Revelation 9:16). The end-of-time prophecies are coming to fruition, she truly believes, and urgently wants us all to realize this.

Does the devil exist?

Yes, for sure the devil is real, very much so, and there are "demonic spirits", who masquerade as light (2 Corinthians 11:14). And there will be an anti-Christ figure, empowered by Satan (the devil). The anti-Christ figure is he who will set himself up in place of Christ, promising to be the saviour of the world, coming to bring peace by governing over us.

The Bible warns us that nobody will be able to buy or sell without the mark of the beast (Revelation 13:17). "Look at how people are being micro-chipped in India and the move everywhere toward a cashless society... the technology and the way we live is all moving toward this," she says.

At the Fall, Adam gave power over to Satan, whom Jesus described as the "prince of darkness". And Satan is the authority figure over this current world we live in. Yet still God is the overall authority, the ultimate power. We humans gave Satan this power in the Fall. We disobeyed God. We ate the fruit of the forbidden tree. Through one man, Adam, we fell, the New Testament tells us – and through one man, Jesus, we will be saved. We all became sinful in nature because of Adam's choice to disobey God (Romans 5:12–17).

Jesus was also tempted by the devil in the wilderness (Matthew 4:1–11). And he overcame temptation, as we must. Jesus often dealt with demonic spirits in his ministry, in a variety of forms.

Helen believes the devil is not stupid and aims for tormenting or attacking Christians if he can – by tempting, accusing, and lying – because they are more of a threat to him as they can expose him for what he is. Jesus said that even demons believe there is only one God, and "shudder" (James 2:19).

God is Spirit, but then other spiritual forces are at work. She believes the Holy Spirit lives within her now, but only because she is a born-again Christian. You are born again and have then a new heart, being "re-born of the Spirit of God".

But before this?

Only the act of being born again allowed Helen to be set free from her sinful nature, allowing the Holy Spirit to now dwell within her. But before this, no. "Being 'born-again' means you are freed from your sinful nature, and by walking in faith, guided by the Holy Spirit, you change." She continues, "You produce what is known as the 'fruit of spirit', and you have a peace that only comes from God. You just desire to do his will. Things that were once appealing to you just aren't anymore." She lists the fruits of the spirit "joy, peace, patience, kindness, faithfulness, gentleness, self-control. These things should increase as you mature in your faith and follow Jesus' and the apostles' teaching" (Galatians 5:22–23).

She tells me of a time when, as a five- or six-year-old child, she stole a ring. Nobody had seen her do it, but she knew she had done wrong and somebody "above" had seen her actions. Her conscience convicted her, and she threw the ring away, knowing she needed to say sorry to somebody/ something who knew of her guilt.

Does this not show we all have a conscience of what is right and wrong?, I ask.

Yes, but Helen believes it also shows we are all sinful by nature. She points out that even two- and three-year-olds can be manipulative and naughty.

"I trust God's Word, the Bible. I do not yet fully understand everything in the Bible!" she laughs. Then sincerely adds, "But the Bible is the complete Truth. I have faith it is right, always."

And the value of prayer?

Helen fulfils with happiness her instructions to pray and to intercede for others. The Bible says that the prayer of a righteous person is powerful (James 5:16). You cannot have a relationship with God without talking to him! She completely believes in the power of prayer for healing and deliverance. It shows we are in a relationship with God if we look to him in our daily life. Many Christians do not realize the importance of prayer. Jesus himself prayed often to his Father. And so must we.

What of the Trinity?

God is our spiritual Father. Jesus is our Saviour, she tells me, who intercedes for us, and we are "clothed in him" as Christians, being made acceptable and righteous in the Father's eyes. The Holy Spirit is our comforter. He (Helen always uses the masculine to refer to the Holy Spirit) helps to guide us, in life and prayer. He may convict us of certain sins, but never condemns us – as the devil does this. He is the "still, quiet voice". He is the seal which confirms to us that we are now God's child, teaching us God's ways, giving us understanding. Helen says the Holy Spirit is always with her. She also affirms that the Spirit is not a "force", neither is he feminine, and neither is the Holy Spirit an "it".

And the future?

Helen clearly states that this last question of mine (the fourteenth) about the possibility of a "universal loving faith", is a dangerous one. An idea that looms in the world at large. *"Beware!"* she emphasizes to me. "A 'universal spiritual faith' is the *worst* future happening possible." If all religions come together as one – as the world tries to unify itself more and more, because of all the troubles, chaos, and wars – then the end is near.

Striving toward "watered down" versions of God, or a universal form of faith, is very much a departure from God's instruction. Such things as "inter-faith" meetings, a move toward a "Oneness" of faith, is a big thing we need to avoid. No one comes to God the Father except through Jesus. As Christians we must preach the good news of Christ as our *only* Saviour. If we entertain other faiths, or other spiritual ideas, as being equally valid, just for the sake of peace and unity, then we deny others the truth of Jesus that will save their souls. "In loving others, as instructed, we must speak the truth in love," she says. And Jesus clearly warned his followers that there would be great spiritual deception, strange teachings and false doctrines ahead (Hebrews 13:9; 2 Peter 2:1; Matthew 24:24).

She tells me how she prays to be kept within God's wisdom and Truth, and his discernment. We now live in a world where truth can be manipulated, personalized, experiential and, at worst *relative*, which it is not. We must beware of joining up with people who believe not in the God of the Bible but in their own made up idea of God, or in other gods. "Stay away from this!" Helen emphatically warns me. "While the world runs after spirituality, unity, and peace in many guises, it misses the only Truth, which is in the person of Jesus Christ and is all in the Bible."

Helen asks me now to quote one of her favourite Scriptures, 1 Corinthians 13:13 (NIV): "And now these three remain: faith, hope and love. But the greatest of these is love."

She earnestly tells me that people like me are in fact a part of the coming of the day of judgment, the end of the world as we know it. Such people love the idea of God, but it is *their* idea, not the Truth of the real God, from the Bible. Beware mixing false spiritual ideas with God's Truth! There is only one Truth: God's.

God wants us all to go to heaven, but not everyone will. She is honestly and compassionately concerned for people like myself (I have mentioned to Helen that I am contemplating the possibility of every one of us returning to God in heaven). Helen tells me that I "seem to be falling for false doctrines which Jesus warns about before his return and in the last days." To Helen "the Lord's return and the tribulation period are nearly upon us." Therefore, she wants to warn people not to fall for the ideas of false prophets and false doctrines – anything which falls outside the Word of God in the Bible. She warns me with love, to be careful.

I hope I have kept to my intention to listen and respect Helen's strong faith. And I have learned a lot from this interview. It is good for me to learn that I can meet and talk with someone whose beliefs about God are so different from my own and am still able to respect and love that other person. I'm not saying this is particularly an attribute of mine. No, not at all! If we want to, we can all do this. To – without too much response – take in the words of people very unlike us in their faith, is unexpectedly not so hard. It has not been upsetting or infuriating I have learned from Helen's deep faith. Her passion and conviction. Her trust in what God can do. Her complete trust in the Bible. It has helped me on my own way toward clarity.

Helen's comprehension of God's Truth is not mine, and we were both honest with each other from the start, but she helps me continue to learn about what the word "truth" can mean to us, spiritually. How powerful, stimulating, and controversial a set of five letters it can be!

*

I just came in from a walk after typing up this interview and heard Bradley Walsh on the radio singing out joyfully "Shout Alleluia, come on get happy, get ready for Judgement Day!" It is a song of delight, about having great peace "on the other side", about all our cares being taken away... and I wonder then what the fear is, in people who warn us of the dreaded "end of the world", when the "second coming" of Christ is set to happen as promised, and God comes to judge us. Because if it really does come, even if it involves some horrid "apocalypse", surely in the end this will be a good thing, as part of God's loving intention for us? Surely all that can ever come about will ultimately be the improvement of our connection to God's love? I ponder on and keep typing...

And as I type I notice some text scribbled beside my notes recording all that Helen said to me. It applies to my own response to Helen, rather than hers to me. It says: "How much do we learn by listening? How much do we fail to learn or grow when we do not listen because we are so sure only 'our' way is the 'right' way? The truth is the truth, but whose is my truth except mine? Can we as humans only ever 'point to' God's Truth? Isn't there always more than our own way of seeing and describing the great indescribable glory of God's ineffable Light?"

All these notes are not clear convictions of faith or philosophy but are part of this mountain journey to understand my/our connection to God. I write this here because quite a lot of Helen's beliefs differ from my own, yes, but – and it's an important but – who am I to say that I am right, and she is wrong? If I am sincere in my holding that none of us can claim to be prime holders of the "absolute divine Truth", then I must follow that without hypocrisy.

I need to ask, who am I to state that someone else's belief (Helen's) – that God's Word as recorded literally and exactly in the Bible, is what all humanity needs to know and follow, or they could suffer great punishment – is erroneous? Would it be like me saying all ideas about truth are equal, but some are more equal than others? Or that nobody can be "wrong" about God, but some people are?

What I am trying to suggest is, we can state that we do not like or do not agree with someone else's ideas of the Truth of God, but can we ever say they are wrong? This is good to consider. I certainly do not yet know the clear answer to this, or even if there is one.

But I am sure that by reminding myself of the aims of this book, I genuinely benefited from interviewing Helen. It did impress on me that we are all on a search for the "answer", and if I ever think I completely "know it"… then I probably don't! So, while I am on my way on the mountain, if I can pause to respect very different answers and directions to mine, this can surely only help me to grow in my understanding? It can teach me not to presume. To be receptive. To have humility.

And I hope that by saying all this here, rather than at the beginning of her chapter, you will already have considered Helen's views above with your own receptive heart and mind. I wanted to keep the tone gentle and perceptions fresh… to then help further clarify your beliefs and guide you on your own way to/with God.

*

As she and I looked through this chapter, Helen and I did go through some testing and very enriching time together, when she needed very much to make sure her beliefs were being put across clearly and correctly. I needed to reassure her that her way of Christianity not being the same as mine, or other people's in this book, is not a reduction or denigration of her own truth, but that without her chapter being included, her own kind of born-again Christian faith would be missing and not heard. Her contribution of beliefs for us to consider, from a very active, living part of the modern Christian church, would be lost. I am so glad she decided to stay with us!

I know that Helen received good help from elder friends within her church community in deciding how she needed her interview recorded and am so grateful for all the work and dedication to her faith which she has shown, working through the text with me and putting Bible references wherever she could – as the Bible is Helen's truth. She reminded me often that her truth belongs not to herself personally, but absolutely to God's Word in the Bible. And I do respect that.

Helen also helped me to contemplate a very interesting new angle on truth, which I shall try to describe for you in the next "interval"…

Jumping Beans!

While we were discussing her own interview chapter, Helen spoke to me about the talks given by Ravi Zacharias[1] (a popular Christian defender of evangelism) whose ideas on "absolute truth in relative terms" helped her to understand and tell me the following:

"All truth is relative" is a statement which could belong either *inside* or *outside* of the "circle of relativity" in which relative truth exists. And either way, it negates itself! Why? Because...

1) If *"all truth is relative"* exists *outside* of the circle, as not a relative but an absolute truth, a universally true statement, then not all truth is relative, because this is not!

2) If *"all truth is relative"* exists *inside* the circle of relativity, as being a relative truth, then it is only relatively true, not absolutely, and so some truth could be relative... but it could also be absolute, or conditional. Therefore, again, not *all* truth is a relative truth.

This is a very interesting set of ideas to really get our brains working. Sometimes challenges like this, where we focus our minds on one puzzle, can help the rest of our being to relax. So, now I will try and put this kind of thinking in a different way, reflecting on the ideas which I have gained from Martyn's interview as well as from talking with Helen and other people involved in the book, in a "picture story" for a mind-puzzle break called...

Not All Beans Jump!

If there is a red box in the world, and only *jumping* beans are kept in this red box, it could be that other kinds of beans are kept elsewhere, in different, blue or yellow boxes. Beans that buzz, beans that lie still...

Now, someone may say "all beans jump" because they are looking at beans only from inside the red box. But not all beans do necessarily jump! This is only a *relatively true* thing to say. If you were looking sometimes at beans outside the red box (say buzzing beans in a blue box) as well as sometimes looking at beans inside it, then to say "all beans jump" you would know to be only a relative truth, just for beans inside the red box.

But if you were always inside the red box and you were always looking at the beans in there, then you would probably think that *absolutely* all beans in this world do jump! You would be wrong. Your focus on the truth would be too narrow. Too "closed". You are only seeing things from "inside your own box".

The one sure thing everyone could know to be absolutely true, wherever they were, looking from either inside or outside of the red box, is that "all beans are beans" (just as perhaps "all truth is truth") of one kind or another... Beyond that, it depends where you are looking from. It depends on your perspective.

Now to me, this means some truth is relative, some truth is absolute and, because this story itself is symbolic in form, some truth is also conditional on how you choose to interpret it. Moreover, as I discover increasingly, some truth is "poetic", containing all these elements, and more beyond.

Some truth is also what we call in the modern world "false truth", meaning people claim it to be absolutely, factually true, when it is not. It is as mixed up and unfounded as its name suggests. And it often comes from a dishonest purpose.

I know – this continues the almost nonsensical word-games... but perhaps it again teaches us something else: that no human words can ever exactly define the great "Divine Universal Truth" – and I use sacred capitals here. Because the very fact that our words are human and limited (like our amazing but also limited minds) makes them neither divine nor universal.

But is it still worth trying? I think so. Because along the way, don't we learn so much? Don't we get closer? Do our thoughts begin to "make sense of" what another part of ourselves already knows?

As I keep coming back to wonder, in my circle of understanding (and as I come to understand more in my next interview, with Jyoti)... is the Truth of God's Love something we *can* clearly and *absolutely* know – not in our minds but in our hearts? Not completely expressed in words (no matter who thinks, writes or sings them) but in a silence that is, yes, enriched by words? Like if we say the word "peace" and then sit quietly with that thought, the feeling it can connect us to, or if we say a prayer such as the "Serenity Prayer" to God, and then just be silent, folded into the effects upon us of that prayer. Or if we repeat to ourselves the three words "God loves me" and begin to feel just how beloved we are?

CHAPTER SEVEN

Jyoti

Jyoti was born into a family whose tradition was Roman Catholic and she attended a convent school in Ireland. Later in life she spent some time in an ashram in Northern India where, unusually, she was initiated into becoming a "swami" which means "teacher". Her name now is Swami Jyotidhara Saraswati, which she tells me relates to "the flow of light".

She is not Hindu herself, nor does she state herself now to be of any one religion. She is, at age eighty-four, open-minded to all (and wise).

What is God to you, Jyoti?

God is something we are aware of, but we do not know what exactly God is. It is "the highest of whatever". The guide to the higher self. We are none of us alone in life as we are all connected by this one great energy of God, which is the highest form of Love.

Jyoti goes quickly to point out to me that the "universe is full of words we need to be careful of". This is because most do not mean anything. For example, what do we mean by "love"? It is different to each of us. All that really matters is an open heart.

It is easy for people to read a sentence in a book, such as a few words about love, but then not really explore what love is and means to their own heart.

Jyoti says, everything is made by God, so good is in everything. But when she says such things as that "God is the highest of whatever", this apparent vagueness serves to stop us using wrong or inexact words which confine love to it being a thought when it is not – it is a feeling.

Who was Jesus of Nazareth, to you?

He was carpenter's son who, amid the mayhem of Jewish history at the time, "liked not what he saw", and reacted as a great inspirer, with good sermons and teachings. A great deal of his "biography" has been made up by the church, so it is now very hard to know his actual life story. However, the myths and legends which help make up the stories about Jesus, do still have a deep truth in them. People of Jesus' day did not really write about him, because the tradition then was more oral – they sang and told stories about him, to pass on his messages and good news.

Jyoti goes on to wonder if the church chose a person called Jesus, who did live at this time, and in many ways made him what he has become to us now. The church added things to his story. She wants to believe he did exist, and did teach great love and kindness, and so she does – she chooses to believe he existed, because why not say it was "Jesus of Nazareth" who taught these great things? But in honesty, his story has been manipulated by the church.

And the miracles?

These stories are probably linked to things that did happen. For example, the "feeding of the five thousand" could have been because Jesus inspired people to *share* the food they had – to practise kindness. Then, years later, whoever wrote about it told it as the story of a "miracle". The meaning is in the teaching.

Was it symbolic?

Jyoti is not too fond of the term "symbolism". She says that the Bible was written by people, holy people, yes, who had insights that could even have been "channelled" from God or Jesus. But we must always take care, be open-minded to truth, while not going "over the top"– accept only what feels right to you, in your heart.

And sin?

"How did sin get into the Bible?" she asks. And answers herself, "because of who wrote it – the 'church'." She puts "church" clearly into inverted commas, as not the church of God, or the teaching of Jesus, but a political power, keeping people "knuckled down". This was not a part of God's message to us. As a child Jyoti was taught strictly that she was born with "original sin" but no, she tells me now, we are born with original goodness!

Heaven and hell?

As a child Jyoti was terrified of going to hell! She was "scared to death" of it. Of that "big bonfire" she might be sent to. But now, she knows heaven and hell are about the way you think and feel inside yourself. When you are a positive optimist, you touch heaven. When you think bad negative thoughts, you send yourself to hell. It is not what others do to you it is what you do to yourself.

What is more, what you do to yourself "touches the wings of a butterfly across the other side of the world." (I love the way Jyoti has here reversed the way I often hear this saying, that if a butterfly moves its wings, it touches and effects everything in the whole world...) She tells me we are all inter-connected, so we need all to take responsibility for how we think, as we affect everything else on the planet with our thoughts.

But what about after we die?

This is something we don't know, so we speculate lots! "What I know," she says, "is that if my spirit disintegrates, it will be a part again of the highest Love." The idea we "meet up with" passed away members of our family, no longer makes any sense to her. We go back to where we came from in the first place. "Life is continually what we perceive it to be," she tells me. "I perceive that we all come from and begin from Love, not dust! And we return to Love, not dust."

The message of Jesus?

Love is his message. If we love others more, often they also love more. If we love those whom we do not get on with, they often become more able to love us. It is simple! We need no "high saluting" concepts for it. We love our children whether they are good or bad – we simply unconditionally love them. In this way, God loves all of us. Jesus asks us to love others as we love ourselves – and to do this we need first to love ourselves. "Love yourself, and then you can love others," she affirms.

What was the holy sacrifice?

Jesus was accused and found "guilty" of a crime that meant capital punishment, and at the time this was by crucifixion. The church has put a lot of "meaning" onto this death, as representing something much greater. They may be right, Jyoti says, but she keeps an open mind. She reminds me again, however, these are all words for meaning. If we keep just coming back to the simple teaching of Love, we are clearer.

Jesus did not have to die to love us, or because he loved us. Love is free! People try to put lots of meaning onto his death perhaps for the very sake of meaning, for the satisfaction of "intellect". But really the phrase "he died for God to forgive us our sins" is all words, just words. There is nothing really for God to forgive, because we are all here on earth at different stages in our soul journey, and we all go back to love eventually.

Are we reincarnated?

"Who knows, who knows?" she tells me, with a smile.

In all religions, all spiritual and religious words, we try all of us to understand our own perception of the "highest of whatever". But there are so many perceptions, so many ways to understand. Others may also be right, from their own experiences. As people worldwide mingle and mix more with their beliefs, this could be good, but causes conflict when we cannot accept the "other" ways of perceiving God.

Jyoti talks about the partition times in India, when Pakistan was "created". Before this time, she says, people of different religions mingled well together, but then the politicians made a terrible conflict where none had been before, by creating a partition, which stressed differences rather than inter-mingling. This happens now in many places in the world.

Words, she emphasizes, are often not the best way to understand love. Jyoti practises silent meditation on the "heart chakra", which can open us out from the heart, with love.

And what of gender issues in Christianity?

Jyoti talks about Mary Magdalene, who was a holy woman, with a lot of influence in her time perhaps; a person close to Jesus. But the church chose to make her out to be a "prostitute", to reduce the "threat" of her having any power within Christianity. They were afraid, so they needed to discredit her. But this perception of Mary is changing.

And the "rising" of Jesus?

Again, these are just words, she says. Jesus "rising" to heaven is an interpretation which makes no real sense, because heaven and hell are *within* us. They are not a place but a state in our own being. Jesus was there in love, in heaven, when he died, as we all are. He did not come back alive to earth physically after he was put in the tomb – this is just an interpretation being made by the church and writers of the Bible. He "returned" in spirit, as Love. And Love is heaven.

The name "Christ" is again a word invented by people to mean something, Jyoti states. Something we are then expected to accept, without really knowing clearly and universally what this word means. This only causes confusion and problems, of misunderstanding.

Is there a devil or evil in the world?

No. There is love, and if someone acts "like the devil" she or he has just closed the door on love. Keep the door open, and you will be guided by what love means.

All negatives we humans create. And we often need to blame everyone and everything for things that go wrong, rather than ourselves. We are all inter-connected. We need to know that.

God is Love, and we are each a part of that Love, so we are each a part of God. What goes wrong is when we have not learned fully how to *be* a part of that Love, of God. How to be with Love.

The negatives in life are not separate from God, no, but they are also not set in stone. They can be changed, as we learn to be with God.

The Roman Catholic Church is full of teachings about the "bogeyman" of the devil or Satan "coming to get you". She remembers this well. But it is wrong.

What is prayer?

Prayer is a bit like talking to your "higher self", Jyoti says. We can ask God to help people, but are better not over-repeating this request, and sometimes it is good to ask for help for people in general rather than specifically by name. We can ideally remember a feeling of a person, or some people, and hold them in our hearts, send them love. Surround them in love. This is prayer. To love from our higher self. Jyoti tells me of her great granddaughter who was born prematurely. Jyoti held her in her heart, and she is sure this love helped her.

What of the Trinity and the Holy Spirit?

Jyoti reminisces on how she used to say to herself "Father, Son, and Holy Ghost" then wonder which of these is God? The idea of the Trinity is perhaps again something used by the church for its own ends. Nowadays, she sees God all as One.

But do you see the Holy Ghost as a more feminine aspect of God?

All words, just words, Jyoti reminds me again. What does "feminine" mean here anyway?

And the future of Christianity, of faith in God?

We each, she tells me, need to choose our own path. If Jesus inspires you – go for it! "I am a being on a spiritual path, whatever that means," she says quietly. "But I am not being flippant. I am open to whatever comes up to guide me." Jyoti tells me about how twice she has been on a pilgrimage to Lourdes, and been very inspired there, in the Grotto. Why? Perhaps because so many people go there, praying, believing. "It was like love had descended on us all," she says. (And I now want to go there!)

Jyoti summarizes for me two strong elements to her beliefs:

1) Keep an open heart and mind.
2) Know that words are not the best way to translate or understand God.

Perhaps we need a new "language" to use for God, in the way the French people have the French language, scientists have physics terms etc... but so far we have no words suitable really for talking about God, to help us clearly understand... so Jyoti prefers to go by feeling.

Often words are just used to "fill up a page", but the big, great feelings are perhaps in truth a part of love that cannot be described or explained in words. Words such as "peace" or "wonder" just don't do it. So, we need to feel them.

I talk to Jyoti about my poem on this subject – called "Track through"[1] – which describes how it feels easier to connect to words such as "anger" or "bitterness" than it is to capture feelings from words like "joy" or "awe".

She replies that this is perhaps because, in contrast to positive word emotions, negative emotions such as "anger" come from a place where we have *reduced* ourselves from the greatness, the expansiveness, of love, and so these feelings are more "in the realm" of the human ego. More "capturable" by words. Easier to translate and describe. (I find this a very good teaching.)

Jyoti goes on to talk about how, if we "hang onto things", it is like hanging on to the branch of a tree. We often don't want to, but we can let go. We can change. Change our minds even. Throughout our spiritual journey we can learn new things from different sources. Jyoti has learned from the Bible, the Upanishads, the Course in Miracles, the Bhagavad Gita... it is all where we are, where we need to be and to learn from, at that specific time in our life.

But so long as our prayers, be they psalms, chants, recitations, whatever, so long as they come from our *hearts*, this is all that matters.

Theories and concepts can mislead us, if we are not careful – take us from the true way, of feeling God's love.

I leave Jyoti's flat feeling more aware of my own rush in life to "know" and describe God; to know just where I am going on the mountain, and I appreciate her teaching that to "go, in love", is the way.

I also reflect, as I type up this interview, on the quote I remember by US farmer, environmental activist, and essayist Wendell Berry, which says: "people exploit what they have merely concluded to be of value, but they defend what they love, and to defend what we love we need a particularizing language, for we love what we particularly know."[2]

For a long time, I have thought that we need only to find a "particularizing language" for understanding God, to then be able to reach and hold the answers... but now I come closer to realizing what these interviews are teaching me – that perhaps we will never be able to find particular words to describe the greatness of God? And yet, and yet, are words all we have for communication, in our own heads, with streams of thoughts, and with each other?

Perhaps we must fumble along as best we can to translate the "untranslatable". And we can value language as a beautiful, even if limited, tool. Human language is good! A gift, a blessing. But even better, Jyoti reminds me here, is the feeling in the centre of our hearts.

CHAPTER EIGHT

Richard

Richard and I meet in his office in Oxford. I have come down for ten days at my old college, St John's, to interview him and one other person, plus to have the treat of a college flat, with time and space to concentrate on writing this book. During my stay, I notice people on guided tours in the city – Harry Potter enthusiasts who want to visit the place where the Great Hall of Hogwarts was filmed: the grand dining hall of Christ Church College.

While in Oxford I listen to the creator of Harry Potter, J. K. Rowling herself, in a television interview. She talks of her hugely popular books responding to a desire in so many of us to know the "unknown and unknowable". Our search for knowledge, even control, of an elusive and all-powerful force. For sure, Harry Potter's world of magic seems to have fed an expanding need in people, a need to believe in something "other", something "magical", which, as Rowling says in her interview "you don't have to believe in… but it's a shame if you don't." As a writer, she responds to the desire in millions of us to believe in something "more than this", which, in the case of Harry Potter, is the magic of wizardry and chance. Many people now look to the "twilight zone" of the occult and obscure, to seek the "extra" which we know deep down fulfils the "ordinary" of life. The extra-ordinary which we could find in the real magic of God. Surreal illusion seems to be more "in fashion", in literature and the film world at least, but time brings change…

Enthused by this idea of God being real, divine "magic", I go to meet Richard, full of intrigue as to what his Catholic faith means to him, and we have a wonderful interview…

*

Richard is a Dominican friar. And a Catholic priest. When we meet, he is wearing his habit (a long white robe). He tells me that his being a friar is his identity in life. His true vocation. He joined the Dominican order in 1995 and came to Oxford to train in what is the largest Dominican priory in the country, Blackfriars. He then moved to Leicester Priory as university chaplain but returned to Oxford to do research for a doctorate in New Testament studies. Now he is provincial bursar at Blackfriars, overseeing financial administration for eighty-five friars. He explains to me that Dominican friars tend to be based in university environments, such as Oxford, London, Cambridge, and now Grenada in the West Indies. Richard is a bursar, university teacher, but first and foremost, he is a Dominican friar, talking and interacting with people about their faith.

And who is God to you?

"God is the Love that sustains me in existence. The reason why there is anything rather than nothing at all," Richard tells me. "And the revelation of God in Christ is that the mysterious reason for existence is not just an impersonal force but is a *person*, who loves and cherishes me, and all of us. Who presents me with the demand to find the lovable and cherish-able in all of us, also."

He goes on to say "Obviously, if God is the reason for everything, then God makes all the difference. But God also makes all the difference because he gives meaning and purpose to life. Why anything matters, is God." (How well said!)

I mention to Richard how I am finding, after interviewing my old friend John who is also a Catholic, that it seems that Catholic followers of Christ are perhaps more tightly bound in loyalty to their church, more unquestioning, than my own experience of being from a C of E Protestant background.

Richard replies that he agrees. He tells me that the "party line" of his church is always what he truly believes. When I first typed up this interview and sent it to Richard to check over, I had written "often what he truly believes" and Richard corrected me that it is not often but *always*. "I'm a Catholic," he tells me. "My personal beliefs are Catholic beliefs." And I continue to listen intently.

Richard goes on to say that the study of Jesus in history is one of the subjects he teaches at the university. And yes, the Jesus of history *is* the Jesus believed in by the church. He was a man of 2,000 years ago, who lived in Galilee and Judaea, ate, joked, moved about as a real person, who was also, and is also, God. The perfect revelation of the meaning of human life. He was God coming to show us how to be a human. But he also showed us that the only way to be fully human is by sharing in Christ's divinity.

It is very important for us to know this is true of the historical, real Jesus. Currently the question "What was Jesus like?" is very popular. We need to remember that those people who were writing about him in the Gospels each had their own agenda. They were not writing modern biographies. However, Richard affirms quickly that he still ascribes to each of the Gospels with full belief.

It is a mistake, he says, to try to see and imagine Jesus as we would like him to be. People often say such things as "Jesus wouldn't have minded" – for example about gay marriage or woman priests – but this is making our own assumptions about Jesus. About how we would like him to act or react. We should not ask such things as "What would Jesus do?" about a problem, as if Jesus Christ is dead. He is not dead! He says and decides things now, through the church, which is his living body. What the church says now is what Jesus would and *does* say. We, the church, as Paul said, are the body of Christ. (I am a little unsure what Richard means by "the church", because different churches do say sometimes very different things, for example about gay marriage, and women priests... but I keep listening.)

The historical Jesus, then, did come to earth to be founder of the church; Richard tells me how much he believes this.

When was the Bible written and why?

By lots of people, over many years, for lots of reasons, he tells me. The majority of the Bible was probably written after 600 BC (which is much later than I have been told before now, and I have trust in Richard's Bible knowledge). Some people are worried by the idea that none of it was even written before 300 BC, but Richard is not at all worried by this, and neither are the scholars who claim this to be the case. The Pentateuch, for example (the first five books of the Old Testament), might have been written between 500 and 150 BC. And why? For both human and divine reasons. Individuals writing books in the Bible did so for their own different reasons. The author of the book of Job, for example, was probably trying to understand the "unknowability" of God, after his own personal experiences. Then the book of Numbers, or Leviticus, were written for religious, political, and theological reasons. They were more "ideological" than personal. It is also possible that not all human motives for writing the Bible books were "pure".

But no matter! What matters is only God's intention. He achieves what he wants to, through humans, even in our mixed up/messed up humanity.

What is the Bible for?

The Old Testament is there to prepare us for the coming of Christ. No Jewish people agree with this, maybe, but Richard sees the best and probably the only way to read the Old Testament... is in the light of Christ.

He compares it to looking at "magic eye" 3D pictures, where we can only see the real picture, deep inside, when we focus correctly and look through it – to see Jesus. He is the clear "explanation" of the Old Testament.

I ask Richard about the time gap between events such as Moses leading the Jewish people through the wilderness, in exodus from Egypt, and the writing down of these stories in the Bible.

The standard view, he tells me, is that the exodus occurred around 1200 BC... but then again, many Bible scholars do not even believe it happened! Richard believes it did and knows that Jews in this time period were very keen on keeping and preserving records accurately, particularly genealogical ones. Hence numbers, statistics, and records of events could easily have been passed down through generations, before things were written down in texts. However, other scholars do say some figures and events could have been made up to fit the story.

None of this is so important to Richard, because the real, important "exodus" is the exodus we all can make, from *sin to life*. To him, it did happen, the exodus in the desert, but the true meaning of the story is still the symbolic meaning. The symbolic meaning of the literal reality! Because this is how God works.

We humans may write completely fictional symbolic stories, such as the magical *The Lion, the Witch and the Wardrobe* by C. S. Lewis, but God makes the real story happen literally, first, and then also makes it have symbolic meaning and teachings... because God can. He teaches us symbolic things from fantastic real events.

Richard goes on to say that, if the exodus of the Jews from slavery in Egypt never even happened, or was a much smaller, less dramatic event, with no parting of the Red Sea but just a walk over a muddy stream, if he went back in time and found this to be the literal truth, then *so what*? This would not change the symbolic teaching from God, as put down in the Bible.

However, if Richard went back in time and found the Gospel stories of Jesus' life to be untrue – for him not to have been crucified and resurrected – then: "I would be totally dismayed," he tells me, very poignantly.

I begin to realize for myself something important on this journey, which is that if I found Jesus not to have been crucified, I would be shocked — because he was a radical spiritual teacher, and this was surely the consequence for him, being executed as a rebel by the rulers. However, if I found that Jesus was not resurrected physically, that he "rose again" in his pure Spirit form, not in a body, then I would not be "faith-shaken" or very disappointed. It would still teach me that all we are is our eternal soul, loved by and in God. The physical is not the crux of Jesus, to me.

And now I also see how many Christians like Richard, in a way I respect very much, do need to and do with certainty believe, that Jesus was resurrected in a body of flesh as well as of Spirit... then I "step over" on my mountain path. To also believe that this was not in the least bit difficult for Jesus to do — if/as he was the divine — to resurrect a physical human body and transform death into eternal life... easy! Because God can do anything... and so, of course, it could have happened.

But do we absolutely have to 100 per cent believe that Jesus came back from the dead, physically, to be able to call ourselves "Christian"? Or is it much more important to believe that Jesus was the divine Son of God, was Christ on earth, and still is, and that whatever he did/does, in the physical or spiritual form, he does to teach us about God's eternal love and grace? All good things to reflect upon...

Going back to Richard talking to me about the Bible stories... he tells me that in the Old Testament, such difficult passages as those on "ethnic cleansing" or about stoning your wife or child if they disobey, we now must read these symbolically, he says, or else we get mixed up. They were originally all stories about purity and protecting Israel from idolatry, and so on. It was never God's intention for them to be taken as an excuse for murder or exclusion.

Richard makes it clear that he is neither a literalist nor a fundamentalist when it comes to the Bible. This is in fact incompatible with Christianity. Even the New Testament does not always take the Old Testament literally. So why should we? For example, Paul said of the text from Deuteronomy "You shall not muzzle the ox when it is treading out the grain" that it had meaning related to Christian preachers, not animals.[1] Paul therefore takes an Old Testament saying and uses it symbolically, subtly, and in a way relevant to the people of his time, as did many of the church fathers. ("Church fathers" is the term for the early Christian theologians, particularly from the first to fifth centuries, whose writings were regarded as especially authoritative.)

What is important is not to ask, "What does the Bible say?" but "What does God communicate to us *through* the Scriptures?"

To understand the Bible clearly requires quite a lot, says Richard. Firstly, prayer. Secondly, serious intellectual engagement. And thirdly, importantly to him, humility toward the traditions of the church.

We need to remember that Christians have been reading and studying the Bible for centuries. The church, the "body of Christ", is over 2,000 years old. And it has been authoritatively interpreting the biblical text for this long.

It would therefore be arrogant for him, he says, to come along and interpret the Bible "anew". New ways are not necessarily better ways of understanding. He tells me it can be risky to read the Bible on your own "from scratch" (which I am doing). This, he agrees with me, is quite a "Catholic" thing for him to say – to advise me to read the Bible with the guidance of the church. (I do take notice and consider what he tells me.)

What about sin and God's wrath?

Richard talks about how the Bible is wrongly construed as the Old Testament being all mean and cruel and the New all lovely and fluffy! There is plenty of joy in the Old, such as in the Song of Songs – about God's love for his people. There is, yes, a shift of emphasis, all because the fundamental revelation of God, in Jesus Christ, showed us how much he loves us. But we must not forget that his love is not incompatible with a condemnation of sin.

Some people may say "if God forgives us everything, then I can do whatever I like, I can do wrong" but no, because we are free to reject God, to turn away from that forgiveness, turn away from God's love. If we choose to do this, then we choose hell, by our own free will. Jesus came to set us free from sin, but we are still free to reject him and all that he is.

Jesus, Richard tells me surprisingly, talks a heck of a lot more about hell than the Old Testament does! He talks about hell a lot, because as God, Jesus knows what hell is possible for humans who reject love. He knows the stark miserable futility of hell.

No, he never said one particular person would certainly go to hell, so we can have hope that hell is empty, but, and Richard stresses this, we must not *presume* that hell is empty! (I find all this fascinating.)

And heaven?

Heaven is to be in the presence of God. To fully experience his love. In this life, we can get a "taste" of heaven, but human weakness and mortality inevitably cloud our experience of it. Hell is simply the *opposite* of God's love.

Could you explain purgatory to me?

Purgatory is a process, rather than a place. It is not a part of hell, but a preparation for heaven (I enjoy this explanation!). Richard continues, if you imagine having a "dirty secret" and then discover that your mum knows and has always known this secret, but still loves and forgives you... then you can feel shame but then feel released and free, because you have the joy of knowing you are still loved, whatever. And then you can move on. This is the process of purgatory. You can also break a bad habit you were trapped in, because that was part of the trap, your shame.

Purgatory is all about healing. Being given the opportunity to heal all the harm done to your "self" over your lifetime. We all do what we choose to do, but we are not always conscious of the choices we are making. So, we need to heal.

And heaven is not necessarily just for Christians. (I am surprised and very happy to hear Richard say this.) "I don't make the rules for God, God makes the rules for me! Put that down," says Richard. "That's a good line!" A Muslim or an atheist who is filled with love and compassion for others has chosen love, so might well go to heaven, because heaven is God's loving presence. Richard is keen not to ever say with certainty who will or will not go to heaven because (as many other interviewees have stated), only God knows this. However, a "Christian" who is deeply full of hate and anger, who chooses not to let God's love heal him/herself, has already made his/her choice – to go to hell. To be in hell.

But, he goes on, everyone who is in heaven *is* a Christian, in that they know Jesus Christ is the Son of God, because they can now see it. The Truth. Sometimes, he says, the light of God – including Jesus – is too bright for us, and as we come out of darkness, we cannot see it at first. So, we need a chance, a place to get used to it, to recover from living in darkness, like when the curtains are drawn suddenly, and we need to prepare ourselves for this vision of God.

If on earth we are not a Christian, we are not inevitably destined for hell. If God wants to save for example a Buddhist person, because this Buddhist is choosing love in their life – even if they are unaware this love is coming through Christ – then "who am I to say God will not allow this person into heaven?" (I find all this very honest and thought-provoking! As so often, seeking the possible truth in what people tell me, teaches me more than looking for the non-truth.)

"However," he continues, if a Buddhist asks me, "What must I do to inherit eternal life?" then I must, and would, say, "Be baptized and live as a Christian."

What was the message of Jesus?

Jesus knew he was the divine Son of God. His message is to reveal God's love. But, Richard tells me, Jesus also had a message about himself. He said, "Trust in God, trust also in me." He came to set us free from our sins. A big part of his message was "I am the one who frees you from your sins." A lot of his teaching was not new – it is in the Old Testament, in Buddhism, in Hinduism... so we do not need God to have become human in order to tell us to be good and kind. But we do need him to have become human so that he could die for us, on the cross. Again, a human martyr could do this, die for people, as a brave, loving gesture, but this man was Jesus, *was God*, dying for us... that is what makes all the difference.

The crucifixion was therefore both a sacrifice and a showing, a perfect revelation, of God's divine love for us. Sacrifice is an offering. What we see on the cross, Richard confirms in an important way, is not God killing a man, but men killing God. Because God as Jesus gives his divine life for us. He also gives divine life *to* us, by pouring out his love for us on the cross, so that we can also have divine life.

This was ultimately the "final" sacrifice, the final offering, and it is also the *only* sacrifice, because every other, before and after this one, takes its meaning from this sacrifice on the cross. We cannot, Richard goes on, understand any sacrifice in the Old Testament by studying it alone, nor can we understand the sacrifice of Jesus by studying those in the Old Testament... only by looking deeper and understanding the sacrifice of Jesus, with all its meaning, can we understand any of it!

Sacrifice is and was the giving of something. Often in Old Testament times this gift was great in the number and cost of livestock. For example, 10,000 lambs were recorded by the historian Josephus, as being sacrificed during the Passover at the Temple in Jerusalem. Sacrificial giving as an act of love, of worship, of repentance, in order to make you "holy". Jesus' death on the cross gives meaning to all this.

Those who talk of Jesus' life being about sacrifice or a revelation of divine Love, are making a false distinction, he says, because it is *both*! He died on the cross to show us and give us his love which is his life, to make us holy also. The popular idea that somehow Jesus' death "doesn't really matter" is so odd to Richard, because why else would he bother? Death does matter!

By dying, Christ changed what death *is*, in a sense, because by nature we are radically separated from God, by our mortality as humans. Death is therefore like a "chasm" between us and God. But when Jesus died on the cross, in perfect obedience to his Father's will, he changed death from being a chasm to a "doorway".

I am really enjoying this so press further... how did death become a doorway?

Because, he says, that is how God chose to pour his love into us. His life into our hearts. God chose this as the way. Partly by revelation but partly by a real change – the sending of the Holy Spirit. Not just at Pentecost, as many may think, but actually while Jesus was still on the cross. The Gospel of John says that when Jesus died, he "handed over the spirit " (or, as the KJV translation tells us, "gave up the ghost") to all of us who choose to accept it.[2]

God could have chosen other ways than by dying, perhaps, but he chose this one! How and why, who knows? Only God. And there is no mechanism to this "doorway" symbol which we humans can find. (I take this to mean, there is no way of us breaking down this symbol – of the death of Jesus on the cross as a doorway for us all into eternal life – into anything more basic than it is.) Yes, it is how it looks, how it was, when Jesus, as God on the cross, gave himself to the hands of men. Literally *and* symbolically. (I do sense in these words some great teaching.)

If Jesus' death on the cross is what God's love for us *looks* like, then, says Richard, it is a great idea to look at the cross! As often as we can.

And gender?

"God is not male," Richard says. "Jesus is a man and he is God, but God is not a man. There, that's Christianity in a nutshell!" he laughs. However, he adds, Jesus did address God as "Our Father" and we should not second guess him, just to attempt to be more "modern". Neither should we ask, "What would Jesus say now about this issue?" That is more second guessing. We can, if it helps us, use more feminine imagery in our theology and worship. We can even say "Our Mother" if we like, but never during the Mass. That would be wrong. If Jesus and the church tell us to say, "Our Father who art in heaven", then this is what we must do.

And what of evil?

Richard tells me wisely that in an important sense "evil" does not exist, because it is the *absence* of God, and so it cannot ever be "present" because it is an absence... like a hole in our sock! But then again, a hole in our sock is still a problem.

Evil is very much a "privation", a lacking. Evil – in the way of thinking very much of Thomas Aquinas, an influential early Dominican friar – is a "falling short".

But Satan does exist, yes. He cannot be totally evil therefore. Because he exists. He has "being". This is a good thing, as nothing that exists can be purely evil. But then again Satan does not exist "enough", because he/it is not good enough. Only God, who is pure goodness, totally 100 per cent exists absolutely.

I find this fascinating and suggest the question: Are there therefore certain parts of us that are not good, non-existent?

Richard agrees with this idea.

He then quotes for me "ens et bonum convertuntur", a saying from Thomas Aquinas, that "being and goodness are interchangeable". He also admits that, during his own life, the "bad" things he has done, mistakes made, weaknesses, have always been due to something being "missing"... usually love.

Satan exists, he tells me, because God loves him. But Satan adamantly refuses to acknowledge that love, or to enjoy it or return it. Satan is a "spirit" and nobody is in more danger of falling into grave wickedness through him than someone who believes there is no such thing as right and wrong. This is a real problem in modern society.

What is prayer, Richard, to you?

"Prayer is an opportunity for God to change my mind," he says. Prayers of "petition" are important, not to try to change God's mind, but so we can place ourselves fully in the presence of God. We need to acknowledge all our hopes and desires, be they right, wrong or even trivial... yes! It is OK to pray for small things, to not hide ourself from God, so that the real person you are is brought before him. Then God can change your mind and heart: can help you so you pray for more important things.

As a Dominican friar, Richard tells me, prayer is not so much a communication of "me and God" but of "us and God". "Liturgical" prayer strengthens his sense of communion with the church, which extends beyond the community he belongs to in Oxford, in both space and time, out to the whole Christian community. He loves to think that when he prays the Divine Office prayer, that same prayer could be being said by perhaps a nun in Bogota, or a priest in prison in Laos, all praying the same prayer for hundreds of years. And some psalms could have been read or said out loud in prayer for thousands of years, and thousands more into the future, in many old and even new future languages. All of them together are praying *in* – Richard here reminds me he says "in" the body, rather than "to", and this difference is important – the invisible body of

Christ. All this reminds Richard that he is not the centre of attention!

As a priest, he tells me, he needs to try to be both charismatic and transparent, when giving a sermon. To aim for the congregation just "seeing Jesus" rather than noticing too much of Richard himself, when he speaks. There are indeed moments during the giving of Mass when he feels full of the Spirit of God, for seconds of bliss. (I see how wonderful that must be.)

And the Holy Trinity?

The Holy Spirit is God, he replies. "The life of God which is the love of God which is God." God's Spirit becomes the power which animates us when we stop resisting. In those rare moments, we are finally free. We finally experience, in some small way, the joy and delight of the Father for the Son, and of the Son for the Father. He points out that he is not saying of "God for Jesus" here but, importantly, of "Father for Son".

Richard now does teach me a very new and exciting idea. That *within* God, these three "persons" of Father, Son, and Holy Spirit rejoice and delight *in each other.* They love each other, within the Trinity of God.

One of the things which Jesus revealed in his lifetime, by his Passion and sending of the Holy Spirit, is that *in God* there is this sharing. This communion of love and perfect delight. It is an eternal Trinity, an eternal "Father/Son/Holy Spirit" communion going on forever, which we cannot imagine... but we can get a glimpse of this inner life of the Trinity, when we experience real pleasure in the sheer existence of another person, feel absolute love, such as for a child.

The Trinity doctrine is not a mathematical formula, or something to frighten people with, it is simply the belief of the church that the *life of God is a communion of love.*

Even without creating the earth, and the creatures and humans on it, Richard explains to me, God would still be Love! God created the world for something *else* to love. But always and forever, before this, eternally, God loves "Godself" as a perfect communion of love.

I find this a fascinating concept. That God as the Trinity is a kind of infinite interactive loving going on eternally, within Godself. The Trinity concept is therefore an amazing potential way to understand God by because, as a non-singular power, God is able to do and to be what God is: to give, receive, and share love. And delight in this! I suddenly realize that God perhaps has to be more than one "element", if God is Love. Because into eternity God has always been loving. And love cannot love alone. I begin to see this now. It is like the Trinity could be a force full of love within Godself, loving the three (or however many) "parts" of Godself, always. And perhaps Jesus the Son coming to earth, telling us he was God but then also loving his Father, and giving the Holy Spirit to us, addressing the three aspects of God, helped us to learn this? And yet, some people say only the church created the idea of the Trinity. But the idea of God being always a dynamic loving interaction within Godself, seems to me a very helpful way to realize God; to realize what God always does.

What of the future, Richard?

He hopes and trusts in God for the future of the church, which he believes the Holy Spirit will not allow to fail in its vocation – to preach the Gospel of Jesus to the whole world. It may be that fewer people are Christians now in the West, but in the rest of the world, there are more Christians than ever before! We plant the seeds, and God gives them chance to grow.

The church does need to constantly evaluate the way the gospel is preached, but also to resist the constant temptation to preach a gospel more "palatable" to the modern world. It needs to remain the gospel of Christ.

The future of the church is the second coming, which may happen today or in millions of years. But the church, says Richard, and every Christian individual must "constantly gaze into the heavens with eager longing" (see Acts 1:10–11) and at the same time always help other humans to live in hope.

Richard emphasizes now to me that, as Christians, we do good works not so that we can go to heaven, but because of a *response* to what God has done for us and promised to us. So, we do good not in an attempt to earn rewards but in a thanksgiving to love, because we are loved. "Anyone who realizes how much they are loved, cannot help but respond with love!" he tells me, happily.

*I enjoy and learn so much from this interview with Richard that I go a few days later to hear him give the sermon at St John's College evensong. He describes the two great laws of God, being shown in the Old Testament in Leviticus (19:18) – to "love your neighbour as yourself" – and in Deuteronomy (6:5) – to "love the Lord your God with all your heart, and with all your soul, and with all your might". But Richard explains that we need to do both. Not just to love our fellow human, and not just to love God – to love Jesus – in a "personal connection" way. We need to love others **and** be devoted to our Lord.*

He uses the symbol of the cross to help us understand this. The horizontal part of the cross we could imagine as being our "outstretched" love toward our fellow humans, while the vertical part could be seen as our "direct" connection to Jesus, to God.

After hearing Richard talk to me about the importance of the cross in his life, this image has a strong impact on me. What a wonderful positive way to see the cross. To live the message of the cross. A message of loving connection to Jesus and to our fellow brothers and sisters. This seems to be just what Jesus taught, and so Richard's aim as a Dominican friar, to have Jesus "seen through him" in a sermon, did at this evensong come true!

I now wear my cross with more joy.

CHAPTER NINE

Brigid

Brigid was born into a family with strong atheist beliefs, but, growing up in the Yorkshire Dales and, as a child, feeling a powerful connection to something that felt very transcendent in nature, she sensed that perhaps an atheist viewpoint on life wasn't quite true, just as much as she instinctively felt that the rather "fear-based" Christian religion she was being taught at school also wasn't quite true. This set her on a path to discover a perspective which might lie between atheism and religion, and she has spent her life since age eighteen (she is now fifty), seeking spiritual understanding. She has spent time in an ashram in India, lived in a spiritual community called the Findhorn Foundation in northern Scotland (where I met her) and has followed teachers of Eastern wisdom such as Sai Baba and Amma, until coming to discover "non-duality" teachings through people such as Eckhart Tolle. Brigid eventually found her spiritual home in the teachings of *A Course in Miracles*[1] *(ACIM)* and *The Way of Mastery (WoM)*, which have Jesus as their spiritual guide.

The Way of Mastery has three main texts, these being *The Way of the Heart*, then *The Way of Transformation*, then *The Way of Knowing*,[2] which is the book that Brigid is currently studying and practising.

Both *ACIM* and *WoM* connect to Jesus by the "channelling" of his divine revelations and wisdom, through living people. The students of *ACIM* and *WoM* believe that Jesus speaks to people directly and the channellers write down his exact words, to communicate them to the students of the courses. It is, Brigid says, simply "divine inspiration" by which the divine can communicate directly with humanity.

For the first part of our two-day interview we sit together in Nanteos Mansion in Wales, which was believed by some to have been one of the resting places of the Holy Grail as a wooden cup fragment, which is now housed in the National Library of Wales. Before we arrive at the Mansion we take a detour to see the cup at the library, and I do feel it is a special relic – not necessarily because it *is* the actual Holy Grail which Jesus drank from at the Last Supper (who knows?) – but because of all the people, from monks to tourists to even thieves, who have held this cup in awe, prayed over it, believed in its powers to heal… just being close to the cup at the library is a memorable experience.

Brigid does not see herself as a Christian, as she says this would define her too narrowly and imply that, for example, she is "not" a Buddhist or Hindu or Muslim. She prefers to say that she sees beauty and truth in all these ways to God but chooses to follow the "new teachings" of Jesus, not in devotion to Jesus as a person (she has no real interest in his biography) but to the pure Truth in his teachings.

Who is God, to you?

Brigid now talks to me about the "new teachings", as she will throughout this interview. She emphasizes to me that really, they are ancient teachings, which may have been misinterpreted or misunderstood or forgotten in the past, and which Jesus is now speaking to us about through the new channellings, to help us realize what he always wanted us to know.

ACIM tells Brigid that "God is the only fact". This means that "nothing else is real", which means that Truth is "purely non-dualistic". To explain she tells me that there is only one "thing", God, and God is all that exists. God as pure Love. This is perhaps far from the human mind's ability to fully comprehend, but we are all a part of God and so we are all a part of that only fact.

The course teaches her an important truth which is that "nothing real can be threatened, nothing unreal exists".

She explains… anything that can decay, like physical matter, such as our bodies, does not really "exist" and is all part of an "illusion", a dream in our minds. We are all really an eternal part of God, of the "nothing real that can be threatened", not as our bodies but as our souls. Therefore, nothing can threaten the God that we are. We are all a part of God, not just Jesus, every one of us is an "extension of God".

And Jesus?

Brigid tells me that Eckhart Tolle called Jesus "one of the earliest blooming flowers of humanity".[3] He was perhaps one of the first to achieve enlightenment, but there have been others since. He was human, like us, but was able to show us the way of what is possible for us all in human form.

And Jesus is still very much invested in humanity now, he is an "engaged presence" now with us, wanting to show us the way. In the new teachings, Brigid tells me, Jesus says that "the Christ" is God's *only* creation. The Christ is the "child of God which we all are". The extension of God, which is all of us, as one thing, non-dualistic.

How do you see the Bible?

Brigid tells me she believes the Bible to be written partly by God, by divine inspiration, but also partly by human egos. It contains lots of "lovely truths and also muddled contradictions". When Jesus was alive, people were perhaps not yet ready or able to fully understand his teachings on a "mass level". So, limited human minds tried to record great truths which they could not really comprehend.

But now, in modern times, we are lucky to have made two important steps forward:

1) the birth, in the 1930s, of modern psychology with Freud, and the growing knowledge of the sub-conscious mind and how it operates.
2) modern science, especially quantum physics, which is able now to research the nature of consciousness.

These great changes allow us to better understand the teachings of Jesus. We can perceive truths which before we could only attempt to interpret, with the concepts we had to hand – truths too big and radical for people to follow, at the times the Bible was being written and revised. Brigid tells me that she has not read the Bible, but when she does open a page of it, she sees too often words such as "wrath" and "smite" and "thwart". This puts her off it as a way of learning the teachings of Jesus, especially when she can now read and follow his new teachings as they are channelled through people in books like *ACIM* and *WoM*. To her, anything talking of sin, guilt, wrath, and judgment is totally incompatible with Jesus' current and past (misunderstood) teachings and the pure Love of God's thinking.

I ask her to tell me more about the "channellings".

ACIM, she tells me, was channelled by Helen Schucman, an American, non-practising Jew and psychologist who heard a voice in her mind saying she needed to write down what was being dictated to her, which she did, for six years. She did not understand it all, but she diligently wrote it down, even when the voice of Jesus stopped mid-sentence and then continued perhaps the next day at the exact same point in the teaching!

Brigid tells me that these channelled teachings are beautiful, "luminous", and in her thirty years of study and searching for spiritual truth, she has never found anything else that for her contains such a heightened feeling of purity. She loves how the teaching never deviates or wavers – even when it is difficult and challenging – from the truth that "God is non-dualistic and is only Love, nothing else". "The purity of this message makes it luminous, to me," she says, with dedication to her path.

A Course in Miracles was first published in the mid-1970s and since then (and no doubt before then too), Jesus, and other enlightened teachers – have channelled teachings through people worldwide, to those who are open and receptive to such dictation by an enlightened soul. The channellers are all very different people and living in very different places, but they seem to have one message, about God's non-duality and unconditional love.

This is also, she tells me, where modern psychology helps us understand God: we see that our sub-conscious mind, whatever it cannot *accept* in itself, it *projects* outwards onto other people and the world. Therefore, the path back to God is a path very much of "loving forgiveness". Forgiveness of our projections onto others. Whoever, whatever, we have judged when we are "triggered" to judge and condemn, Jesus teaches us that the path of forgiveness is to "embrace your miscreation", with the love of God that you really are.

To change your mind and choose again, to love and forgive both yourself and the person/thing/event you are judging, so that every time your mind "contracts" in judgment, away from what is in front of you, your forgiving mind can now perceive all of this with love.

By doing so, you are *realigning* your mind to the one holy truth, to think as God thinks, and thereby to fit your mind "into heaven", which is yes, a state of mind, and not a place.

Brigid goes on to tell me that the language of *The Way of Mastery* she finds easier to follow than *A Course in Miracles* – which is more heavily cloaked in biblical language. *ACIM* is a very beautiful, poetic text but *WoM* is for her more accessible and straightforward. She confirms again that she prefers reading and studying *WoM* and *ACIM* teachings than the Bible, because for her they are unadulterated teachings and "the purest I have found, not like cloudy water... why wouldn't I choose to drink the purest water I know of?!"

The channeller for the *WoM* is a man called Jayem – originally John Mark – who in a sense embodies the teaching because he was once accused of a sexual crime with a child. Jesus teaches, Brigid emphasizes to me, that *everyone*, even icons of evil such as Hitler, is in truth Christ. This is a difficult truth to realize, but it is totally non-judging, and non-discriminatory. It therefore encourages Brigid that Jesus chose such a person as Jayem to channel his words. This teaches and shows not that "Jayem is imperfect and yet a channeller" no, but that "Jayem, as with all of us, is the perfect Christ". To see him as imperfect is only an illusion. It is an illusion to think that whatever anyone has ever done or said or thought could in any way tarnish the purity of the Christ that we are.

So, we are all perfect in truth, and Jayem illustrates this teaching because to Jesus he is perfect, now, as we all are – all of us being the Christ. Seeing any imperfection in anyone is an illusion of our minds only. If we find judgment in our mind about him or anyone (as I admitted to Brigid I did feel), then we need to forgive and change our own mind-set, our misconception, our illusion, and see the reality of Christ in all of us.

We do this by 1) forgiving ourselves for judging and 2) liberating the person from our judgment, by loving them as Christ. This will then enable us to change our mind and think like God, that all beings are the Christ, which is pure Love. We will also see that "separate people" do not really exist, like Brigid, myself, Jayem – no, we are all really one, as only the Godself really exists.

What do you believe about "sin" and guilt?

"Sin does not exist!" Brigid states. The new teachings of Jesus are very specific about this, she tells me. Guilt is an illusion of the mind because, if we see ourselves or others as sinful, we are misperceiving ourselves or the person before us, seeing only their "illusory personality", not the Christ that they, and we, are. Sin and guilt do not really exist, only in the illusion. "I'm not saying bad things or people don't happen," Brigid tells me, "They do, but only in the illusory judgmental world, where we perceive people or things or events as good or bad, but the teachings say we need to perceive through the eyes of God, and love others as they really are. You do need to see that nothing really has happened, except in an illusory world. You need to try to see the truth behind the form." (I keep listening, writing, and learning as we continue with this.)

"We need to distinguish between action and thinking," she explains. "On the level of the illusory world we do need to take action against 'wrong-doing' for disciplinary purposes, yes, but with our mind we need to try to perceive with love and understand the deeper truth that all we see is a reflection of our own mind and that we are all ultimately wholly innocent. And what is more, you cannot *act* in error, if your mind perceives with the Love of the Christ. We can at least aspire to this."

Brigid goes on to tell me that the main gist of Jesus' new teachings, the truth of which she believes was perhaps "fudged" somewhat in the Bible, was to teach us to train our minds away from perceiving with *fear* toward perceiving with love. All negative mind-sets and emotions, she explains, such as anger, hatred, bitterness, vengefulness – they all stem from this fear, which is at the root of all negativity. It is the wrong thinking of our ego, our erroneous perception that we have a separate self, a separate identity from the Godself.

The new way of thinking brings Jesus' teachings more in line with Eastern spiritual philosophy, which can see the physical world as only a *relative*, not an *absolute* reality. Such "new" teachings of Jesus have not "come from nowhere", she says. The idea of an "illusory" world has been with Buddhism for centuries, and Jesus as an enlightened being was perhaps influenced by such Eastern philosophy. Moreover, quantum physics can now step in to help us, being in line with such thinking in that it defines matter as mostly being "empty space" at an atomic level – and because form is mostly space, some quantum physicists believe that "matter" is therefore much more *malleable* to "thoughts". This scientific idea aligns to the Buddhist sutra that "form is emptiness, emptiness is form".

Brigid is inspired that these various new ways of thinking are now coming together regarding the "spaciousness of reality", and the power of the mind to create "reality". She tells me "Jesus teaches us that 'nothing exists outside of the mind.'" And this is where modern psychology also comes in, because just as quantum physics teaches that the world is only "relatively real" and we create the world around us with our thoughts, so psychology teaches that anything we judge and cannot accept in our self, we project out and see outside of ourselves in the world.

For example, she goes on, if we say to our self that a person is "mean", this is because we are projecting out onto another person the lack of kindness which we cannot accept in our own sub-conscious, and which very much needs to be loved and forgiven. Therefore, if we perceive the "mean" person with love, we are in truth forgiving and loving this "meanness" in our own self. The part of us which we could not know or accept we see in another, because we deny it is within us.

Also, if on a deep subconscious level, we believe ourselves to be unworthy and unlovable for example, then we unwittingly create scenarios where we encounter people who seem to reflect our unworthiness back to us by treating us disrespectfully. We can repeatedly forgive all this too: the "others" for their seemingly unhelpful treatment of us, and ourselves for misperceiving ourselves – so in this way the mind can be gradually healed and returned to a loving state.

And the ultimate purpose is perhaps to learn to know that none of this in truth matters! Because it is not really real, it is all an illusion. And when we aim to align our mind with God, then anything can happen. To aim to become connected and non-judgmental, the consequence of which is unknowable, but can only be good. Our human mind needs correction and "purification" because it has been conditioned by fear, by the world we live in. Our thoughts need to be corrected not because we are "bad" at all, or sinful – quite the opposite – but because we need to *realign* ourselves back to think like God.

The experience of God is available to all of us because we *are* God, every one of us, anytime, in all circumstances. Nothing from God needs to be "earned", Brigid emphasizes. It is instantaneous. That is why, she tells me, it is important to her that her *knowing* of God, which she is working toward, is not a "belief". It is an "experience". This experience is not easy to mediate through the rational mind, but we do need to purify our mind in order that we are able to ultimately transcend erroneous and conditioned thinking and so experience God. But we are all God *right now*, and nothing, she reminds me, can make us "more" or "less" God!

When the mind is fully realigned, she confirms, then it is a living *felt* experience, not a belief or a theory or a metaphysical idea. When we are One, when we know we are One in God, then we live in this enlightened state of Oneness – as Jesus did – and we know it as our everyday reality.

How do you interpret "heaven" and "hell"?

These are, she tells me, states of consciousness experienced in, or outside of (post death), our physical bodies. We can choose to perceive either heaven or hell, with our own mind. Heaven is "a lived experience of complete Oneness with God and all that is", while hell is fear and separation from this Oneness.

Because we are all a part of God, we each have powerful minds, which we can use to choose repeatedly fearful thoughts, and put ourselves "in hell", or to train our minds to repeatedly think loving thoughts and ultimately attain a complete unshakeable Oneness with God.

Such a heavenly state does not "require" an awareness of Jesus, as many other mystical traditions can lead to this. Brigid tells me "There are many paths up the mountain, yes, and we are all of us heading back up to God, as we cannot go anywhere else! We are going back to God as this is the Truth of our being, ultimately, but some paths back up the mountain meander a lot, some are more direct."

She continues, the way to God is not dependant on Jesus, but his teachings such as *A Course in Miracles* and *The Way of Mastery* are, for Brigid, so pure, so non-dualistic, that in them Jesus has given us a path which is very clear. "That we are all part of a Oneness, nothing real has two sides or many parts, nothing real can decay, and nothing is real except for God, God being Love."

But what happens after we die?

She tells me with enthusiasm that modern research into phenomena such as near-death experiences now provides a massive amount of very persuasive evidence about this. Medical science is developing fast and we are experiencing more and more people being brought back from death (with the use of defibrillators in particular) who describe their experiences of being conscious despite being beyond the physical body. Their reports are shockingly uniform. From psychological research, hypnosis reports, even hypnotic past-life regression… these all provide anecdotal but very uniform descriptions, as real experiences by "living" people, of what happens after death.

It seems, she continues, that we still have a sense of "self", even without our body. People report how we each go through different stages in the afterlife, of learning and purifying and growing, until we are ready to return to another life stage on earth, as a human being again. And this is repeated many times. People describe it as like a long process of perfection of the human soul, through learning intense lessons in the dense physical stage of having a body, until eventually we are ready, at the end of these incarnations, to finally let go of having a separate "identity". Perhaps ultimately it becomes so problematic to us, to be a separate entity or soul, so much a suffering in that separated-ness, that we happily relinquish this and merge back into God – which is all we have ever really been! We begin to see our separateness as the cause of our suffering, and very much want to merge back into all that is.

Interestingly, Brigid now tells me that the emphasis on "suffering" might be more of her own personal perspective at her current stage of learning. Others who have a greater insight might call it more of an "intense experience" to be in a physical body, where we can learn so much. They might say that they are not "suffering" in a body but simply aiming to become more and more aware, after a series of intense physical lifetimes, of being "completed" and ready to let go into God's Oneness.

But when we do let go and merge back into God, this is by *our own* choice always, as we each create our own reality in our minds, and we come to want this more than anything else, not "have to" or "need to" want this, but *come* to want it, naturally, every one of us, when we are ready.

The body can be subject to extremely difficult and limiting experiences of pain, hunger, cold, illness, and death, so it can therefore give us a more intense experience of our separation from God. This can all gradually teach us to aim to transcend these limitations. The soul is free from such *physical* limitations, and so upon death we feel a greater sense of our being *un*limited – a sense of freedom which it is possible to be aware of even while we are alive.

However, Brigid tells me, the limitations of our being are not completely removed upon dying. We may have removed the physical but not the *mental* limitations upon our soul – such as guilt, grief, anger… we may, yes, feel closer to the Oneness of God but may not go "straight there", unless we have become enlightened in our lifetime. We still need first to free ourselves from mental and emotional limitations, which we can most effectively do in another lifetime, as we gradually perfect our human soul.

The majority of people who describe the afterlife from their near-death experiences, she tells me, talk of being with very loving presences who are incredibly understanding in that there is no place for a concept of judgment or punishment. The only place for such ideas is in our human minds.

Later that day, after we have watched a webcast session for students of *The Way of Mastery*, Brigid explains for me what she means when she says that even after death our souls can still be limited by mental baggage or "parts" which need letting go of, or "digesting", so that we can be truly free.

She explains that to her, the human soul is not the same as the Self of God. The soul still has parts to be loved and healed. These can be "put into the arms of Jesus" to be embraced and then gradually released from us. (The words of a lady who leads the web session are "If you can notice it, it is not you!") Only God is your true Self. Your soul is within God, but due to an erroneous "dream", it is under the illusion of being separate from God. It dreams that it is a separate entity, which is all untrue. So too is the illusion of having fearful and "contracted" parts of ourself, which take many lifetimes to heal and which, as a soul, we at last choose to release in order to "subsume" back into God's Oneness – both the fearful and contracted parts and the many lifetimes are all ultimately untrue and unreal as we are always *only* God.

It is important to Brigid to explain to me that all of it, even the "afterlife" of the separated soul, and the physical, mental, and emotional limitations of a human life, the "outside world" which we create and live in, they are all *illusions* of the mind, erroneously thinking it is not completely one within

God. As soon as we choose to know this, we are on the pathway to knowing ourselves as free, and real.

Until then, we *think* we are subject to the physical laws of the world, like being in a body we cannot leave and re-enter at will, or not being able to heal a sick person with simply the power of a very pure and unconditionally loving thought. But, because the soul is in truth unlimited, when we identify wholly with this – as Jesus did – then we can surpass all the physical laws. And so, Jesus could heal the sick, raise the dead, perform miracles. Brigid tells me that the course says, "I am under no laws but God's". And Jesus knew this. God's true laws supplant completely any physical laws and so "miracles" are really a natural occurrence for the enlightened soul. This is the state we eventually choose and very much want to merge back into: the unlimited Oneness.

Brigid now stresses to me that, despite the complexity of all that she is going into with me, the quantum physics and so on, the main thing Jesus teaches, then and now, is that every moment of your day, when you notice yourself being "triggered" emotionally or mentally in a negative way, with negative feelings or thoughts, we can always remember to choose again, and perceive differently, and see with eyes of love. The eyes of God.

She stresses that she knows she is limited still in what she is able to comprehend and explain of all this and is not 100 per cent certain if she is representing the teaching of Jesus as he truly means it – perhaps even in a year's time she will be able to be more accurate. But for certain the teaching is to transform the fearful ego of the "individual" human mind into the love and peace of the Godself which we all in truth are.

Could you explain to me more of what Jesus teaches in ACIM and WoM about forgiveness?

Forgiveness, Jesus teaches, is not really "I forgive you for what you have done to me" but is the undoing of your own mind from its misperceptions, because nothing has really been done to you that can truly harm you, only in an illusion, which doesn't matter! Because in truth everyone is the perfect Christ – both the person you are forgiving, and also yourself.

Brigid tells me that the *experience* of this kind of real forgiveness is so important to her, because "I feel the gradual undoing of my mind's misperceptions. Since I came to *A Course in Miracles* in 2009, and through this process of radical forgiveness, I can honestly feel there is less fear and more peace in my mind in a lived, experiential way…"

ACIM teaches that "the world is an out-picturing of an inward condition". Jesus says that if there is chaos in your mind, there will be chaos reflected outwards in your world, and conversely, if there is peace within your mind, you will find peace in the world around you. You will see around you and find in your world what is inside you.

I can feel my inner hackles rising at this suggestion, due to the children I have seen suffer in my lifetime, but I know that Brigid will soon clarify what she is saying, and she does...

ACIM teaches, she tells me, "I am not a victim of the world I see." This is explained in three important ways:

1) Because you are God, and God is not a victim.
2) Because the world you see and live in is just an illusion your mind creates.
3) Because you create your world and lifetime to teach you necessary things... so you can also "un-create" it. You can change it. And this is empowerment.

Brigid is drawn by how unwavering *ACIM* is in this teaching. Yes, it seems a hard truth, but it is true, she says, that we create our life experiences through our thinking, and perhaps by the choices of our own immortal soul, to learn what we need to in this and every lifetime. Our soul then comes here for experiences that are seemingly "good" and "bad", in order to learn important things for our enlightenment. "Something you judge as being 'bad' may happen to you," she tells me. "I don't deny this. But this doesn't stop it being true, the teaching that you have created it, to learn from." But remember, she adds, that the soul cannot really be hurt, and our "worldly experiences" are not really real, but are there for you to learn from, without any "punishment" being involved.

What's more, we can only *truly* forgive people doing "bad" things to us, when we understand that this world is all an illusion. Only then can we forgive in the complete sense Jesus wants us to, because we need to understand the action has not really happened, because it is all a "dream" we have created with our own mind, as an out-picturing of things which we need to heal inside ourselves. And because we have created this, we can let it go more easily, which is empowering!

We can release what we in truth create. (I struggle on to comprehend this way of understanding and am enjoying the challenge very much. I sense a very new language and mind-set, rather difficult for me to feel comfortable with, but the discomfort is in itself a teaching.) Brigid tells me that this thinking about life and reincarnation as our own soul's desire to learn is again more in line with Eastern teachings, which she believes Jesus may have been aware of, perhaps from his own past life experiences.

So, how do you understand the crucifixion?

As Jesus now teaches, she tells me, if we have peace inside of us, we can find peace in the world outside of us. So, yes, Jesus was crucified but he identified so fully with God that at the very end of his life he transcended all the pain and suffering. He showed us that it is possible to transcend all suffering. He tells us that he looked at a Roman soldier who was banging nails into his hands with such love that the soldier stopped and walked away from his job in the army and never gave allegiance to such an external worldly authority ever again. This shows us the healing, transformative power of forgiveness.

And what of gender in relation to God?

"In Oneness there is no gender, there is no two or more of anything! There is only One, only God" she replies. This is why there is no duality of "lifetimes on earth" and "the afterlife" really, and no "good" or "bad", because all that really exists, is God. This simple truth takes us humans a lot of learning, a lot of lifetimes perhaps, to come to know. And when we do, we are enlightened. We are free. We are One in God – which is all we really ever are!

The Resurrection?

Jesus said, all through his life, as he was getting closer and closer to God, that he wanted strongly to demonstrate that death is not real. The message of the Resurrection is what is significant here. Jesus wants people to focus much more on this than on the crucifixion. Death is not real, is the teaching! We are eternal, in God. He rose from the dead to show us this.

What do the terms "evil" or "devil" mean to you, Brigid?

There can be unhappy beings which exist both outside of a physical body, or inside a physical body, and they are stuck in fear, and so have a very negative energy. But I don't think there is one being called "the devil" as a personification of evil, pitched against the goodness of God. "That's not to say I don't believe there can be possible 'devils' in the universe," Brigid tells me. "Fearful beings, yes, but the malice, cruelty, hatred in them and in the world is purely a result of fear in the mind."

Absolute Oneness is the ultimate reality of God, but evil does arise, in our illusion. It is therefore a "relative truth", a relative reality. In this world, damaged people exist, and so cruelty exists – but it is all in a dream-world of illusion. The pure, ultimate level of reality is only Love.

Any act of seeming evil arises from a lack of awareness of love's presence and is a result of fear. This is not an evil *cause*, as in "the devil" existing as itself in the world and creating evil, but rather it is a *consequence*, of fear, a "child of fear", which is an illusion. It is caused by our limited human minds, which are "dreaming" that it is possible to be separate from God and pure Love. This is actually impossible, because we *are* God! Fear in the mind perceives an erroneous separation, and therefore what our mind sees, reflects these fears and illusions.

When you move away from fear in the mind, she continues, and move back toward God, then you cannot help but manifest a holier, more loving, relative reality. You are more "surrendered" to God, and so God can do more goodness, through you.

What is prayer?

Brigid tells me that *ACIM* teaches her that one of the highest forms of prayer is the aligning of your mind with the fact that you are dreaming an illusion of being separate from God, and that really you are at home in God always. Therefore, to ask for things to happen in the dream-world that is not real, is perhaps not so much what Jesus would ultimately teach. A truer form of prayer is in just allowing the mind to rest in the experience of that knowing, moving toward the alignment with being at home in God.

So, for Brigid, maybe a higher form of praying is to say something like "This is an illusion and I am safe, we are all safe inside it, so Jesus please help me to see everything, whatever arises, with love and forgiveness."

The new teachings in *WoM* and *ACIM* also say that the mind is immensely powerful, and therefore the way to heal a sick person is not to say "Please, God, make 'X' well", but to perceive that this person is the Christ, and so to know that they can, as the Christ, suffer nothing. So, you heal them by aligning your own mind with the Truth, which is that they are only ill in an illusion, in a dream. Because your own mind and their mind are also really One, as no separation in Truth exists, it follows that by aligning "your own" mind to the Truth – of no illness really existing – then you can heal them. You can do anything, if your mind is truly aligned, which is what Jesus did. What he showed us is possible.

She tells me that *ACIM* teaches her "The Son of God can suffer nothing, and I am the Son of God."

Can you describe what the Holy Trinity means to you?

Brigid tells me that so far, she hasn't come across so much in Jesus's "new" teachings about the Trinity. The focus is more on Oneness really. But her own personal understanding is that ultimately love is a *state of being*. It is therefore more of a noun than a verb. So, there is no "other" within God's Oneness. "Yes, on a more relative level there is God and Its Creation (the Christ) but ultimately God and Its Creation are exactly the same and therefore are purely one thing," she says.

I note to myself how I struggle to use the word "It" for God, but respect Brigid's language choice, and we continue...

"Ultimately God *is* Love, with no need for something or someone for God *to* love, perhaps? Love simply 'extends Itself' maybe?... I remember once someone saying to me that we are 'God Godding Itself' and I really liked that idea... I cannot put it exactly into words... I don't think I really *can* understand the nature of God very well at all – it's just way beyond me, so I am only guessing here obviously!" she says honestly.

When we talk on the telephone as I am typing up Brigid's interview, I comment to her that her chapter of answers does have quite a few "maybe" and "perhaps" words in the language...

Brigid replies that this is how she wants to be recorded, because it is dangerous for belief systems to ever be "rigid" and "definite"... we all are on a journey toward understanding, and as we progress, even after a short time, we can change in the way we understand God. To say "maybe" is to be essentially honest!

"The blocks we have in our way to understanding God as pure Love, and ourselves as a part of that Love, are what *ACIM* and *WoM* help us to unblock. But ultimately maybe there is no 'relationship' to God in terms of a trinity, because even this would be 'dualistic' or 'tri-alistic'." And God, to Brigid, is completely non-dualistic.

But she goes on, there are for sure two levels to our understanding, and to the teachings she follows. Yes, we do have a *relationship* with God, with Jesus, in a relative sense, but beyond this is the *absolute*, rather than the *relative* reality, of only pure Oneness.

Now Brigid tells me of another new teaching in *ACIM* and *WoM*, while stressing that this is also an ancient teaching, which Jesus spoke of 2,000 years ago but the lesson was not fully understood back then, perhaps. This new teaching is that the Holy Spirit is "the Great Comforter" – an aspect of our right-mindedness which is eternally connected to God. Jesus describes it as a "still, small voice" or the "Voice for God" which speaks comfortingly to us in the dream of separation. Jesus and the Holy Spirit are ultimately the same thing, but the Holy Spirit is an aspect of God which can guide you in the illusion. Brigid finds it helpful because God can be so unfathomable! The voice helps "call you back" to God. It can try to reach out to you when you are lost in the illusion of fear.

"In this sense, the Holy Spirit and Jesus are also more 'personal' for me," she says, "because for me God is so abstract. God is an 'It' to me, rather than a mother/father or a he/she, and so the Holy Spirit and Jesus very much help 'bridge the gap' between me and God."

Just before I finished writing this book, Brigid contacted me to say she needed to clarify her description of the Holy Spirit because, from studying *ACIM* more deeply, she came to realize more fully how vitally important the Holy Spirit is in the Course's understanding and practice of *forgiveness*. By this, when we are triggered emotionally by challenging events or people, we realize that we are thinking with the "egoic" part of our minds – simply *because* we are judging what is – and then we can choose instead to think with the Holy Spirit – which is really another name for the "Holy" part of our own minds. With the Holy Spirit in us we see that we are never really a victim of anything, because we have created an illusory dream of all that is happening to us, and we remember that we are truly One with the eternal, unchanging Oneness of God. In "reality", Brigid explains, nothing has happened, and so whoever or whatever we see in front of us, which triggered our responsive emotions, is in truth entirely innocent.

She now understands that the Holy Spirit has an intrinsic role in this forgiveness process, because as we hand over our minds and thinking to the Holy Spirit, we allow the Holy Spirit to gradually undo our ego, and therefore the "dream of separation" which it created. She goes deeper now and explains that *ACIM* teaches how the Holy Spirit can undo the need for "cause and effect", and is able to "collapse time" for us – because through our learning to forgive we need less time in which to learn our "karmic lessons", which are the consequences of our thoughts and actions through numerous lifetimes. So, as we align ourselves to the fully forgiving Holy Spirit, our minds can return to complete wholeness, peace, and enlightenment. She tells me "Ultimately, according to *ACIM*, even time and space are dissolved by the Holy Spirit and then there is only a non-localized, eternal, always-now."

Finally, Brigid, what do you see and hope for the future of your faith?

Brigid tells me her studies teach her that a universal *theology* of God, to be agreed upon by everyone, is impossible, but a universal *experience* of God, to be shared by everyone, is not only possible but is essential.

We do, as humans, need lots of different theologies, because we are all different types of people and are at different points on our journey of returning to God. No faith is therefore "wrong". They are all needed for who we are and where we are on our path.

"When it comes to Jesus," she tells me, smiling, "he is my *big cheese*! But I can see there are and have been loads of other great spiritual teachers on earth. It is a danger to think that one teacher or religion has a 'monopoly' on truth. All relative truth theologies are important, for the diversity of humanity on the planet. But hopefully they all point us to the same ultimate experience – of knowing that separation from anyone or anything is an illusion, an impossibility, because there is only love."

God, she tells me again, can only create like unto Itself, which is an *extension* of God (that is us; life in all its forms). But because in our minds we still believe in fear, we create little "universes" with the power in our minds which God gave to us. But we do this *via* the fear in our minds, which does not really exist!

Even in this illusion of only a "relative reality", the glory of God can still be perceived, in the beauty we create with the "right-minded" part of our minds and we can therefore "see" beauty around us. But whereas God uses God's power to only create the purest love, the fear in our minds "sways" us in our illusion to create such things as tragedy, illness, war, and death. This is neither real nor is it God's creation; it is ours, in our illusion of a "relative reality".

Brigid stresses to me that she is still coming to understand all this, as it is not easy and takes time and work to understand inside ourselves, but she continues to explain, we are connected to God and Truth in our minds, so we can create beautiful experiences and things in life. We also hold fear in our minds, and so create and encounter negative experiences and things... still *all* of this is an illusion in the world of our dream universe, because *no dualism* or separation ever ultimately exists![4]

I come to understand that Brigid is explaining to me her increasing knowledge that any time we see or experience things in our life which have an "other" or an opposite, such as good/bad, pleasure/pain, hope/despair, health/illness, even life/death, or earthly life/ the afterlife... this is all a "duality", and so is all a dream... as all that exists, is God – and ultimately, God, being Love, can have no opposite.

*

This has been a fascinating and stirring interview, which has helped me see many things from a new perspective and given us so much to reflect upon. A new "language", even mind-set, with which we can perhaps come to understand God. And a developing awareness of what "Oneness" can mean, when we refuse to waver from what we see to be the truth of non-duality. I have gained by doing my best to listen to Brigid's choice of words as she talks about her dedicated pathway to knowing God. We have different ways of understanding the "dark" or difficult side of life, but her own way, when I dare to listen, teaches me to think afresh and helps clarify – rather than confound – what I do believe.

Perhaps you also have found words or concepts in this interview which "stir you up"... how do these ideas affect you alongside those for example of Margaret or John or Helen? Can we listen to them "alongside" each other, rather than "in comparison"? Can we find in all of them understandings and "languages" for getting closer to God which are good to contemplate or even experiment with using? Can we listen to them with a truly open willingness to change or be influenced, to however small a degree? Do we find new reflections or ideas that "go well" with us? How do they make us feel about the One Love, about Truth, the Trinity, about our own comprehension of reality? When they "raise our hackles" does this perhaps show us more than a disagreement? Can it show us the detailed, sometimes challenging way to a deeper awareness of our own faith?

Another way in which listening to Brigid has really challenged and helped me to see where I am "stuck in the mud", is in her ability and enthusiasm to "cross over" between, and so bring together, the worlds of spiritual and scientific study. Often when she talks to me about "scientific evidence" for her knowing of Truth from quantum physics and from detailed research of beyond-death experiences, I feel my hackles of resistance rise... Why? Because I am "boxed in"! Struggling in my mind to accept the practice of taking faith into the world of science. And yet many modern spiritual thinkers are doing just this. They are using their minds "outside" and "between boxes", which is something I do believe in, and hope for, as you will see in the next chapter.

So why do I – and perhaps you also – resist allowing my understanding of God to be helped by a scientific understanding of our life on earth and beyond? I have no good answer for this, but meeting with Brigid on the mountain points and encourages me toward a new way of walking. I need to move now with a less "entrenched" perspective. To "walk my talk" and truly cross paths, bringing together science and spiritual philosophy. As I find in the next meeting with Andy, such new thinking can be a fuel to us, empowering brave steps forward....

CHAPTER TEN

Andy

Andy is a research lecturer (and now an associate professor) in applied ethnobiology and conservation at Oxford University. He is a tutor for human ecology and conservation in Human Sciences (which was my own combined-subjects degree). This is an institute in the university that teaches about understanding humanity by utilizing many different approaches, with the underlying aim of helping us live more sustainably on the planet. The degree itself reminds me of the intention of this book, in its standing that by learning from a panoramic vision of humankind, we can gain so much. Unfortunately, as education and much of society insists upon becoming narrower in specialization in one specific subject or interest group, the more open, wider-angled stance struggles for both funding and recognition. "One-subject" thinking reduces and over-concentrates much of our culture, and minds. It threatens to make our thinking stagnant, our knowledge valued as a product, rather than a process. But the fresher approach of correlating and interweaving our mindsets holds increasing importance, in our complicated but fascinating world.

Andy is a Jewish convert to Christianity. He was born into a liberal Jewish family, and after his bar mitzvah at age thirteen swapped any engagement with religion for a love of birds. He always felt there was a "more than this" to life, but that religion was too "anthropocentric" for him – it seemed to focus too much on humankind and not enough on the planet!

He came to faith through the 1990s because of, ironically, studying all the books of the famous "atheist" Richard Dawkins. By reviewing his own notes on evolution and ecology, to prepare himself for teaching human sciences students with perhaps no specific biology background, Andy came to a new way of seeing his own subject.

He felt stirred up by the *Selfish Gene* ideas of Dawkins (in his now famous 1976 book, Dawkins takes a "gene-centred" view of evolution, rather than views focused on the organism or the group. He proposes that the more two individuals are genetically related, the more "sense" it makes for one to behave selflessly toward the other, and that altruism really has a selfish motive, for the long-term survival of the gene[1]). Andy saw that these ideas held within them an "atheist rhetoric" which made a caricature of Christianity, a constant "drip-feed" of personal beliefs from Dawkins himself. So he thought he would study the religion which Dawkins so denigrated... and he began to read "science-faith interface" books....

Andy was baptized in 2000 and when I met him he was preparing to be ordained as a deacon in the Church of England! In 2017 he had been professed as a Franciscan tertiary. This means becoming a member of the Third Order of the Society of St Francis, an Anglican society which has three orders: the monks, the nuns, and his own third or "tertiary" order (the secular Franciscans, either as laity, or, as Andy was soon to become, members of the clergy). I was more than intrigued!

So, Andy, who is God to you?

God is the "necessary ground of all being". Necessary as in not at all hypothetical. Who loves and sustains all of creation. We can look at God from the view of theology or philosophy, he says, but Andy's personal *experience* of God is his key guide. From this, he totally challenges Dawkins' belief that "faith is not evidence-based" – because that is what this is, namely a *belief* which Dawkins has. It is not a scientific proven "fact" which Dawkins can claim to know, not at all. (As you can gather, Andy has very strong beliefs in opposition to Dawkins' negative view of God and religion. And as we progressed through this interview, I came to see Andy's fresh ideas as fascinating...)

When was the Old Testament written?

Andy tells me it is indeed important and relevant that we do not know when exactly all the Bible books were written! This is all a part of the "mystery" which comes into our search for Truth and which needs to be a search; he would question anyone who claimed to "know the whole story", the "literalists" who find no mystery there at all.

A lot of the Old Testament was written down during the Babylonian exile (c. 597–537 BC) with a sense that what is in it comes from much earlier traditions. It was perhaps written during this difficult time to help give the Jewish people something to "hold on to". Many scholars search for when specific books, such as the book of Job, were written. But it is not good to be simply told and accept things about the Bible as "certain". This does not blend with the "mystery" of it all. And this is also true of science! Very often things are not really "proven" facts, even though we may like to say and believe they are.

The Bible *must* be seen symbolically. Its strength is in that. But this does not mean that a "committee sat and thought it all up". No. Was Jesus Christ a flesh and blood person? Yes. Did things written about in the Bible actually happen? Yes, but that statement needs a lot of qualification, and its meaning or exegesis ("critical explanation or interpretation of a text, especially in scripture", says the *Oxford English Dictionary*) is at least as important as its historical factual validity. Did God literally make Eve from one of Adam's ribs 6,000 years ago? No, but does it mean that Eve is the female part of humanity? Yes.

God inspired the symbolism. Metaphor and symbol are plentiful in the Bible. Indeed, *all* language is in itself a metaphor (I love this idea!) because it *represents* something and because all words can have a deeper meaning. Allegory is there in the Bible as much as in poetry. So, does this mean the things written about cannot also be true? This depends on what we mean by truth. What we mean by "reality".

We must not be superficial in our understanding of the Bible. Very much of the "science versus faith" debate, he says, is based at this superficial level. In the "foothills of understanding". But Jesus himself said "[there is] so much more I'd like to tell you, but you are not ready yet".[2] We may be becoming increasingly ready, as our knowledge of the universe and our place in it grows, but whether we yet have enough wisdom to really understand what it all means is another matter.

Therefore, to ask the question "Are the Bible stories literally true?" reduces the great complexity of the Bible to a trite simplicity. It is, he laughingly suggests, what Dawkins might ironically call, a "non-question". Too simplistic to be worth asking.

The Bible is about our evolving understanding of God. Bound up within it is our own sense of understanding and, yes, misunderstanding of God. Our relationship with the divine. We can see this kind of "wrestling" with understanding in the wonderful book of Job.

The real character of God is expressed in our notion of the crucified God, of Christ. Andy tells me that Martin Luther, 500 years ago to almost the day of our interview, spoke the phrase "the crucified God", which expresses, and which *is*, God's humility as Christ.

Likewise, we need to also approach everything about our faith with humility. We do not *know* the Truth, but we can approach the Truth. Andy recommends to me the Bible passage (Philippians 2:1–13) which says that

God so loves, is so bound up with, creation, body, and soul, that he will do anything for us consistent with the good. The cross is this profound demonstration of God's love for us.

Andy confirms however that he sees no "error" in the Bible, in that nothing is in there by mistake. God wants whatever is there to be included as it is. But some misunderstanding and correction is expressed. For example, the Anglican and Catholic Bibles are not entirely the same! The Bible contains fallible but wise, guided, and yes, God-intended, human choices.

Anglicans very much believe in reason. The "four pillars" of faith are Scripture, tradition, experience, and reason. If a belief will not stand up to reason, then it is weak as a belief. For example, if we know fossils can be 200 million years old, then the literalist biblical belief that the world was created "6,000 years ago" cannot stand up. We must not be too simplistic. We can find real security not in dogma, he says, but in God. Andy now begins to unfold for me the very interesting idea that we need to rebuild our relationship with God which we lost *through* our evolution, on our way to becoming "fully human".

He explains: a crucial stage in this evolution was when, about 2 million years ago, *Homo habilis* (the precursor to *Homo sapiens*) developed bigger brains. This was most likely caused, at least in part, by sexual selection – females choosing more intelligent males. Thus, allegorically speaking, female humans "gave" to the lineage of *Homo* knowledge and intelligence. We could see from this the story of Eve in the Fall giving knowledge to Adam, as in all of humanity. The female "part" of *Homo sapiens* gave us – by sexual selection – the fruit of the tree of knowledge. Thus the "rib" of humanity gave us intelligence – the potential for wisdom – by choice. (When I was typing up this part of the interview, I looked up the Latin term *Homo sapiens* and, of course, it means "wise man".)

We need, Andy excitedly tells me, to see this story in Genesis for so much more than the superficial way we see it now. It is God-inspired. It is a great allegory about our spiritual evolution and unfortunately the common focus on the "anthropological" or man/woman aspect of the story has overshadowed its deep theological meaning.

I suggest to Andy does he mean that we needed the "fall" of receiving greater intelligence and knowledge, before we can one day become our full potential as humans – in the same way that teenagers need very much to grow and struggle through into maturity?

Andy says yes, that's it.

By having bigger brains, we can now have knowledge of good and evil. Women, Andy explains, as "Eve" have suffered for this development in our evolution by now having pain in childbirth – because of the larger size of our heads, the cranium of our skull, passing through the cervix. But this is all an inevitable consequence of our necessary evolution.

And who created the "serpent of temptation"? God did. To enable us to move along on this journey to becoming fully human. But, Andy says, we do need to beware of "theodicy" ("the vindication of divine providence, in view of the existence of evil", as in showing God to be justified or "blameless" for dark events), which includes the idea that God might cause bad stuff, or collude with evil, only for the causation of some greater good. "Temptation", as in sexual selection – by hominid women being more attracted to intelligent men – both caused and allowed the Fall. This was the "moving onwards", on our way to developing a new relationship with God.

No, the writers of Genesis did not know all this! But God did, of course. The writers were inspired by God to write Genesis as they did. To Andy this is a precious truth, and it reminds him that objectivity is only one aspect of reality. What we call "facts" can change as we advance in our understanding as humans.

What are heaven and hell, to you?

"They are on this earth, now, and I am unclear on more than that, after life," says Andy. "As a nun once said to me, 'We can believe hell exists, but we don't have to believe there is anyone there!'"

However, he adds, "Vengeance is mine, saith the Lord!" Yes, there will be justice, but how, who knows? "God always surprises me in my life and does things not in the way I would expect."

When we study Jesus, in Christology, the studies can be wonderful and interesting, but when we talk about heaven and hell, the approach is often far too simplistic, silly, and unjust. We need to ask, "What is justice?" We need to understand the fallibility of our frail human nature, for which God is ultimately responsible. And to see that the justice coming is God's justice, so will not be what we expect, or even necessarily what we want, from the viewpoint of here and now. "If I have a vision of Hitler dancing with the Jewish and Romany children he murdered, his eyes streaming with the pain of his realization of the Truth and of their suffering – is this the justice I want or expect for such monstrous evil? No, probably not. But is it a beautiful and just reconciliation in Christ? Yes, well maybe it is."

Andy is confident that justice will be a beautiful reconciliation. Jesus did speak of God's judgment, yes, but in a way which we do not yet follow. It needs to be seen in its context, which is "the most profound expression of Love, by the Prince of Peace".

So, if ever your theology or understanding of God conflicts with this concept of peace – then you have got something wrong.

Andy tells me now how he distrusts people saying they know this or that to be 100 per cent true, but then there *are* some fundamental truths which he does 100 per cent believe! And one of these is "God is the necessary grounding". God is what makes and sustains everything being possible.

Moreover, he continues, the beauty God creates on earth *is real*. It is not just that we perceive it to be this, in our biological response to what we see. Our physiology finds the real beauty which is already there. Beauty is embodied, incarnated in the earth, and Jesus Christ is the incarnation of this beauty, wisdom, and truth of God.

But why does God do so much for us? Because we could destroy this planet if we do not come to realize our true place in the world. Our place in *relation* to what truly is. And our search for God is in this. Jesus came to teach us that it is all about this relationship. The same is true of evolution and ecology, he says… it is all really about relationship!

The crucifixion was necessary, cosmologically. Judas himself was "necessary" to bring about the "plot". Jesus even said to him "go and do what you must".[3] We need really to focus on the meaning of the crucifixion, which is this – who is Jesus? He is God. We crucified God, but it was God who made this necessary for us to do… because it *bound us up* with him, through this evil thing we did. The evil act was necessary for our own salvation. If we think we understand this in our heads, Andy suggests, well we probably don't. It's too big. But stand at the foot of the cross, and just know.

The crucifixion was an expression of God's solidarity with creation. It was God showing that he knows there is suffering on earth. If you create a material universe, God knows that there will inevitably be conflict, as we all have the seeds for competition within us. But (and this was when Andy's ideas became very new and exciting!) evolution is itself the *resolution of conflict*, theologically.

What do you mean by this, Andy?

That evolution is not just the Darwinian ideas of the undergoing of conflict and competition in the battle for survival of the fittest. God knows that this is there, and that he created it. But is God happy that we suffer so much because of such conflict? No.

Therefore, God created the evolutionary process of *understanding* as a way of reducing this conflict. And so, biological and spiritual evolution could be seen anew, as a process not of creating conflict and competition but of *resolving* this conflict.

We need to look, Andy tells me, for a deeper theology to our evolution. The superficial debate about "creationism" versus "evolution" is so missing the point. Evolution is coming about from the resolution of competition, by us each finding our best place in life. To find our "niche", our true identity, within God, is to build peace and create harmony, which is what God wants, and we need.

Evolution through resolution, through understanding who we are.

This was a remarkable interview, in which I received just tasters of some of the great ideas inside Andy's faith. To see evolution as a peace-creation process rather than a conflict-bound one, is such a new way of looking at life, and at God's purpose for us. I knew that we had only touched upon the surface of his ideas, and I came away feeling sure that here is one more person who has found their "niche" with God – as a challenging scientific thinker and Franciscan tertiary, soon to be a wonderful priest.

*

Increasingly I learn from these interviews that many of us do not like other people saying they know "absolute truths" about God, because of the genuine risks of "absolutism" becoming exclusive, literalist, and narrow-minded, but at the same time we often still hold tight to some "absolute truths" ourselves! Such as my own, and many people's belief, that God is Love. And Andy's belief that God is "the necessary ground of all being".

Do we need to let it be when other people describe God differently to how we do ourselves? Or do we need to argue passionately for our own concepts of spiritual reality? Or perhaps both! Do we need to find a balance between being arrogantly over-righteous and liberally over-vague? Between saying we are certain who God is and saying that none of us/all of us do?

Talking with Andy has helped me see how provocative and at the same time exciting it is for anyone in the world to claim they "100 per cent know" the abstract reality of any spiritual and non-factual truth. Moreover, and importantly, perhaps, even scientific "facts" are only known to a limited extent... because with time our grasp of factual truth does itself change. Even Einstein's equations, just like the flatness of the earth, become contested. Recently I watched Interstellar *(2014) where the "flat lines" of time and space were "folded up" so that someone could travel through them, in the "extra" dimension of love... so who knows what "facts" will be ours to grapple with in the future?*

Just as Richard Dawkins does not "know" there is no God, or even that all genes in our DNA are "selfish", neither, I have realized, do any of us mentally "know" God's complete Truth. Not even from reading the Bible. But, so long as we stay humble and acknowledge the "other" location for our real knowing, in what we say is our hearts but is really our souls, we can enjoy growing in serenity, courage, and wisdom (as the Serenity Prayer, below, encourages), as we move along on our way home.

For me, Andy has shown the courage asked for in the Serenity Prayer in his brave quest to find new ideas, to "change the things [he] can" in the realm of evolution studies as well as in spiritual thinking. He has also shown the "wisdom" asked for in his dedicated searching and finding of fresh perceptions, which results in new understanding.

Andy and Brigid have both shown me the excitement of efforts to use our minds in a "de-compartmentalized" way to grasp truth. I begin to appreciate how much good creative thinking can come from forming networks of concepts which interact, rather than knowledge being weighed as a summation of singular memorized facts. Indeed, it is in the network itself, the process of interactive relationship within a whole matrix of wisdom, from which great new ideas can be born. And it is only by looking and feeling for new ways, new concepts – such as Andy's idea that spiritual evolution takes us toward resolution of competitive conflict – that we can help our human race move on. Move toward becoming peace-makers, and so to "evolve" in our souls.

The Serenity Prayer

This popular prayer is often used in drug and alcohol recovery programmes, and many people make it an integral part of their lives, to help us feel supported and empowered by God's grace. It has been attributed to Saint Francis of Assisi, Thomas Aquinas, Cicero, Saint Augustine, Marcus Aurelius… but probably has more humble, modern origins in being written or popularized by twentieth-century American theologian Reinhold Niebuhr… perhaps the truth is this prayer belongs to us all.

Lord, grant me the serenity to accept
the things I cannot change,
the courage to change the things I can,
and the wisdom to know the difference.
Amen.

CHAPTER ELEVEN

Tim

Tim had been a minister for the Methodist Church for two years when I met him. His circuit covers Stainton, Shap, and Penrith in Cumbria. Before this, he had been in senior management in the motor industry. He was born into a devout Christian home, but this was something kept "on the side" for Tim, as he saw religion as something of the head, not the heart. For all his life Tim has known a strong urge to "achieve" but also felt that his "success" in business was not enough – that real achievement needed to come from somewhere other than himself.

He began to feel called to the ministry but denied this feeling until he knew he could no longer refuse his vocation and, supported by his very loving wife, Tracey, they gave up their farmhouse and downsized radically so that Tim could study theology at Durham University, moving on from there to study for ministry in Birmingham. It was here that Tim began his real search for truth, and learned he needed to look wider, to question and enquire more, before he could go deeper.

A tutor helped him see this wider searching in the symbolic image of the cross, with its wide "asking arms" as well as long deep vertical connection to God. He learned to now never simply say "this is the truth", because "who am I to say?" He saw that his own beliefs are very much influenced by the context of what has been "fed to him" during his own upbringing, and his own "truths" are therefore conditional, not fixed. Tim began to see that there is no real "black or white" to truth, but more of a wide-reaching "grey", which is for us to explore and begin to understand.

Who is God to you?

Tim tells me that this is one of the most interesting questions of them all, because we think it is a basic thing, but it is in truth so very hard to answer! "God is the 'Other' that is greater than me," he says. Not a man or a woman but a life-force or Spirit behind all that is. Something/someone that has created and caused it all to come into being. Therefore, there is some meaning/intention/point to it all. "God sustains and holds us all and is far bigger than any of my understanding!"

"The more I read the Scriptures, I can't get away from God being love," he says. "God wanted relationship. To bless and relate, to share... he is the God *of* relationship. I only find purpose and contentment in my own life, when I know I am a part of a story of love and relationship."

He goes on to tell me that he hasn't studied other religions in detail, but in his studies of the Bible, weaving through it all is the relationship God wants with his creation. If you embrace that, you find purpose, contentment, and meaning in your life (I already feel that Tim is putting in simple terms the crux of a lot of wise words!).

What about the history of Jesus?

He tells me that much of the life story of Jesus is no longer up for debate. More was written in historical times about Jesus than about Julius Caesar! No one can doubt his existence in Palestine. He was written about after his death and no doubt the writers knew the Old Testament intimately. They could see in it things "pointing'" to Jesus coming, from their interpretation of the stories and prophecies therein, but how much of the story of Jesus and the New Testament Gospels were "shaped" by the Old Testament? Who will ever know?

For example, in Psalm 22:1 we have the words "My God, my God, why have you forsaken me? Why are you so far from helping me, from the words of my groaning?" Perhaps these words prompted Jesus himself (who knew the psalms) to actually recite "My God, My God, why have you forsaken me?" when on the cross about to die (Mark 15:34). Or were these words fed later into the account, to fit with the psalm? Who knows? And Tim is not sure it really matters.

What matters is that we understand that Jesus, who was/is God divine, was part of a much bigger story, and this link to the prophecies shows us this bigger story. The person of Jesus was a *thread*, a divine thread in the one great story. The Bible is about this great truth of our relationship with God, his willingness to love us, our response to this... and all the time Jesus is for us the prime example of this story, this divine relationship which we can have with God.

When was the Old Testament written?

From scholars' research we can say that much of it was written during the captivity of the Israelites in Babylon, for forty or forty-five years around 587 BC, or after this time. Two generations were trying to make sense of their identity. As with many Eastern cultures of this time, an orally passed down tradition was then accurately written down. Leviticus, for example, sets down laws and commands in such detail, because this was how people back then expressed their faith in God. Why? To articulate their belonging and how they "fitted together" in their relationship with Yahweh because, as with people of all faiths, this is what we want – to have a story of belonging.

Paul's letters were the first things written in the New Testament, and we need to remember there was no original intention for a "new" religion. The early Christians were Jews. They saw Jesus as the Messiah and saw that the kingdom he was bringing was not after all domination of Jews over all other people, but something very different. As the early church grew Paul and others like him began writing letters to "fledgling" churches all over the Roman empire, to encourage and challenge them in articulating this new faith. People such as Matthew, Mark, Luke, and John began to put down eyewitness accounts, to help others see Jesus' message.

We could see it as the Old Testament being one nation's struggle to understand God, and the New Testament being a continuation of this story, the ultimate expression of God's intention for all humanity – in Jesus.

Throughout history we have tried to understand our relationship with God, and God then came as Jesus, to show us in real life flesh and blood what God means and intends for us – what God's true nature is.

And it is a relationship focus – thus repeatedly Jesus said things such as "remain in me" or "I am the vine"[1] – on which the fruit grows, or withers if it is not connected to the vine – or "apart from me you can do nothing".[2] And parables such as the Prodigal Son tell us not about an "errant son returning" but about God's nature to love and embrace and forgive. How he teaches "love one another even as I have loved you…"[3]

No, this was not a "new" message brought by Jesus, but a message from God lost in among all the rules and commands of the Old Testament. The message had been there, but Jesus came to show and point and remind us of it clearly: to reveal God anew.

So, can we say stories such as the nativity are "true" stories? Was Jesus an immaculate conception? "I don't care!" says Tim. This is not important. What matters is the message within the story. A virgin birth was at the time of the writing of this story seen by the people as the sign of a divine incarnation. This is the point! What matters is that Jesus was believed to be God, not just a "good man". If Mary was a virgin in "reality" this has much less importance for our focus than the fact Jesus came to bring relief to the poor and help the oppressed.

The first to see Jesus were a lowly, despised class of shepherds. The angels said to them "this will be a sign"... and the sign was the very good news that a baby born into poverty, with the excluded all around him, is God! The Old Testament message that the Messiah would be "Emmanuel", meaning "God with us"... came about to mean the God of all of us, including the poor and lowly and despised. Truly the God of all, with us all. That is the good news!

Is the Bible the "Word of God"?

This, Tim says, is a difficult question. Written by God? No. People trying to make sense of God? Yes. So, when a psalm is written about killing foreign babies, such as, in Psalm 21, "You will destroy their offspring from the earth, and their children from among humankind",[4] or King Saul is told by God to obliterate a whole other nation, this is not being written by God but people trying to understand their relationship with God. The whole Bible is the story of God's desire for this relationship with creation.

A repeated pattern occurs of humanity failing in this relationship, falling away from God, then God forgiving us and trying again, and again, so we come back, we fail... until Jesus comes to us, whom we kill, and still he says "Father, forgive them!" Jesus is the reconciling of all creation into an intimate relationship with Godself.

"And the Bible gives me all I need to begin that relationship, and then grow in it," he tells me. "It is inspired by God." There is so much more we can learn that is beyond the text on these pages, yes, but the Bible points the way. It reveals something of the nature of God. So, too, Tim adds, does seeing a sunset, or a newborn baby – they also help reveal to him the incredible nature of God.

The Bible is not totally "inerrant", no, but it is the story of people making sense of the God who made us out of love. Every page is about how humanity responds to this loving creator, in good ways and bad. The Passover story in Exodus is therefore both celebrating a great thing – the Israelites having been freed from slavery, and the Jewish people on their journey to have a strong relationship with God – but it is also about millions of Egyptians dying. This part of the story is not about God's message or purpose for humanity; it can only be seen as Jewish people trying to make sense of God's purpose for them.

What about the wrath of God?

Tim tells me how we need to remember the culture from biblical times, of both Old and New Testament. In the East then, cultures were full of religious creation stories, flood stories, the needs of people to both please and appease their gods or else vengeance would be executed. So the Jewish people were no different from their peers. For the Roman gods and Greek mythology of this time, all the same rituals of appeasement were there. The tradition of sacrifice was definitely not just Jewish. It was everywhere. One big difference was that in other cultures, the likes of a flood story would usually involve everyone being annihilated, whereas in our Old Testament version, the righteous Noah is saved. With our God, salvation and hope exist.

In those times sacrifice even of children was not uncommon, says Tim. The "eye for an eye" rules of the Bible were actually given to bring about more fairness, more equity, rather than more ruthlessness. Therefore, if someone stole your sheep, it was the given law of God to take back a sheep, not a full herd. The biblical times were harsh, destructive, cruel even, and killing was not uncommon, but the Bible tries to understand God within this context, in the light of what people knew and experienced in life then. And even in the Old Testament the new light is one of *hope*.

The orphaned, the oppressed, the marginalized could still have hope to be accepted and received by God. For example, Tim tells me, Ruth in the Old Testament was a Moabite, not a Jew, who was taken back to Palestine by her Jewish mother-in-law, where she was accepted, treated well... then became part of the ancestry of King David himself! Even the Jewish ancestry contains a foreigner who was accepted and loved.

And yet still we continued, the Jewish people continued to fail in their calling to God, as they strayed "away and back... away and back" as God forgave and tried to recall them again and again (I tell Tim this "away and back" phrase reminds me a lot of a shepherd calling out to his sheepdog as he tries to bring in a wandering herd).

The theme of judgment is still there in the New testament, Tim says, because judgment was still strong as a religious theme in the culture of the time. But the idea that God's wrath was "appeased" by the crucifixion is not how he interprets the Bible texts. This interpretation is read and falsely supposed into it. In the same way, he tells me, the hymn "In Christ Alone" by Stuart Townend has a line in it that speaks of the "wrath" of God being "satisfied" when Jesus was killed on the cross. This is so beyond Tim's understanding of the crucifixion that he feels unable to sing this hymn.

We always need to read a text in the Bible with reference to the context of what is written before and after it. We need to place a piece in its setting, rather than read it in an isolated, possibly then false sense. And we need to never forget that there are far more references in the Bible to love, than to any sort of righteousness or judgment.

Furthermore, he tells me, the word "judgment" in its ancient Greek form (the language of the New Testament) comes from the root word "crisis" which means "to decide". To make a decision. So, yes, there will be a decision made by God, a "judgment" on what happens to us. Remember, he says, "God is God and God will get what God wants!"

Tim believes, as a result of his learning from Bible Scriptures, that God decides and has ordained that all of creation, every one of us, will one day be restored and reconciled to an eternal, amazing relationship with our creator, our Lover, God. The Lover of us all. Hence the bride and groom symbolism in the Bible. So, is anyone going to be eternally in damnation? No!

However! Hell is talked about by Jesus more than heaven, in the Gospels. He calls it Gehenna, which was the place where very lowly people were burned and criminals were dumped, after they had died. It was literally a "rubbish dump" for people, and this was Jesus' word for hell. It was a figurative use of a word to describe life "where" we might choose to go without God, without including God in our lives.

The phrase "eternal life" is used in John in 3:16 to mean not life forever in a place, but life with God, from above and beyond us. So it can be right now, if we are now with God. As Tim says, "I am in heaven right now because my life is infused with God. I am in relationship with God." That this life in heaven could go on beyond his lifetime on earth – hopefully. But, he tells me, this will not just be for the chosen few, it will one day be for all of us. God gets what God wants and God wants all of us responding to him, as soon as possible!

Tim is not concerned about the "next life", because there is little point – all we know is this current life. But he is certain that when it happens, it is for everyone. The biggest shame about Christianity, he tells me, is that faith is often being seen as an "entry card", a "way in" to heaven for eternity… or rather even a "way out" for avoiding hell and damnation.

"If the value of Christianity is concerned with where we go when we die… then we've missed the point of it, and of all the Bible tells us," he assures me. "Faith is for now! And the value I get from my faith is what it brings me *now*."

And the "song" of Jesus?

That God is the God of Love. That the "heart" is the greatest thing. That the unrighteous can be righteous. The excluded included. We need to read the Bible "crossways", so that we see pieces of Scripture and what Jesus said, fitting in with a recurring message and motifs that have a few common themes. The Bible therefore becomes its own "witness", its own evidence for the teaching as a whole – not in bits. We can imagine being in a court looking for truth, and we do so by looking at the whole body of evidence, in full context with its connected parts.

What do you see in the rising of Jesus?

People writing the Gospels, and people who witnessed his death, were trying to make sense of what had happened. They needed to use the language and metaphors common at the time. In Roman times, judgment and justice and sacrifice were popular motifs. A lot of the metaphor in the New Testament is trying hard to grasp the reason for Jesus being killed. But really it is all trying to show God as saying, "Whatever you do to me, I will still love you!" That whatever we do, God stands by us.

When I ask Tim to clarify for me if he does believe that Jesus rose from the dead, he tells me "I certainly believe in the physical Resurrection of Jesus from death. Because of his Resurrection – and his conquering death – there is hope for us all."

But the idea of "punishment" of Jesus for our sins implies that God has "limitations" to his love and power and ability to be our God. It implies that God would have *needs to appease*, and this makes God limited by our human concepts! But the truth is, God loves us despite what wrongs and bad things we do. He loves us no less. We can do no worse than crucify our God, and yet he still loves us.

The original message of early Christians was this unconditional love of God, but then the church was changed by mortal human nature, and by ruling powers who needed to bring in a sense of threat and punishment. For the early "desert fathers" of the church, punishment of our sin was not the message of the crucifixion. This came later, with the likes of St Augustine. And our faith still all comes down to our own conditioning within our culture, which is now beginning to question this idea of a punitive God – which is good!

Is gender still an issue within the church?

Tim tells me he works for Cumbria's "Churches Together", in an ecumenical steering group for people suffering domestic abuse. He tells me a lot of perpetrators of abuse use patriarchal nuances within the Bible – such as the husband being "head of the household" – to excuse their foul behaviour. And likewise, victims of abuse use these nuances to persuade themselves to stay in a relationship. All this must change. There is still a lot of work to do. We need to understand the socio-historic setting of the Bible texts and move on.

And what is the "second coming"?

Jesus comes repeatedly to those prepared to receive him, Tim tells me. It will not be a "one-off" thing for Jesus or God. But he does hope that there will be a time when the world and creation are more as God wants and intends for us – reconciled to God. He tells me that in Romans 8:22–23, Paul speaks of how "the whole creation has been groaning in labour pains... while we wait for adoption, the redemption of our bodies." Then one day, God will get what God wants for us, and there will be a new life for us all.

Terrible "childbirth pain" may be going on for humankind, but there is hope! Yet this hope for the future is not what drives Tim in his faith. God being in his life right now is what matters to him.

Can you describe to me the Eucharist?

The Eucharist does two things for us. It helps us firstly to remember. Jesus said, "Do this in remembrance of me."[6] Secondly, the word "remember" in its original Greek form means to "make present". So it brings to mind and also makes present, Jesus with us. For Tim, it is the love of God and grace and mercy of Jesus, coming to him, showing him how much he is loved. The bread and wine help him recollect and receive this mercy and grace once more afresh, because this loving gift to us was not just on the cross but is given in every Eucharist.

What is evil or the devil, to you?

As much as there is good and loving in the world, says Tim, there is evil and hate. But is this a being, a force? He doesn't know. Part of Jesus' message is to seek and choose the forces of good and loving. There is a lot written about the devil, probably in metaphor, but it is not a "sleep loser" for Tim. He feels "covered by the grace of God" to protect him. Not as a "forcefield" to completely shield him against evil powers, but God is greater, and God's love will win in the end.

And what does prayer mean to you?

At its core, Tim tells me, prayer is very simple for him. His own marriage is a healthy, strong, loving one, because he and his wife share and communicate very well. That makes their relationship work. It expresses their intimacy, sharing their joys and sorrows. And the same is true for his relationship with God. He shares his feelings and listens, intentionally and consciously. He senses God's wonder, his presence, and is open to God telling him things.

We all pray and communicate with God in different ways, he tells me. Some need more discipline and "liturgy", others, like Tim, love to pray outdoors while walking the dog in the beauty of the Lake District. Whatever works! But intimate honest communication from you to God and from God to you, is the key to a close relationship with God, through prayer.

What is the Trinity to you?

"Another hard question!" says Tim. The word "Trinity" is not in the Bible. And yet even in Genesis, in the Old Testament, we have different distinct "dimensions" to the description of God. The Spirit of God is said to "hover over" the waters during creation.[7] If God is all about relationship, and if God is Love, then love can only express itself in relationship to another. As he tells me, "God's character is love as is manifest within Godself."

Jesus Christ was pre-existent before he was made human. In John 1:1 we are told "In the beginning was the Word, and the Word was with God, and the Word was God." So, we have from John's Gospel a description of the divine, even before Jesus was made man, as two dimensions of God and the Word. And we have the third dimension of the Spirit as described in the Old Testament. Then Christ Jesus was born and so we have the three "persons" of the divine, God the Father, Jesus the Son, and the Holy Spirit. This came to be known as the Trinity. Essentially, because love is God's character, God needs to have a way of *being* that love. Even before creation existed, God's existence as love was in relationship. The idea of the Trinity does help us to understand this.

I am very excited as I hear all this, as it builds upon my interview with Father Richard in Oxford, who first introduced me to the strong concept of God's essence being a "Trinity". That is, a multiple being, within One being – because it is a pre-supposition for God as love to have something or someone to love, to be able to give that adoring love to! To share it. Here again I meet someone who tells me that love as a relationship is what God is. Not love standing alone, originally bereft of any being to be love with, but an active, dynamic loving power, which has always and forever loved, and now also wants to love us. Somehow this idea of the Trinity seems now not to be a staid old "church powers" idea, but a modern, vitalized way of understanding God as containing God the Creator and Christ the child, created by God, as well as the Holy Spirit, which you and I can be blessed by. That same Spirit which hovered over the waters at the beginning of creation, can now empower and connect us with the grace of God's love, and with God's purpose for us to love others… it is all very alive!

And how great it is to meet people who can help us to comprehend this: to allow us to see God through fresh eyes.

And Tim, what of the future?

"God is doing God's work, with or without us!" he tells me. The church has always been both a blessing and a cause of harm and division. God will do God's work whatever, but Tim hopes very much that the church will learn to focus more on what unites rather than what divides us.

Jesus' last prayer, before he went upon the cross, was that we all might be one, that the world will see who really sent him to earth. Tim's Christian unity hope is not that we all become the same, as one church, but that we celebrate what we agree upon. Contradictory doctrines should pale into insignificance over all of us knowing about God's eternal love for us, and sharing this in our world, which so desperately needs such love.

He hopes that the church will work hard, to the exclusion of all other concerns, to give out the good news of God's love and relationship with us. The news that there is a much bigger story happening than our single lives, and that we are all a part of this much bigger story, every one of us. That God is calling us to this relationship with Godself.

"There is hope!" Tim says. "The angels came to the shepherds and said they brought good news of great joy for *all people*. The joy is that faith is for all. God is with us, loving us all, not just the chosen few."

As we part on this morning after coffee and so much bright, intense talking, I feel filled myself with "good news". The news that people like Tim are the new hope of the church, the ministry to help us all come into a relationship with God, filled not with guilt, fear, and unworthiness, but with fresh understanding, active involvement, and secure excitement about being loved.

*

In a sermon Tim gave at church one Sunday, he told us about Betsy Ritchie's account of being present during the final days on earth of John Wesley (1703–91), the co-founder of Methodism, whose great preaching, often outdoors, helped many working-class people's hearts turn toward a new way of Christianity.[9]

She tells of how, with almost the last bit of strength left in his frail body, Wesley cried out, "Best of all, God is with us." And then, to assert this faithfulness of our promise-keeping Jesus, and to comfort those weeping around him, Wesley lifted his dying arm in a token of victory, raised his feeble voice for one last time and, with a holy triumph not to be expressed again, repeated those heart reviving words:

"Best of all, God is with us."

We need no more words really. God is with us, in every step we take.

PART TWO

Challenges and Discoveries

I Felt You And I Knew You Loved Me
TRACEY EMIN[1]

Challenges and Discoveries

And so, I come to the end of my eleven interviews, having met with these inspiring people each at their own unique point on the mountain. They have all taught me so much. Listening to them has been a challenge and a joy. Every one of them has helped me to see things from new angles, to widen the panorama of what words such as "heaven", "Holy Spirit", and "Christ" can mean. I hope they have also helped you.

It came to be that I interviewed some people from the same church denominations, but this can help us understand further that even within one spiritual group, we can each have very different personal understandings of our faith. Some people are adamant that the "personal" does not affect their beliefs about God's Truth – but I dare to say now that none of us can 100 per cent deny our subjective perceptions in life. I interviewed these eleven people and have tried very hard to record just what they told me... but it is impossible for me or anyone to hear the words of others without "interpreting" and so altering them to some even minute degree, in our own brain. That is why we are human!

Perhaps it is true that two people from faith groups which teach a need to "only believe what you are taught", by the Bible or religious leaders or whoever, will be incredibly similar in their beliefs, but will they be identical?

Margaret and Martyn are both Anglican, John and Richard both Catholic, Carol and Helen both born-again Christians, but you will have seen, like me, just how different as well as similar they are in their understandings of God. How we can belong to groups with a certain pattern of thinking, but still hold onto – indeed can do nothing else but – having our unique individual way of "getting home". That's exciting! That's our "pilgrimage out of exile".

And I believe it is often *language* that both connects *and* separates us.

For example, I think of the *differences* in how I follow Brigid's and Richard's way of understanding God as Love... for Brigid primarily as a noun, a state of being, while for Richard more as a verb, of loving. But then their *similarities* in understanding the afterlife... for Brigid as a time for "digesting" negative illusions, the parts of our ego-mind and emotional fears which need to be "let go of" to purify our souls, before we can again join the Oneness of God in enlightenment, and for Richard as a time in purgatory where we learn and can also be purified and gradually forgiven, before we can join God in heaven. For Brigid this happens over many reincarnated lifetimes, rather than just in the afterlife... but how much do our different "spiritual languages" here hide the clear, strong thread that weaves between them?

Brigid talks of God being a "non-dualistic" One, of only Love existing, and so evil is an illusion in our mind of the absence of this Love. Richard talks of evil being like a "hole in the sock". Thomas Aquinas taught that it was a "falling short" – again an absence... the teachings of long ago meet up and correlate quite easily with the teachings of modern times, if and when we are willing to allow this, and to "see through" the different vocabularies used – the different "mind-sets".

To move on healthily in our approach to fuller awareness of God, I believe we need to recognize and respect the languages and mind-sets of modern times, just as much as those from the sacred past. Either one without the other would be a waste.

And yes, we do need to appreciate the *differences* in "particularizing languages" used... the difference in *tone*, especially in degree of focus on judgment. How much we insist upon us needing to "earn" God's rewards (either by our good faith or our good deeds) or describe us as being "always there" in heaven, just not always knowing it. Such different senses of focus and intention *do* matter.

Ironically, I believe they matter on the "surface", in our human choices to take one or another direction, where feels best to put our steps... but deep down do they matter not a jot? Perhaps understanding this riddle is all part of the adventure.

It may be true that our spiritual journey can be held back, come across hard obstacles, if the path we choose (or are pushed into choosing) is one which leads us into dark caves, down scree slopes, or over precipices. It is also a risk that we choose a path which puts others into difficulty or danger. Ultimately, we will all find our way, but the clearer path, with an enlightened focus – literally, "a path in the Light" – is surely a good one to discover and walk along. And to encourage others to join us. But which path is this?

*

Before I press on to answer the fourteen questions in my own "interview", I could perhaps give you my main impression of what each of these eleven interviews has helped me to see more clearly. This in no way encompasses all that they have shown me (which is more than I ever expected) but is a start.

Margaret taught me about our journey to God being a "pilgrimage", and about the meaning of prayer in a fresh, upholding way. She also taught me about God's grace.

Bob taught me about the deepest truth of God's love being eternally inclusive and unconditional – what this really could mean, this universal "Oneness", without boundaries.

Carol taught me about the strong need for justice in some Christian people and challenged me to think about what justice means. She gave me insight into a way of trusting in the literal truth of the Bible: how God can easily create miracles.

John taught me about the power of trust in the "mystery of faith", and about Catholic loyalty to the church and the holy sacraments. He showed me a good example of devoted Christian life.

Martyn taught me about the meanings of truth, of exile, and of living for God in the present moment. He reminded me of the Christian responsibility for active service.

Helen taught me about the value of a personal relationship with Jesus, and how much absolute faith in the Bible teachings can infuse the whole of our lives. She showed me what the words "born-again" can mean – born into a new life with Christ.

Jyoti taught me about the importance of the open heart, and of God's love being a feeling, an experience, not a word. She reminded me not to complicate God!

Richard taught me about the vital truth of the Trinity, as the eternal process of God being Love and loving, and about the value in the symbol of the cross.

Brigid taught me challenging ways to understand the "non-duality" of God, confirming to me that Love can be all that exists, and that as we come closer to knowing this Truth, we come closer to "merging back" into the reality of God being who we are.

Andy taught me about the importance of new thinking, of looking for fresh ways of understanding God's universe and purpose for us all, and of the possibility that God's intention for us in evolution is to progress toward our potential for greater harmony, rather than competitive conflict.

Tim taught me the value of listening to and following the wise
truths in our heart, putting together all that is sourced from
Love, and how when God's love is put into practice, it is a
loving relationship with the divine.

You will see these are just some of my impressions of what has struck me
in these interviews – a consequence of my own needs and questions, my
personal life experiences, the "context" of my own belief system, mind-set,
language choice, and my certainties about God. Likewise, different things
will have stuck with you, I am sure – different strong impressions, whether
challenging, changing or simply informative.

It may be helpful for a few moments for you to reflect on what these
impressions are… what do these eleven interviews each say most clearly to
you? Could you perhaps jot these down, as I have? This may enable you to
form ideas and feelings about the next steps you will take as you connect
with God, and in deciding if Jesus could help you. It may also show you that
listening openly, even to people who we do not "agree with" on the surface,
can itself be a great teacher… I hope so.

We can keep reminding ourselves to listen with a *willingness* to change
and be influenced by others, rather than to always change and influence
them. This is such a valuable tool on our journey of faith. And in life itself.
It is great to want to make our world a better place, but it helps a lot to
be able to *receive* and then process other ideas, rather than try to offer all
the answers. This may sound simple, but it requires some real discipline at
times, to resist jumping in with "OK, but *I* know what is right."

*

The next part of the book contains my own discovery of faith – all developed
and challenged by these interviews, as well as by my life so far. I began this
book with strong but vague feelings about God and now I have, at last, some
clear beliefs. Of course, our beliefs never stand still (if they are healthy!)
but this exploration has helped me find my way now, on the mountain, as I
hope it may for you.

After my chapter of answers, written mostly on Iona (and in a slightly
different order to the other interviews, to fit with my spending Eastertime
on the island) we will look at deciding if we really want to call ourselves
"Christian" – what this means to us and if it feels right for us. Then we
will finally ask "What next?" in terms of where we can go actively with our
faith, and where Christianity could go… if we choose. If we listen. If we
dare.

CHAPTER TWELVE

Jacci on Iona

I grew up in Lancashire then went to study at Oxford University. Just before my finals I discovered I had a brain tumour, which set me off on an intense, sometimes frightening, journey of learning about healing and love. I then studied to teach yoga, went travelling, and together with a friend set up a charity (The Kianh Foundation) after meeting some children who taught us a great deal, in the disabled wing of an orphanage in Hoi An, Vietnam. I then developed an auto-immune disease called "scleroderma", then melanoma skin cancer – but despite all this I am still here!

In all my years of struggling with health I have gained increasing faith in God loving me, and feel incredibly lucky for this "holding". I now live in a converted Non-conformist (early Methodist) chapel, and when I moved here with my husband, I had no idea that Jesus would become so important to me… funny how life works! In 2016 my first poetry collection (*A Whole Day Through From Waking*) was published. This encouraged me to follow what really matters to me now in life – active spiritual faith – and so I began the adventure of exploring Jesus-connected beliefs, which has created this book.

I have now come to Iona, this very special island just off the Isle of Mull in Scotland, to sit on beaches, in the abbey, chapels, hotels, and cafes, to begin to write down my own responses to the fourteen questions. Iona is where the idea for the book began, and it feels the perfect place to have my answers come to me, after a soul-stirring and enjoyable eighteen months of searching.

So, I am here as the "twelfth disciple" in the book, and for sure my own beliefs have not been diluted or muddled by listening to all the others. No, the very opposite – they have often helped me to see my own direction.

When I do not quite see, I ask Jesus to guide me. I hope the same for you. I have brought with me to Iona none of the reams of notes which I have made from my reading and thinking about things along the way. All I have is my faith and my pen and paper. I have no idea really at the beginning of this week what I shall write, but I trust!

I have also developed some ideas since I returned to the mainland, as I keep learning from inspiring people/events/writings which I connect with along the way, and so the crux of what I believe, which is ever-developing – as it is for all of us – is here…

Who is God, to me?

This was written firstly while sitting on my favourite beach, North End, Iona; a turquoise sea.

My core belief is this: *God is the Love that we are.* God is all that truly exists. And so, Love is all that truly exists. God's love is the great paradox of non-duality which contains, within the "Oneness", all dualities (of doubt and trust, sadness and joy, hope and despair, pleasure and pain, anger and peace and so on). We could imagine two overlapping circles crossing, to create the symbol of a fish.

All we truly are, every one of us, is this Love. I recently watched the classic 1940 film *Grapes of Wrath* and in it the itinerant ex-preacher (Jim Casey) says two things which capture my own beliefs… basically that everything living is holy and that our souls are not separated, but rather all belong to one big soul.[1] What does this mean? Firstly, in our deep soul, we are all the pure Love of God, so we are all holy. The deepest desires of our soul – when we can find and dare to listen to them – are the desires of God. For us to be Love.

Secondly, we are not truly separated other than by the physical boundaries of atoms. Our separate bodies have souls (which may involve some temporarily individual soul existence), but our tiny souls are all a part of one big soul, which is God. I think of a Being with trillions of "tendrils", all moving and pulsing with life, but all connected as one Being… and the Being enjoys life through these tendrils, just as God enjoys life (and suffers life) through us. We are "separated" in different bodies and forms, but we *circulate* the molecules which make us as we live, eat, breathe, make waste, die, and so we are joined as One. God is us and the more we know this, the closer to the comfort of home we are: the closer to "Truth".

Why did God differentiate from One pure Love to create our universe, our so varied creation on earth? I do not know! But I do not believe it was an illusion, or a "mistake", at all. I believe all of life is God's way of expressing and reflecting the flow of Love as an energy that God is. A divine, all-knowing conscious energy of Love.

Life involves great challenges, caused by natural laws and by free will, which God chose to give us. God is in all the "trials and tribulations", the light and the dark times. I see and respect that. And when we find the Light of Love within us (find the "Christ" in us), when we learn to forgive, then the dark is inevitably put out.

I once met a boy called Khanh, who has cerebral palsy, in an orphanage in Vietnam. His ability to forgive inspired me so much it stays with me each day. There is a poem at the end of this book about the grace which he showed me is possible for us all to contain.

God is the Love that we are. All of us. We are each a tiny part of the "mountain" of God, so we are all the mountain. Or, if you like, we are each a tiny speck of leaf on the "Tree of Life" of God, but we are all the Tree. We can say more easily "God is me" than "I am God" because God is me, you, the creatures around us, the rocks, the footprints... and then so much more!

Images help me to begin to comprehend who God is, but God is truly beyond *all* human words and explanations. For every school of thought or religion or image or belief that tries to "define" God, we none of us can fully describe that which is beyond describing... and God is so much greater to us if we accept this mystery.

As I move along finding my own interview responses here on Iona, and then upon returning home, I come across some texts which I have added to my reflections or else placed at the end of some sections, to help clarify my answers to the questions. Here is one of them: it is the first verse from the hymn "God be in my head" by Henry Walford Davies (1869–1941).

> God be in my head, and in my understanding.
> God be in mine eyes, and in my looking.
> God be in my mouth, and in my speaking.
> God be in my heart, and in my thinking.

Who was Jesus of Nazareth?

As I begin to learn answers to this, I develop more questions. But the only important truth to me is that Jesus was God incarnated in a person, *as we all are.* However (and it is a divine however!) Jesus was fully aware of this, fully holy. Aware of this from birth? I do not know. We know so little of his early life. But he came to show us what we all can be – he came as the communication of the Truth of God to humanity, as "the Christ". He was, as Jesus of Nazareth, God in mortal flesh. And as the Christ, he will be this communication to us forever.

I feel comfortable with the idea of "the Christ" as the part of God which extends into us to "save" humanity. I know really that the Christ is another name for God. Some people use other names but with the same message of truth, to help them connect to divine Love. This truth is not exclusive to Christ followers, but I believe that anyone who finds the Truth finds Christ, in whatever human terms they wish to use to comprehend this. I comprehend through "Christ", who is here to save us from something which has nothing to do with being punished for our sins. Christ is here to save us from *not realizing* the Truth of who we are – not knowing the Love that could be the driving force of our lives. For that reason, Jesus Christ is my Saviour. My "Messiah".

Jesus of Nazareth was/became Jesus Christ. And he showed us what we all can become. He said to people who were really listening to him "all this you will do, and more". (John's Gospel tells us that he said, "Very truly, I tell you, the one who believes in me will also do the works that I do and, in fact, will do greater works than these, because I am going to the Father". John 14:12–14)

Jesus was not the "only Son" of God. To say this denies his purpose. He was calling us all back onto the path home toward becoming sons and daughters of God, holy people actively living out and expressing God's love. He was not saying "only in me", as in some unique human being for us to put onto a pedestal so high that we never believe we can reach this state of loving. No! He was very much saying "be the Love that I am".

He was a rebel, but a Jewish rebel who tried to bring his people back onto the path which they were losing sight of. He advised people to go back to the values at the core of their Judaic religion. "Get back onto the path home", he was saying, passionately, to his people, and to all people. A calling, a mission, which he was willing to suffer greatly, even be murdered for.

Was he "born of a virgin"? I don't know. I believe in the capacity of God to make the wonder of the nativity miracles true, if God wanted to do this. But the deeper meaning for me is in the poetic value of this miracle story... the symbolic teaching of values such as inclusion, humility, trust, and very much saying "yes" to God. The nativity story is true in a way we find hard (but are perhaps finding easier) to grasp and be settled with now. Truth from a wider, deeper perspective which involves many layers, all linked together. We are beginning (again) to see that truth is not just in the literal factual. Jesus was and is exactly the Christ. This is the only "exactitude" I need.

God who came as the Christ into humanity. And is still here. I pray and talk to the image of Jesus of Nazareth, but deep down I know I am praying to the Christ that is within him.

*

When Jesus asked him, "Who do you say I am?" Peter answered, in Mark 8:29 "You are the Messiah".

My NRSV Bible tells me in the notes that this could also be read as "You are the Christ."

Who wrote the Bible, when, and why?

I don't know my Bible well enough yet – I'll be the first to admit that! It's not so long ago that I was one of the people who open the Bible, see random words such as "slaughter, kill, stone" in the Old Testament and even sayings linked to Jesus such as about "hating your family" or "using your sword" and quickly shut the book. But more recently I have found some humility, seen that this is a book containing profoundly sacred teachings. So, I opened my receptive ears, to listen.

It helps me to understand that both parts of the Bible were written (and officially selected) in very different times, politically, religiously, and culturally, to our own. Just as the context of our environment in modern times helps to create the way we think, speak, feel, and write, the same was true then.

Both Old and New Testaments are fallible *and* sacred. The Bible is holy, in that it is often (but not always) teaching God's message of loving Truth to us. It is also a library of human words and ideas. These words are brilliant, challenging, regulatory, wise, but they are also human, and therefore inevitably limited by our human capacity to know and describe.

I do not believe that the Bible is entirely God's "Word" in that God wrote it, through somehow "breathing the words" into people. God allowed and enabled humans to write it, and for it to therefore be a text to interpret, to question, to grow with. It was not seen in the early church as a "dictation" to be followed word for word. Some people believe that the Bible is to be read as exact literal Truth. I respect this belief, but I do not hold it. I believe God wants us to use our free will and hearts to discern and learn from the Bible. And to be brave enough to say when the words in it do not follow the Love of God.

Some Christians say that the parts of the Bible which talk of vengeance, jealousy, rape, killing, violent favouritism, or just plain cruel judgment, are parts which are still divine (because they are in the Holy Bible) and we just have to "study more to understand their divine meaning". As if, with greater understanding of God, we will come to comprehend why it was written you should stone your new wife to death if she is "proven" not to be a virgin, or even to stone your "rebellious children" who are drunkards or gluttons, or for the Israelites to slaughter every inhabitant and burn down cities such as Jericho, when they crossed over the River Jordan to gain their "promised land" (in the book of Joshua). That with time and wisdom we will come to know the divinity in these words… I strongly disagree with this. Some words in the Bible are not the "Word of God", no matter how long we may look. They are the words of human beings, trying (perhaps understandably) to keep order, health, and prosperity among a specific group of people at a specific time in history: to bring clarity to their own religious/territorial history. We need to perceive the difference.

As I write this about the Holy Bible, a childhood church-attending part of me fears that my words could put me in danger of hell-bound punishment! But this is all just that: fear. Fear instilled often by people who do not want others to differ from their own understanding of the Bible or of God. I need to say that God is very much *in* the Bible, in the hearts, minds, and souls of the humans who wrote it but, just as religion is not God, neither is the Bible.

Many people say that we must not "pick and choose" which parts of the Bible to follow without question. I believe it is time to look again at this statement and ask, "why not"? Indeed, we already *do* "pick and choose", because we no longer stone people (thank God!). We no longer tell a widow, if the brother of her late husband refuses to marry her and help perpetuate her husband's name by making her pregnant, that she should pull off his sandal, spit in his face, and declare his own family to now be known as "the house of him whose sandal was pulled off" (in Deuteronomy 25). Indeed, such behaviour may now be perceived to be madness! Most of us do use sense in choosing which words in the Bible to follow exactly. Those who say they do not still seem to pick and choose which words to follow literally, and which to skim over.

We also choose sometimes to take words such as the religious laws laid down by Moses, and now follow them symbolically for their teaching, rather than literally, as was perhaps once intended. So, a law to leave a few olives on trees, or sheaves in a harvest field, or grapes on a vine, to not glean all but leave some for the "aliens, orphans and widows"[2] – we can now learn from this to be kind, not over-greedy with our wealth. And we need to all be honest about this use of our sensibility.

It is a great loss to simply close the covers of the Bible (as I know many people have) and call it out-dated, vengeful, or prejudiced. But to open the book and really find God's Word in there, we need to be brave with our honesty. There are verses which will never ring true to the Love of God, for me. There are others which I can be amazed by, which teach me deeply. But we do need to use our gifts of intelligence and intuition to finds these teachings… and so to keep moving forwards. God wants us to be active pilgrims making our way up the mountain home, not robots.

Being honest, I believe it is possible that Jesus' life could have been made more dramatic or "prophecy fulfilling" when it was written about years later, in the Gospels. But this does not spoil who he is to me. When the New Testament was being written Christ was *there* in the people who were writing it, encouraging them, guiding them with his Word, and sometimes they were aware of this, sometimes not. Sometimes they understood him, sometimes they misperceived and muddled things. Sometimes they listened to God, sometimes they followed their own human egos. And the end result? Well… there *is no end to it!* Because Christ is *still* working in us, hoping we will hear God's Word inside us… it is up to me and you how conscious we are of this. How much we dare to listen.

We can recognize the Bible's origins in humanity as a *richness*, rather than a weakness which we need to pretend is not there. Anything written by humans needs to be valued in its *im*perfection. To be understood as we see best, using our own (and our churches') spiritual conscience.

But if we are unwilling to consider this "human side" of the Bible, and its context of development within Jewish and early Christian histories, then we could rob it of its true power. We could allow this avoidance of reality to put many people off reading this great book, so sadly deter them from finding Christ in its pages. Likewise, if we choose to completely ignore the Bible in favour of only reading "modern texts", I now believe we will miss out immensely on a wonderful piece of human writing which is in many aspects an important *representation* of God's Truth.

*

Recently, I read in Deuteronomy of Moses giving warning to his people, before they crossed over the River Jordan into their promised land – a land not even he was allowed by God to live long enough to enter, because of once disobeying his Lord. He warns them of God's terrible curses of skin boils and a hunger so desperate they would eat their own children, if they do not "behave", and I sense just how urgent this need was, to make a new start for the Jewish people and their faith, leaving wicked and fickle ways behind them.

I then realized, from listening to people like Richard, that the text of Deuteronomy, indeed the Pentateuch of the first five books of the Old Testament, was written many hundreds, perhaps even a thousand years *after* the events and law-makings which they carefully record took place. So, not only were these strong religious laws, warnings, and promises needed at the time when they *occurred*, they were also very much needed for the Israelites at the time when they were being *written* about. This is so important to grasp.

I believe that by seeing the divine poetry *as well as* the human rule-making, the true Love of God as well as the territorial anguish and determination of the Israelites, the passion of the early Christians as well as the state/church needs for order and conformity – then I find more hope, wisdom, and teaching in the Bible; much more desire to read, study, and love it, than I ever did before.

> ...but test everything; hold fast to what is good...
> *1 Thessalonians 5:21*

But can you say the Bible is symbolic and also holy?

Yes! The Bible contains many stories which are symbolic, pointing us to their meaning by the images which they put into our minds. Jesus himself used this technique brilliantly in his parables. In the days of Jesus, and of the writers of the Old and New Testaments, using symbolism as a way of reaching for God's Truth was an important tool for the teaching of very deep things in a simple way. But this did not make the symbolic stories superficial, or any less "true".

I believe stories in the Bible such as the making of Eve out of Adam's "rib"; seven pairs of every kind of "clean" and one pair of all "unclean" animals being put into Noah's ark; the coming of "manna" bread from heaven for Moses and his hungry people... these are all well within the bounds of being both symbolic stories *and* physically happening in "real life", because God can do such "magic" if God chooses. God has no bounds. Some stories (such as of the manna bread, even the great flood) may also have roots in real events. But I focus on the symbolism in these stories; I choose to believe that God intends them to be learned from symbolically without them needing to have happened as told… and this makes them no less profound. Indeed, this enhances their meaning, for me. To "rob" them of their poetic truth somehow robs them of their teaching purpose.

It is also important to be honestly realistic, that we cannot say the words of Jesus as recorded in the Bible are always his actual words. They were written down, for example in the Gospel of John, a long time after Jesus had died. They are passed-down words, perhaps very well preserved by oral tradition (which was a much more popular and careful way of passing down records then than now), but we cannot say for certain that they are the words spoken by Jesus. And does this matter? No.

It only matters in that we need to keep this honesty. Not to allude to a greater literal truth than really exists. Because this is misleading. The more valuable truth is that the words written down by John, and of other writers in the New Testament such as Paul, who never met Jesus, are often inspired by Christ. So, the times when the Bible reads "Jesus said" and tells us of great compassion and justice taught by Jesus, to me they "are" the words of Jesus, passed down from him, because Christ is actively guiding the writers as they listen within themselves and put down the text. This is not always true, but when it is, it is true to the Word of God.

We need to see Christ as not gone away but able to inspire all that happens, then and now, in our writing of the Bible and in our understanding or contesting of it – the developments and changes within the church are a "movement" as well as a "body". We can comprehend how, if writers of the Gospels altered in some ways the literal "truth" of Jesus' life to give the text more symbolic value, they still did this in a way Christ was aware of, as the living Christ. So, this is all a part of the Truth of Christ, in a deeper way than simple accuracy of facts.

And again, we can ask if factual accuracy is the only "truth"? One of my favourite artists, Hughie O'Donoghue, said that even though memory is rarely accurate, it is "invariably true".[3] Why? Because (like the art of painting) memory represents how we *feel* about things, rather than what we know. What we remember in the Bible about the story of Jesus, even when this varies between Gospels, and what we remember in the Old Testament about the journey of the Jewish people, of our spiritual "ancestors", is all true in the *memory* of the faith.

In the past, perhaps people did "need" miracles as a way of helping them imagine and believe in God, more than they do now; in John 14:11 Jesus says, "Believe me that I am in the Father and the Father is in me; but if you do not, then believe me because of the works themselves." People in the modern world are generally more "sceptical" about miracles (thinking about them rationally, rather than poetically) as well as perhaps being more able to think about God in abstract as well as "image-bound" ways. I personally can believe in Christ without a single miracle of Jesus' life *needing* to be literally "true". And I emphasize the word "needing" here, because of the difference between needing miracles, and believing they could happen. Miracles do not feed my faith. But for sure some people do still very much need the impression of "real" miracles to keep their faith steady and growing. I understand this. It is no less of an understanding and certainly not a weaker path to God.

To be clear, the miraculous things Jesus is said to have done could *without doubt* have physically happened. As the Christ he could heal the sick, raise the dead, calm storms, walk on water... be resurrected himself from the dead... I dare to say "easily". He was fully conscious of the Christ within him. He was God. But we can look for the huge symbolic value in all these stories for finding their most important teachings... about unconditional all-inclusive love, humility, trust, loyalty, kindness, striving for justice, contesting prejudice, and being born-again to embody God's holy Love. To only be swayed by these events having literal truth as miracles, we could perhaps lose their deeper truth, in symbolism.

I noticed recently how the description of the baptism of Jesus by John the Baptist in the River Jordan is described differently in the Gospels of Luke and Mark. Luke says that the Holy Spirit came down upon Jesus "in *bodily form* like a dove", as in physically in a body (Luke 3:22, my emphasis), whereas Mark describes it as the Spirit simply descending "like a dove" upon him (Mark 1:10). This slight difference in words shows me that symbolism and literal physical "reality" are very much intertwined in the Bible. But beneath and wrapped all around them is their true purpose – to teach us using the effect of the words on our hearts.

What do you make of God's anger and wrath in the Bible?

Written after joining in the first part of a Stations of the Cross walk around the island, on Good Friday. People from the Iona Community, volunteers, visitors, inhabitants of the island – together we walked and paused at special sites, to remember the time Jesus walked to his death, carrying a cross. There is now a pause in the walk, and I am sitting quietly in my room.

My strong belief is that the concepts of punitive "wrath" or "spite" and so on in the Bible are concepts of the human mind, perhaps as we try to understand God. But they are not of God. If you believe, as I do, that God is pure unconditional Love, all loving, you cannot then include in *any* of your comprehension of God, wrath and a need for vengeance!

Such terms (as Martyn and Tim helped me see) limit God by implying that God "needs" some retribution for our wrongs, to then be willing and able to love us. On the contrary, like the father of the prodigal son who welcomed him passionately back home with humility and total forgiveness, even *before* and without even asking for an apology, I believe this, and more, of God. If we want to come "home", God wants to welcome us, with only Love.

Yes, I agree, in the Bible Jesus does talk of hell and judgment, but I can only believe what is in my heart, which is that God knows we are human and make mistakes, but still calls us home. Calls us to come out of this false state of weakness, of distracted "sin" and limitation (which is "hell"), into the goodness that we truly are.

Sometimes the Bible threatens God's punishment of sinners so that certain powers could keep just that – their power. Warnings also come from those who genuinely wanted the writings now collected together in the Bible to help them keep their people healthy, aim for virtue and not fall into chaos. But does God want to preserve a hierarchy of the fearfully guilty and pompously righteous, of "select few" and "outcast", "hell-bound" and "heaven-due" – does Christ, did Jesus? No. All the evidence and conscience for me is, no.

To me, Jesus only talks of the dark so to point to the light *already lit* inside us. And we cannot be hypocrites. We cannot say "God is Love" but then say "God will send harsh consequences" or "God only allows the faithful ones into paradise and condemns the rest to eternal torture"… because not only do we insult the Truth of God, we also put people *off* the God by whom they could be blessed, off the Christianity to which they could belong. Because many now cannot bear the tangled nonsense of such teaching.

I believe people have moved away in their hearts from the church when they have "seen the holes" in statements which are ridiculously contradictory in some sermons; some saying even in the same preaching… "God loves every one of us"… and then… "God seeks retribution from those who sin". Unconditional love *only* forgives, *without* condition. God does "judge", but in a divine loving process which we humans cannot yet comprehend. God may do things to teach a beloved child, to show them the way, even strongly challenge them, but God does not vengefully punish, full stop.

Mercy is the meaning of God's grace.

So, what are heaven and hell to you?

I have come to understand that all "rules" about getting into or being kept out of heaven, are surely human-made. God wants us all, and will get us all, eventually.

Yes it may take longer for some of our souls to be close again to God in what feels like paradise because we die weighed down by our "baggage" of fears, distractions, and resistance, but somehow, eventually – who knows what will happen next to help us get there – I do believe we all go back to the Oneness, because there is ultimately nowhere else to go! Best of all, we could begin to realize while we are alive here on earth that we already *are* home, in God. To stop searching and realize that we are found, that wherever we are on the "mountain", feeling fulfilled or feeling lost, we are always a part of God. We belong. To realize this, is heaven.

Hell is, in the way I think Jesus most likely described it, like a "rubbish dump" for souls who resist and deny God's love so much they refuse to come home, refuse to know it – because they have been so afraid and unused to love on earth. I don't feel Jesus wants us to believe God or himself as Christ will "send us to hell". But we may be in such a bad state when we die that we feel we are in hell, as our soul resists the Truth of who we are. And such resistance all comes from fear... fears that we learn to adopt with our human minds because of the lives we experience on earth, in the environments which we are born into, or which we create for ourselves.

Hell is not being aware of the Christ in us, even after we die. I need to reconfirm here that people of other religions or no religion would use different language to describe "the Christ", but reconciling our soul to divine Love means the same in any way of thinking. When we die, human concepts of faith lose their relevance. What matters is if we can let our soul know God's love. To feel a soul-sucking absence of love, no perception or recognition of it, is when we are full of lacking, full of fear. This is hell. On earth or after we move on.

God's love is there always. The fear does not really "exist" – it is a dark "hole" rather than a "presence", but still we feel it. It is like thinking you are in a pit of snakes when really you are in a pool of warm water, but still you think you are in with the venomous and strangling snakes... so it feels like you are in hell!

On earth, hell can be felt as loneliness, unworthiness, guilt, insecurity... all a hollow hunger. But we do not need to ask or earn our way for God to love us and let us be in heaven, either when we die or when we are on earth. I believe heaven in God is waiting, and when we "open up" to realize this, we are there. We are "born again". Newly alive. But when we are tightly closed to this love we are in hell; we are "dead" as souls. Still God wants us and tries to help us wake up and come to life again.

While we are on earth we can open and close our hearts to peace, or to letting agitated anxiety take hold of us – because we are human. When Christ was here as Jesus of Nazareth, he was also a human. God chose to be born a human being. And so he did sometimes feel "dark" emotions such as fear, fury, sadness, and grief. He experienced human temptation. But in the end, he overcame all this, because he knew the divine Love that he was. He knew trust. He felt safe in God.

All our souls do want to return to God. To be at peace. But our human ego, which is like a little selfish child, is fearful of its own vulnerability – perhaps because it knows deep in the unconscious that it is finite and will end, unlike our soul, which is eternal. Our ego can tempt us to make choices which will boost its power, make us feel "victorious", give us "high status" or a strong "identity", all because our ego fears the truth that none of this will really matter when we die. But the more we listen to this craving, the more we can resist the Love within. We can gain false values, false ideals, become twisted in what we see before us.

God knows all this. God *gave* us our human minds which create our egos, as well as giving us our "easily tempted" bodies – the body and mind are even perhaps intrinsically connected to our soul, in a way which we are still to fathom. God wants us to be humans, or we would not be! Just as God wants us to live on planet earth – to become Love here and now.

And after we die, do we still have a personal identity or are we all just "One"? Do we retain a boundary around ourselves (even if this is just a dotted line!) which makes us the soul that we are? I choose to think so. I choose to think that God gives us individual souls for a reason, gives us human egos for a reason, gives us minds, feelings… but how we go from being an individual soul to being totally "at home" in the Oneness of God, I do not know – and probably never will, until I die. I like to think we each keep an "identity" as a soul, but that is because I still have such a persistent human ego, wanting to stay existing as Jacci! When I one day let go of this, perhaps then I will be truly happy to be One in God; will want to let go of being a "droplet" and just be the ocean.

Perhaps this turning away from focus on judgment is a new way of faith? I think of the words we are told are by Jesus, in Luke 5:38–39 "But new wine must be put into fresh wineskins. And no one after drinking old wine desires new wine, but says 'The old wine is good.'" The NRSV Bible notes say that some ancient manuscripts read "the old wine is *better*" or do not even contain verse 39. Is this a teaching about new ways of thinking and believing, both then with Jesus, and now? Is the "new way" to act from the faith that we can *all* reach for the state of heaven by waking up to God's presence within us, by becoming "Christ conscious"?

And when I speak with people who are adamant that God judges us in a limited "human" sense, and eternally punishes the children who go wrong or who lack Christian faith, I try to ask, would a loving parent do that? What greater love and mercy is God's? It is time to ask ourselves – why do we "need" to believe in *anyone* being sent to hell, so much?

If people are cruel in this life, if they remain cruel when they die, they will not need sending to hell – they will need God to help them find their way to heaven.

Luke 17:20b–21 says Jesus told the Pharisees:

> The kingdom of God is not coming with things that can
> be observed; nor will they say, "Look, here it is!" or
> "There it is!" For, in fact, the kingdom of God is among
> you.

The Bible notes add that "among you" could also read "within you". Yes, among and within us all is heaven, waiting.

And the "song" of Jesus?

In Mark 12:29, before he tells us the two great commandments on loving, Jesus says:

> "Hear, O Israel: the Lord our God, the Lord is one..."

And in Matthew 22:37–40, here are the two jewels:

> '"You shall love the Lord your God with all your heart,
> and with all your soul, and with all your mind..." You
> shall love your neighbour as yourself.' On these two
> commandments hang all the law and the prophets.

"One unconditional love" is the song of Jesus. The message, the Word, of the Christ.

His message to me is also very much "I am with you always".

I have a book which has an image on the front cover of my favourite painting (mentioned previously) of Christ – "The Light of the World" by Holman Hunt. The book title is *I am With you Always*. I often look at this when I am feeling fragile, confused, or afraid. The painting is based on Revelation 3:20 "Behold, I stand at the door, and knock: if any man hears my voice, and opens the door, I will come in to him, and sup with him, and he with me" (KJV).

Christ stands in this painting outside the door to the human individual's heart, which is overgrown with weeds, and there is no visible outside handle. This implies that Jesus may knock but it is up to the individual themselves to open the door of his/her heart and trust in the Light of the World, with his symbolic lantern, to guide them through and out of the darkness in their life.

Yes, Christ is there waiting in us already, but we do need to very much *dare to listen* to Jesus knocking on our heart door and open it. As this book journey continues, I begin to understand how much our listening needs to be not only to other people, but intently, personally, to the Christ inside us. When I remember this knocking, this constant Light, I feel safely guided, no matter what I dread. And, I very much believe that we can all learn to *be* the Light of Christ. Then we can see who we are.

We can follow Jesus' teaching to love God and so love our fellow humans, our planet, ourselves... because God is fellowship. We cannot love God if we do not "also" love each other and love ourselves... because the "also" is a false word here. There is no also! Every living thing, every human being, every bit of earth, is a part of God's loving – and Jesus came to teach just how lucky that makes us.

The song of Jesus is, to me, to become "Christ conscious". And to feel appreciation that we have Christ as the guardian of our souls – which makes our souls eternal, invincible. When I think of the words, "I am with you always" I feel more able to climb the hard slopes. Part of a big family, pulling me up. Empowered to know Love as an energy so much greater than was possible when I did not know what I belonged to. Because, although God is of course "more than" any one of us, we each have a *share* of God's loving power within us. We are pulses of the Light.

The song of Jesus also contains "warnings" which are dramatic and arousing, even shocking (fitting perhaps with the style of his preaching at the time), to help alert us, so that we do not miss out on this superb opportunity. And if we ever think or are told otherwise – told to believe Jesus warns we could be *sent* to hell as punishment for our sins – I believe we need to stop and think again.

Jesus' song is to assure us in our times of horrid darkness that when life is terrible, Christ's Light is with us, just as much as when life is superb. I saw recently a quote on the wall of my favourite Oxford café (Georgina's). It was reportedly said by the incredible Stephen Hawking (1942–2018) when he was coxing for a rowing team as a young man – but I believe he could have stated this at any stage in his life. He said, "Life would be tragic, if it weren't funny". To me, this means that yes, life can be painful, frightening, "unfair", but how great it is to know that even in the lowest and darkest places and times of our lives… if we can find it… there is light, even humour. And the greatest Light, is the "highest of whatever" that we share in Christ.

In Romans 8:38–39 we find these empowering words from Paul:

> For I am convinced that neither death, nor life, nor angels, nor rulers, nor things present, nor things to come, nor powers, nor height, nor depth, nor anything else in all creation, will be able to separate us from the love of God in Christ Jesus our Lord.

Here is a poem from my new collection (*In the holding*). Many tragedies remind us of the potential horror of our mortality. That is not to be denied or dismissed. Suffering, especially when caused by injustice, can be terrible. Our human emotions in times of dread can change continuously. But the meaning of this poem is that faith can hold us up, in a constant secure knowing, deep in our souls.

It's not the same

we can turn around fear to hope to grief to joy
all in a burning forest
but faith stands alone,
the tall stone that reaches above the smoke,
does not exchange itself
or find relief in cindered leaves –
to feel, when all other feelings have given up
or fled,
and with each breath know you are safe.[4]

The crucifixion?

It is Good Friday still and I am sitting on a pew in the Abbey, having now completed walking all the Stations of the Cross on the island.

It has been a strange, disturbing day. I was moved at the "station" or stage on this walk which brought us to the island parish church. Here we remembered Veronica, who wiped Jesus' face. We were each passed a warm wet flannel and we offered gestures of the same tenderness to people around us, touching their faces or hands gently, quietly, as this woman possibly did for Jesus.

It reminded me that the crucifixion continues to teach us, to this very day, to show each other more kindness. Avoid being fickle or running from helping our fellows in trouble. And it made me realize that the crucifixion of Jesus is no real surprise to me. *Of course*, we did this to him, to God as Christ on earth, because we were, still can be, weak and misguided humans. We often act from a selfish desire that comes from the fear in our egos. And God, even Jesus, knew this would happen. It upsets me now that I do not find it shocking that we crucified the Son of God.

As we walked up the road toward the Abbey, we went to the old cemetery of St Oran's Chapel. At the gateway, a woman and her daughter were singing to us and this brought home something else which upset me. I suddenly became very aware of the dread I have inside, of an upcoming hospital visit to see if my brain tumour has again returned. And I asked Jesus to keep me safe, keep guiding me through whatever happens next. Then I scolded myself for selfishly asking Christ for support even on the day we are mourning his crucifixion! Even as we walk behind someone who is re-enacting Jesus carrying a wooden cross on his shoulder toward a cruel death, I am fearfully worrying about my own.

But then the women singing to us at the gate were remembering the women of Jerusalem who cried at the terrible treatment of their beloved Saviour. They sang of how Jesus replied to them "Daughters of Jerusalem, do not weep for me, but weep for yourself and your children."[5] So, even at his painful time of death, his concern was for the state of us, his beloved humanity – for our future suffering. He had the capacity, as Christ, to do this. Even though we killed our God, he loved us through it all. This is what the crucifixion says to me – that even though we as humanity killed him, Christ still loves us, still holds us.

Then as we walked from the Abbey to finally re-enact "laying Jesus to rest" in the "tomb" of St Oran's Chapel, I realized with more guilt that I do not feel specifically terrible about the death of Jesus himself. It seems to me a death both unsurprising and in a deep way one tragedy among many. I come to understand that this means to me that just as Jesus suffered human pain and despair on the cross, Christ also suffers in each of us every time we suffer the pain of torture or of bloodshed, in war, terrorism, cruelty, abuse. When we suffer injustice, Christ also suffers it. When we perform injustice, we perform injustice upon Christ – this is what I realized today.

Whenever we are selfish toward life on earth and our fellow humans, when we are not inclusive in our loving, when we do not listen to each other but impose our will upon others, then Christ suffers for this, just as Jesus Christ suffered on the cross.

Christ did rise "above" the pain in his last moments on the cross, but as Jesus the man he suffered pain, humiliation, and thirst before this, and in us he can suffer. This is a hard truth, a real responsibility to realize and keep in our hearts – that whenever we make a choice between selfishness or compassion, punishment or grace toward our fellows, we are choosing how to act toward Christ.

*

But what about the crucifixion and our repeated image of Jesus as a "lamb of God who takes away the sins of the world"? How do we challenge, comprehend, or try to change this image? How can we understand this "bloody sacrifice"?

It is important to keep remembering that ritual sacrifice was current, and very much believed in during the time of Jesus. Many cultures, including the Jewish people at this time (and so perhaps, I do accept, including Jesus of Nazareth) held great faith in "paying ransom for wrongs" or making offerings as a display of devotion. By killing things or giving up things which were precious to them, often shedding a lot of the blood of others, the people making such sacrifice believed this could afford them favour with the divine. It was the way of living then.

Therefore, when Christ was willing to die for the teaching and people he loved, it was understood as a sacrifice in the sense not just of "giving his life for us" (as, for example, the people who die for their loved ones in war and tragedy now) but also of giving his life to "pay the debt" for the sins of humanity. To some this translates as Jesus paying for and so "purifying" the sins *only* of those who believe in Jesus being Christ. To others this was a ransom paid for all human sin. To then be forgiven by God.

But to believe this, you need to believe that God a) needs our sins to be paid for and retributed, in order to get over a brewing anger, and so forgive them; b) accepts the death of one as payment for the sin of another; and c) that a big ritual flowing of blood is a form of "cleansing". I don't believe this. Do you?

I don't believe that killing a lamb pays for your sins and helps them to be forgiven. And I certainly don't believe that killing Jesus as a "lamb" of sacrifice would do this.

We need to bravely look again and question the belief that the crucifixion enabled God to forgive us our sins... because I have much greater respect in God than all this. I see God as far beyond such limited human understanding and rituals and language. God *only* loves. God forgives us, but to be able to enjoy this forgiveness we need to find our capacity to feel the loving of God. To "be" it. That is our human challenge. To dare to recognize and welcome and live out this Love. Surely that would make us "righteous" and good, because we would want to be.

Jesus' dying was the "ultimate" in the ritual of sacrifice (powerful in his time), enabling us to see that such a ritual is needless. That it is finished with. That rather than Christ making a sacrifice *to God*, for us, God has made a sacrifice *to us*, a sacrifice of Love, as Christ – so the ritual has come full circle. Therefore, the sacrifice we can all make now is in a soul surrender to the power of God's loving. Jesus did this, and he showed us the way. This is my truth. It may or may not be yours. But I so much hope it is worth considering?

When we ignore a need for love, wherever it is, inside us and in the world, we ignore Christ. But we cannot hide from what God asks of us. The crucifixion is therefore to me a symbol of when we turn our backs on God, not just on the day we killed Jesus around 2,000 years ago, but every day now, when we do not strive for justice and act for mercy.

And the Resurrection is a symbol of something else – of what is possible when we realize and act as God's love. God sacrificed Godself, not someone or something else. But the only reasons, to me, that Jesus Christ sacrificed himself and died for us on the cross, was to show us how completely he was a part of God, how greatly he loves us, and how, because he is the *living* Christ, he would and does continually rise again, as life eternal.

What of the way the Atonement, as the death of Jesus, is described in Christian theology as being "the reconciliation of God and mankind through Jesus Christ"? Yes, I agree so much. But not because Jesus was sacrificed to pay the debt for our sins. No. Because he showed us the endless capacity of God as Love, as God dying in human pain for love of us on that cross, completely connecting to us and rising again for us as the greatest ever teaching, the greatest reconciliation in our history.

The Resurrection of Christ

Easter Sunday, a very sunny day, sat on a big stone looking out at the bay behind Iona Abbey. Everything looks fresh.

Jesus rose up from the dead. I believe this in all ways now. And it does not surprise me. But it does excite me!

Jesus was the human Christ. Even the "human" part of him was affected by the fact that he was Christ. That's why he could perform miracles. I realize now that my earlier statement that his miracles were "possible" needs to be clearer – I believe that if Jesus Christ did *not* perform miracles, it would be stranger than if he did! He was the conscious Christ, so of course he could surpass the laws of nature. And he wanted not just to surprise us with what is possible (for us all) but to teach us how we can get there… as a new way of being.

In the same sense, I would be more shocked if Jesus did *not* rise from the dead. He raised Lazarus, yes. He raised the daughter of Jairus, yes (Mark 5:37–43). He said to his disciples that he would rise again. And did he rise "in the flesh"? Yes, but in flesh fully infused with Christ. The human Jesus could not be separated out and untouched by the full divinity within him – surely? This is the essence of his non-duality, his Oneness.

He rose as a body fully aware of God. So, to ask "was that body purely spiritual?" misses the point. Could Mary or Peter "touch" Jesus after he was risen? I believe so. But does this make the risen Christ any different than if Mary had reached out and her hand passed right through him, as purely Spirit? Not to me. The importance of Christ rising is to show us something far greater than all this "limitation by definition" – that the Christ in all of us never dies. So, human mortality (human "weakness") is no longer a barrier between us and God. Here is our great reconciliation. Our coming together. We can realize through Christ's rising that death is not the end. The final fear is "finished". What an astounding revelation!

Christ rose not to impress us with a miracle, just as he never performed miracles while he was alive to show us how "uniquely magical" he was or to create a "Jesus fan club". He was not vain. He was not full of ego. No, he did all this – he came back to life – to share his message of Truth with us of what we are, in Christ: eternal.

*

At the Easter Day service at the Abbey we sing to celebrate how the living Word comes out of death's dark silence. And this reminds me that Christ is the living communication of God to humanity. And every time one of us "hears Christ", hears the Word within us, then Jesus rises again. Jesus as a "human" rose from the dead. But as Christ he rises continuously.

So, we sing in praise of a great day of new beginnings. This day. Today! We sing of Jesus Christ touching us and so calling us "back to life", anew.

> Jesus looked at them and said, "For mortals it is
> impossible, but not for God; for God all things are
> possible."
> **Mark 10:27**

Here is some beautiful poetry (which may have influenced the great poem "And Death Shall Have No Dominion", a modern psalm against dying written by Dylan Thomas). These original words are found in Romans 6:9–11. They speak of a new, eternal life for us all, in God. A life of no sin because all that we can be in God, in Christ, is Love.

> We know that Christ, being raised from the dead, will
> never die again; death no longer has dominion over
> him. The death he died, he died to sin, once for all;
> but the life he lives, he lives to God. So you also must
> consider yourselves dead to sin and alive to God in
> Christ Jesus.

I see another teaching here, which is that Jesus died to show us that human sins and weaknesses, our mortal, ego-constrained human life can die, can be crucified, but the power of Christ is not touched by this. His dying and rising enabled death to no longer have dominion over us. We can know the power of God's love; overcome sin, weakness, and even death, by inviting Christ into us.

And the Eucharist?

I love to share in the Holy Communion. It is a ritual in which I enjoy the liturgy, the recited words which have been said for so long, all around the world. Sometimes I go to join in the Celtic Communion service at my local Anglican church, St Andrew's (where I also go to quietly light prayer candles). And the Communion feels like I am joining in with people around me as well as from long ago and far away, in the Celtic lands such as Iona. People coming together to remember the Christ whom we love and are humbled by. It is a remembering of Jesus' sacrifice for us all, and his own humility.

Are the bread and wine *really* the body and blood of Christ? This means, do I believe in "transubstantiation", which my dictionary defines as "the conversion of the Eucharistic elements into the body and blood of Christ, at consecration, only the appearances of the bread and wine still remaining"? It depends what we mean by "really". The Christ is Spirit. The Spirit can become physical substance whenever and however God chooses. In the Risen Jesus Christ. In the wafer in my mouth... it *is* the body of Christ, to me, because it is the presence of Christ, with me. The body of Christ, both in the Communion bread and in the Risen Jesus can be physical and "touchable" but this is still not the same as the physical which you and I touch or exist as every day. Christ is "more than this", wherever Christ is. And when/if you or I ever become fully conscious of Christ, we too shall be "more than physical". That is how Jesus was able to raise people from the dead, to rise himself from the dead, and to be present now in the Communion bread and wine. It is a dimension we do not comprehend yet, even though it is a potential within us.

Jesus was just as much flesh as Spirit, and therefore the Communion wafer is just as much the "body of Christ", and the wine his "blood" as it ever can be... to argue over "is it *really* his body?" is to totally miss the point. Misunderstand what is real. The Eucharist is sacred, the most "real" that is. A very special blessing.

*

Mark 9:23–24, after being asked if he was able to heal a sick boy:

> Jesus said to him, "If you are able! – All things can be done for the one who believes." Immediately the father of the child cried out, "I believe; help my unbelief!"

Gender within Christianity

This is an important question for me, and what I write here is not in line with some traditional Christian beliefs. But if we listen to different ideas, even if we don't agree with them, the aim of this book is that we can still be prompted to think afresh, to "open up the box" of our own way of believing and see how this new idea sits within us. That's my hope!

I heard a woman Anglican priest being asked why she stayed within an institution which is so "misogynistic and patriarchal". She replied that the real way to change things is from within. Not to leave and aggressively criticize, but to stay and be determined to work toward what is just. How much I now agree with her. (I also later note the importance of the words "from within"... because of course the greatest change we can ever make is at the level of who we are. Then work outwards...)

Is the Bible patriarchal? Yes. I know there are lots of "good women" in the Bible. Very important and recognized women in the story of Jesus, but we cannot pretend that it is not the males who are foremost... as Father, Son... even the Holy Bible, when writing of the Holy Spirit uses a masculine pronoun "he". And I do totally understand why the Bible is written as it is, from the time and culture to which it belonged. And why the church and powers that be (male, predominantly) have kept up that patriarchy. "Men in/women out, where it counts", is an exclusivity of long-held and deeply embedded tradition.

But it is time for renewal. Time to remember honestly whom Jesus was close to, whom he trusted to be among his most important witnesses, who was there for him both at the cross and at his tomb, who did not desert him or be fickle in loyalty to him. Women. Women like Mary Magdalene. The two stages of the Stations of the Cross which moved me the most on the island walk were related to women – tending to Jesus, crying for him, faithfully loving him. This nourishing, caring feminine aspect of the Christ in *all of us* needs to be recognized, and cherished.

It helps me to remember that God cares for me as a mother does her child, and then some! That when I am afraid or weak, God will not only protect me and give me courage, but also hold me in her arms and tend to my cries. To fully connect to God, we need to know God as our Father *and* Mother, and then step beyond this to realize that God is neither and yet all of these, because God is only Love, the power with no opposite, which contains all opposites. Our One creator, nourisher, and protector.

When I say "protector" I don't mean that God as our almighty Father will stop any harm ever coming to me or you, no, but that when hard times do come, as they will on this earth, God is there to hold us strong, to face the gales together. And as our Mother, God is there to help when the gales knock us down. To say, "Come on, get back up, keep going, you're doing grand" and to remind us that no matter what, even if we cannot get back up, in this life, if we have now to pass on, God is there for us, eternally.

Jesus was a man, of course... but he could just as easily have been a woman. He was a man who came to bring change in a "man's world". To be listened to back then, the Christ needed to be made human in Jesus the man. But women were crucial witnesses and supporters of Jesus. Not just in Mary his mother and Mary his loyal companion, but also in the background, encouraging his mission, probably with meals, good conversations, and with comfort (Mark 15:41 tells us about people around the cross of Jesus "there were many other women who had come up with him to Jerusalem").

*

What is most important about gender in God to me, is that the Christ *in* Jesus, the Christ in us all, is not feminine or masculine, but God. And God has no gender. You may have noticed in this book that (except in Margaret's chapter, in respect of her request) I have not used the capitalized pronoun "He" very often for God, because it goes against what I believe, to make God only a sacred Him. If I had to believe in God as singularly a "He" to be a Christian, then I could not be a Christian.

I read back over these last few paragraphs and am happy to see my words "*our* Christian faith"... because I do want to call myself a Christian. I know that now, and I believe that Jesus does understand if I do not want to use the word "Father" as continuously as he did. Jesus lived in one time, one context of environment. I live in another. Sometimes I do connect to God as my Father, yes, (and love to say the Lord's Prayer, especially with others) but when I really connect to God as One divine Love, words of any gender are irrelevant.

God is God, not a he, or a she, or an it; we can just say "God", it is quite easy! I believe the words we use *do* matter – they are how we think and communicate with each other. We have seen hopefully in this book how crucial our choice of language is to the formation and expression of our beliefs, and then our actions. Continuous use of masculine words like "Lord" and "King" and "Master" is not "just words". They belong to a whole cultural concept and religious philosophy... it is a masculinization of our world. Our spirituality. And we all suffer for it.

When we do this, we limit the divine to being humanized – someone "like us"... like our own leaders who are, and for so long have been, mostly men. God is so much "more than this". We need to step forwards and leave behind such reductive terminology. We can do this. And not be afraid to do so. What we could call the "beyond-humanizing" of God is vital to the future and our developing spirituality. And if we are to evolve spiritually, then a great way to evolve is by *example*. Jesus helped us to evolve as humans by the great example he set. If we want Christianity to become less patriarchal, more harmonious, then we need to live as examples.

Yes, being conscientious about the language we immerse ourselves in can be a real challenge! At church I struggle very much with hymns about us needing to "crush the enemies of God" and of God's "angel army". The hymn book and the Bible are abundant with such aggressive, conflict-based terminology. But I no longer walk away because of this. I keep singing, even if I miss out or change certain words, and if a hymn gets too much for me to bear, I just sit down in quiet protest! I understand our history and try my best in writing, song, talk, and action, to work by example toward a lighter future, in which we honour the caring, feminine aspect of God within us all, women *and* men. To hope we can together find a way to renew our language of faith, stop unbalancing God's truth and move along – evolve.

*

Extra notes written when home.

"Virginity is an ancient symbol for sacred purity in women, reaching far back in time before Jesus was born. So the two Marys seem to have been used to symbolize either complete holy worthiness or disreputable unworthiness – the non-sinner and the (forgiven) multiple-sinner."

These words above are were written during my time on Iona, reflecting on how I saw Mother Mary and Mary Magdalene. I want to show you here how much listening can help us to grow! Recently, just when I was thinking that I had "worked out" my understanding of these two crucial women in the life of Jesus, when I felt a close connection to the powerful guidance of Mary Magdalene, but the Holy Mother seemed just too pure for me to align with – listening changed me.

By reading an online daily meditation from Richard Rohr[6] I suddenly came to realize that the Mother Mary can be understood as a representation of Mother in a whole new way… our "Mother earth" has been worshipped by pagans for centuries in female fertility goddesses, as the producer and nourisher, the creative spirit in us all. Mary links us to these powers. I do not mean that Mary did not really exist, but that she helps us, symbolically, to connect to this creative force.

Not only this, but I now see that creation once said "yes" to God and so the first "incarnation" of the divine came about, in our physical universe, our life on earth. Then the second "yes" was said by Mary, who welcomed and held bravely the incarnation of the Christ inside her womb, to create the baby Jesus. Now the third "yes" is waiting and beginning to be said, as we invite the third incarnation of the divine, and say "yes" to the Christ within us all.

As I read the words of Richard Rohr, as I listened from deep inside, they changed me and changed my life. I found at last my connection to Mary, the mother of Jesus, as a fertile, creative symbol of what happens when we say a brave *"yes"* to God.

What does the Trinity mean to you?

Written firstly on Port Ban beach, occasionally walking along the shore and picking up amazing multi-coloured pebbles.

How do I best perceive the different "aspects" or "Three in One" states of being which help me as a little human, understand and describe the great divine?

1) God – Creator; Mother/Father; unconditional ever-present all-encompassing Love, containing me and you and all in Oneness.

2) The Christ – an extension of God into all humanity; a communication of the Word of God's Truth into us; Christ who is "knocking on our hearts" and waiting for us to listen, to become "fully human", as the Love that we are.
   Jesus – a human being who was fully aware of the Christ within him, fully "Christ-conscious".

3) The Holy Spirit – the Spirit of God throughout everything around and within us; that which connects us together in "fellowship"; another "aspect" of God as our Advocate teacher, who comes to help us understand and practise the Truth in the teachings of Christ, now that Jesus is passed on... as our guide, who "intercedes".

Richard and Tim really helped me to understand the *relationship* aspect of God within the Trinity – how Love, as an action of lov*ing*, involves "giver" and "receiver", and so, since time began, God has loved by being able to give and receive love between God, Christ, and the Holy Spirit within the Godself, and indeed share it... but yet, God is a multiple within a One!

God is God is God.

Love is active. When I practise visualization-meditations and want to imagine peace, I can sense this simply by imagining a creature such as a swan completely at peace upon a lake, or a buttercup in the sun, but to imagine love, I need to think of and feel the love of *one for another* – a bird for her fledglings or my own love for family – this true feeling of love can be imagined and sensed in me only as an exchange *between* one and another.

But! I need to remind myself of this… these are all words. I also hold to what Bob and Jyoti helped me to understand – the Holy Trinity words are human words for a simple truth which our minds struggle to pin down with labels (like a butterfly). God is only Love.

In a sense, really trying to listen to these two ways of comprehending God's Love, helps me get a little closer to understanding the answer beyond them both. We struggle to speak the truth, and perhaps we then come to quietly listen? This reminds me of the quote at the beginning of this book, by Epictetus the stoic Greek philosopher… about us having one mouth but two ears.

*

Some notes added at home.

Recently, during my scary time over the possible return of some brain tumour cells, on my way to Newcastle Infirmary to see my consultant, I visited Hexham Abbey, to say a prayer. I went over to a place for lighting prayer candles, in front of an icon painting of Jesus called "Christ Pantocrator". The postcard for this icon has a quote from Colossians 1:15–16a on the back: "He is the image of the invisible God, the firstborn of all creation; for in him all things in heaven and on earth were created".

This is a fascinating letter written by Paul to the Colossians, because it suggests that *everything* that is created is contained within the Christ (I remember Brigid talking of the Christ in this way). He writes that all things "visible and invisible"[7] are created as Christ the extension of God and that "in him all things hold together".[8] Also, the beautiful words, that Jesus Christ is the "image of the invisible God". Christ in whom "the fullness of God was pleased to dwell"[9] and through whom, in Jesus, God could "reconcile to himself all things".[10] By showing us what is beyond human sin and mortality, through the giving of his life in complete forgiving love of us on the cross, and by rising from death to life again, Jesus Christ brought us all the chance of this "fullness".

When I need a personal connection to God, I pray to Jesus. And I say to myself, as I did in Hexham Abbey that day, the words of Jesus "Abide in me as I abide in you" (John 15:4). I pray these words as if Jesus is talking to me, telling me how connected we are, and then I repeat the prayer focusing the other way around, as myself talking to Jesus. So, I "abide in Christ" just as Christ "abides in me". And my growing awareness of this helps me to cope with pretty much anything.

I went on to the hospital, knowing that if I was told "time up" or told "free to go on living" (thank heaven the latter) I could be safe in my faith in Christ, no matter what.

*

Jesus said "No one comes to the Father except through me",[11] meaning, I believe, except by becoming the Love of the Christ. Not by putting Jesus on a throne but (if we choose this way to God) by following him, with dedication. By a long-held, over-idolizing tradition of holding the Christ up as being "above us" and *only* in Jesus, we so reduce and limit this Holy Truth within the Trinity. We deny its power.

We need not "detach" the Christ from Jesus; no, not at all! We can connect to the Christ more easily *through* Jesus, as he helps us by being God's personified "living image". That was his purpose in many ways. To be the communicator, the hand of God physically reached out to us. But we do need to see the deeper truth, which is that Christ is fully present in Jesus, but waiting in us.

*

Notes again from my time on Iona, sitting in the ruins of the nunnery, founded in 1200, which was a flourishing convent for 350 years. Some local schoolchildren are playing 'tig' nearby.

I sit here to ponder the eternal "be-loving" of God which is represented by the Trinity. I enjoy pondering this "verb sense", this interactivity of God's being. That, even before the universe was created, God was busy loving!

Very often in my answers so far, I have found myself putting layer upon layer by saying, "God is One but God is a Multiple within a One" or "Jesus is Christ but the Christ is not only in Jesus" or "God is Light but the Light is also in darkness"... because I think God is like this. God wants us to see that the answers are wrapped up within and around each other, the levels to true understanding are like steps spiralling up a mountain... but then, at the top of the mountain we find that we were always already there, in the greatest "circular answer" there could be – God is closer than our breath. But perhaps many of us need to go climbing before we can accept how easy the way "home" really is – before we can let go of all the limiting feelings and restrictive concepts in our minds, to feel one simple connection in the breath within us, which has always known.

*

Notes from home on the Sunday when we celebrate Pentecost — the coming of the Holy Spirit to the apostles.

I have been today to church and listened to a great sermon by Tim about the Holy Spirit and what this means to us. And for hours now I have been wrangling with a persisting need for clarity! What do we mean by the Holy Spirit? Much more importantly, what did Jesus mean?

Tim told us how the Hebrew word we translate or transliterate into "Spirit" is *ruach*, which is in the Hebrew Bible, meaning "breath" and "wind" and "spirit". Jewish rabbinic literature also talks about *shekhina(h)*, which is a word not found in the Bible, but which means "the indwelling, divine presence of God", the *shekhinah* which settled in the tabernacle, where Jews believed God then lived, in the Temple, and which can "settle" in us now, as we can become "temples" of God.

I read and find "while a wind from God swept over the face of the waters" in Genesis 1:2 in the Old Testament. In the notes we are told that this verse could also be read as "while the spirit of God". In the Hebrew Bible this is *Ruach Elohim*, hovering over the waters of early creation. Yes, I can see that the Holy Spirit is the part of God which breathes life into us all. Genesis 2:7 says God "breathed into his nostrils the breath of life, and man became a living being". Moses, in Numbers 27:16, calls God "the God of the spirits [*ruach*] of all flesh."

I can also understand the Holy Spirit as the glorious *shekhinah* of God within us. The celebration of God's presence in our very life as we breathe God's air.

In Hebrew, *Ruach Yaweh*, the Spirit of God, is what empowered Jesus with the Holy Spirit "descending like a dove and alighting on him", in his baptism (Matthew 3:16).

And, to me, Jesus meant all this *and then some*, when he talked to his disciples (who became the apostles) about how the Holy Spirit would be coming to them, after he was gone. When the Pentecost did happen, and the apostles were lit up with the flame of the Spirit and able to speak in tongues (to communicate with people of all languages, and so spread the teachings of Jesus), I find something extra in this description to that of the Holy Spirit so far. I find connection to the Christ.

In John 14:16–17, Jesus called the Holy Spirit "another Advocate, to be with you forever", (or, as my NRSV Bible notes say, a "helper"), to help people learn, as the spirit of Truth. Jesus also said that *he* was the way and the Truth. In John 14:17 he says to the apostles that when this helper comes they would know him because "he abides with you and he will be in you", just, as at another time, as I considered earlier, Jesus also spoke of himself, the Christ, saying "abide in me as I abide in you" (John 15:4). What could this mean?

In this enlightening fourteenth chapter of John, Jesus went on to tell his disciples that he would not leave them "orphaned". These three verses are worth telling here (verses 18–21):

> I will not leave you orphaned; I am coming to you. In a
> little while the world will no longer see me, but you will
> see me; because I live, you will also live. On that day
> you will know that I am in my Father, and you in me,
> and I in you.

Jesus knew his teachings would need more understanding, so he said that when he was gone, the Father would send the Holy Spirit as an Advocate "in my name". I think this is very important.

I understand it to mean that Jesus told his followers that a helper, a divine part of God, sent by God, would carry on guiding them after he was gone, and so would continue Jesus' work on earth. The helper will be there to help us all to come to know the Christ within us, should we ask for this help. The Holy Spirit therefore *continues* our chance to be reconciled to the divine Love that we are, if we follow the guidance we are offered by this Spirit of Truth. Because Jesus was departing from earth, he promised the help of the Advocate, to carry on his work.

I use the words "becoming Christ-conscious". Some people prefer to focus on "receiving the Holy Spirit" – but I see now how these words are so inter-connected that we barely need to separate them. Jesus said, "I am going away, and I am coming back to you" (John 14:28). The Holy Spirit, which Jesus spoke of coming in his name, which came to the apostles at the Pentecost and comes every time we open our own awareness to Truth, is the helper for our becoming Christ-conscious.

So, to me (how my words struggle to define and limit this!) the Holy Spirit is always there, in the "breath of life" on earth, who connects us all in fellowship, who is the "indwelling of the glorious presence of God", the *ruach* and the *shekhinah* – *and who now* comes to help us know the Christ – just as Jesus did when he was alive. The Holy Spirit and Jesus Christ are interlinked as they both come to "save us". They both ask us to welcome them. They are both already within us.

And, of course, they are One.

*

Jesus talking about the coming work of the Holy Spirit:

> He will glorify me, because he will take what is mine
> and declare it to you. All that the Father has is mine.
> For this reason I said that he will take what is mine and
> declare it to you.
> *John 16:14–15*

And Jesus' promises of the Holy Spirit to his disciples (John 14:16–17, 26–27):

> And I will ask the Father, and he will give you another
> Advocate, to be with you forever. This is the Spirit of
> truth... You know him, because he abides with you,
> and he will be in you... But the Advocate, the Holy Spirit
> whom the Father will send in my name, will teach you
> everything, and remind you of all that I have said to
> you. Peace I leave with you; my peace I give to you...

Paul, writing about the help of the Holy Spirit for our communication with God:

> Likewise the Spirit helps us in our weakness; for we do
> not know how to pray as we ought, but that very Spirit
> intercedes [for us] with sighs too deep for words.
> *Romans 8:26*

The devil, evil... do they exist?

Port Ban beach again, in a little nook by the rocks.

I am sitting here on the beach, a very secluded place with today not a soul in sight. The sea is calm, the sky blue. But just as I was about to write this, a cloud came over me. I began to think about the disease which might again be developing in my brain. I remembered the warning given me by Carol, how the devil loves it if we don't believe in him, because he can then sneak up on us… and I look about. But no, there is no devil here. I am nervous to be writing this now, alone on a remote beach, but no, there is no devil here…

What there is, is nature.

To me, I am not afraid to accept and be grateful for the natural laws which God instilled to create our earth and the living creatures and plants upon it. That is, birth and death, construction and destruction, dark and light, order and chaos…

But also, to accept the truth that we cannot have the bodies we live in and often enjoy, without the reality of our biology which also encompasses the risk of disease. We cannot have days like this, with no breeze, without the natural forces of our weather which can also cause devastating hurricanes. That is life on earth. And I believe very much that God chose to create it as such. This way, on our planet, is how life and death are meant to be. A hard truth for me sometimes, but a truth.

What's more, God created humans. God knows us, knows we have childish nervous egos and selfish desires. That we are easily afraid of losing our own identity and so can react dramatically to any sense of danger to our ego's survival – be it mental, emotional, or physical. The "I" will do so very much to stake a claim on earth, on our life.

God knows all this. God is not, I believe, very surprised by the errors (and achievements) we make as humans and have been making for millennia. I cannot go along with the concept of God being "in despair" about the mess we made as ancient people, so deciding to flood the planet and start again or, when the Israelites behaved a bit like a human yo-yo, going to and from God's loving Truth, that God was at all shocked by this. And of course, God knew what we would do to Jesus.

*

People say, "How can there be a God when there is so much suffering, so much evil in this world?" This is a heartfelt and very understandable questioning of God's existence. What answer would I give to this? That God does not intentionally *cause* suffering or evil, but yes, God has created for us a world where suffering and evil are possible. As possible as joy and goodness.

God chose to give us the natural powers on earth by which we live. And God chose to give us free will. This gives us so much capacity and potential. We can gain wisdom, we can choose to do great, creative things. God can "enjoy" life and love through us. But we can also choose destruction and a diminishing of God's purpose for us. God gave us the freedom and capacity to do either, for God's own reason. This freedom is a truly great gift to us *but* of course, as God knows well, it has risks. It can lead us into the dark.

But what is the dark or the "badness"? I believe "nature" on earth is a force which *has to contain* a negative, destructive harmful element within it. The laws of physics and biology and chemistry which we live by *enable* us to live because of the chance within them for chaos and destruction. For "entropy", as in the chaotic breaking down of order, as well as for order and harmony. This is the necessary "denying factor" if you like, of life itself.

So, disease and disability, pain and suffering, disaster and tragedy are not the work of the devil or a punishment by God but an inherent part of life on this planet. I accept that. I even learn and grow to know God's love *within* that suffering. To not believe this, to think that when I am ill God is "not there" or worse still, that "evil" has the upper hand, or I am being "punished", would to me be the real failing.

And when people are bad or "evil sinners", I see this not as the work of some demon force outside of God – because nothing is outside of God. I cannot say I believe God is everything, a whole Oneness, and then "cop out" when things look nasty! The bad and the sin of us are done when we do not know the Love we contain. We are distracted by other emotions. We can be afraid to know such great Love, perhaps because we have been hurt in our lives, or because it seems so big and all-encompassing, outside of our ego's control. Perhaps some of us do not dare hold what we are too afraid to lose?

God's love can be scary, being so unconditional. We may even feel unworthy of such loving, especially if we have heard the voices of criticism too much in our past. We can listen to our selfish (frightened) ego inside, to our mis-perceiving minds or to influences like drugs and drink, that can twist our mind-sets. We can learn behavioural patterns or even damage our brains, so they become prone to denying love. Or we can listen to other twisted minds and be corrupted. We then do harm, to ourselves, others, and our planet. But still God knows, is not surprised, is not unforgiving or condemning us. God gave us all this complicated, challenging, and yet potentially wonderful life we have as humans, and waits for us to hear the true voice. To listen.

Christ waits at the door and knocks.

We may take all our life (or many lifetimes) to hear that gentle knocking, to open the door of our hearts. But God has known this all along. What God wants is for us to be *reconciled* to Love and will keep waiting (in us) until this day comes. God calls us to make our planet and our existence a loving success, not a tragedy. Asks us to be re-awakened. This re-creation is born from the old but has always, in Truth, been God's love.

*

More notes written on return home.

It is good, I think, to consider more what the word "reconcile" means. It is a verb, an action, meaning "to restore friendly relations between" or "to settle" and "to make or show to be compatible". How valuable an action. It originates from the Latin "re-" as in "back" (expressing intensive force) and "conciliare" as "bring together". To reconcile us with God is to *bring us back together*, intensely, with God's love. And at the church service yesterday, a lady read something which said everything so well, about the action of Christ in this, from 2 Corinthians 5:16–21:

> From now on, therefore, we regard no one from a human point of view, even though we once knew Christ from a human point of view, we know him no longer in that way. So if anyone is in Christ there is a new creation: everything old has passed away; see, everything has become new! All this is from God, who reconciled us to himself through Christ, and has given us the ministry of reconciliation; that is, in Christ God was reconciling the world to himself, not counting their trespasses against them.... So we are ambassadors for Christ.... For our sake he made him to be sin who knew no sin, so that in him we might become the righteousness of God.

*

I believe therefore that no evil truly exists on earth, because all that exists is God. But there is yes, a desperate lacking, a "non-love", evil "holes in our socks" as Richard put it, that need to be filled with love. And there could be "demons" or "devils" as in tortured souls on this earth, or in the next life. These have voids of love-lack, hungry hollows that are evil, because of fear, but are still *capable* of becoming filled with loving, of reconciling to God. I realize now, which I did not before, that we do need to be aware of the dangerous voids of evil. But evil, like the dark, is an absence, not an existence. When there is (as Leonard Cohen put it so well in his song

"Anthem"), a small "crack" in the dark, then the light can get in. Love fills and so denies the existence of evil.

There is no singular personification or realized being of the devil which is an absolute opposite to God, because God has no opposite. God is the only One which has no, but contains all, dualities. Troubled demonic souls could exist, but they are still God's children, and God is still waiting for them to know this. To stop refusing. They may be horrifically wicked "sinners" but they still have the goodness of God being turned away inside them. They cannot *exist* as souls and be 100 per cent evil (as Richard told me), and so they can still be saved; still be reconciled to Love.

When I say, "they may be sinners" I really should say "we may be", because the sinner is of course not necessarily someone else! How careful we should be of scapegoating, or of holding up emblems of evil such Hitler, Myra Hindley, Judas Iscariot, even Satan. This is our attempt to project and personify evil outside of ourselves. We can all sometimes be lacking in love, feel a void within us that is fear, and this can lead us all to selfish even "wicked" destructive ways, hurting those around us and damaging our planet. But we each of us can at any time choose to listen bravely to God's message within our own soul, saying "do not be afraid, for I am with you, always". "Satan" or "the devil" cannot purely exist or completely have any of us, because we all belong to God.

*

A friend I made on Iona at the very start of this journey, as we sat around the fire discussing heaven and hell, is Reverend Susan, a Presbyterian minister from New York. When I asked her in an email about who goes to heaven, she replied with memorable words… "We all go to heaven eventually, even if some of us need to be dragged there, kicking and screaming!" We all go.

So, I am more aware now that threatening "holes of non-love" can be there for us to deal with in our lives, but, as a hymn line which contradicts all my "non-gender" ideas about God, but which I still often sing to myself says "Dear Lord and Father of mankind, forgive our foolish ways"… and God wants to forgive us, even though we can be fools. God loves us forever. We can be fools who dance with an evil lacking, but we never cease to contain within us the greatest good of all.

More of the above hymn, by John Greenleaf Whittier (1807–1892):

> **Dear Lord and Father of mankind,**
> **Forgive our foolish ways;**

Re-clothe us in our rightful mind,
In purer lives thy service find
In deeper reverence, praise,
In deeper reverence, praise.[12]

What does prayer mean? Is trust enough?

Port Ban beach – still! I don't want to leave!

When I hope and pray now about the coming results of my scans, I do something which utilizes my reserves of faith: I trust in God. I acknowledge and accept that whatever God intends for me, is best for me. This is not easy! I won't pretend it is. Especially, to accept that what I hope for (being well) may not happen. But there is also something very powerful in this act of acceptance: it confirms to me that I gladly surrender my life to God. It outlines and concentrates my faith.

The same is true with my prayers for others. We can ask in hope for those whom we love to be made well or get out of dark times. We can communicate to God in this way, or personally to Jesus. We can "hold people up", as Margaret so beautifully described to me, hold them in God's love so that they can become more aware of God's mercy; God's grace. We can also very effectively send people or living things, places and situations, love from inside our own hearts. This is such a powerful way of sharing God's love from within us.

But in my core, I believe in surrendering to God, knowing that God is the One who ultimately *is* the universe, and we can ask to guide our life. By choosing to say, "Please God, let me surrender completely to your love", this to me is the greatest prayer of all.

There are aspects of prayer which I do not yet fully comprehend – how there can be the potentially chaotic forces of nature (health/disease, fortune/disaster) and of human choice (both good and wicked, tormented human souls sometimes performing acts which have horrific effects upon others) yet still beyond all this, the "over-all" power is God. This is beyond me. But I do believe it, in a part of me that is not my mind and has no words.

So then, if things go the way I hope, I trust in God. But if things go another way, I trust in God. Because all there ever is, is Love, and so all we can ever truly be, is safe. Easier to say or write than to live out as a fragile human being, with full confidence? Yes, for sure! But I know that to live with this trust is possible. This is true faith. To believe God will always make "everything OK" and provide us with plenty and keep us healthy, is not honestly true. Not even if we pray for this, for ourselves, for our loved ones, for the world. Not even if we are "good Christians". To say so is to me a false hope. A false promise. A "conditional" faith. But to absolutely trust that God will always love us and keep our souls safe, to believe in God's love no matter what happens to us in this life – that, for me, is the way.

"Is trust enough?" is really a non-question. Because ultimately trust is all there is.

*

As I return from the beach and head toward the Heritage Centre Café, walking over pebbles and rough tracks, I become clearer of something not to forget – that surrender to God is not a *passive* thing. God gave us free will to choose how we live but if we say we "give our lives to God", and ask God to guide us, this does not mean we should then opt out of making any responsible, even difficult choices for our actions or our words. Surrender is not like being a prisoner! We need to be busy followers of Jesus. Busy pilgrims. As I arrive at the café for a toastie, I realize how prayer itself is very much an active connection with God – a way to feed our souls.

*

More notes from when I returned home, still seeking to clarify my beliefs on prayer.

At a Bible study group meeting I attended recently, an elderly gentleman preacher (Mel), was there. He very much reminded me of my late grandad (Frank), who was himself a Methodist preacher. We were talking about prayer and I said that I do find it quite hard to ask God for things now, because I believe so much in trusting to God with my life. I was thinking of a poem of mine called "Cumberland Infirmary Dermatology Unit, 1pm". It was written days before a scan to test for skin cancer cells and includes the lines:

> I prayed more,
> uttered *I ask, I ask*, then added
> *I trust, I trust*, until I wasn't sure
> which came first – or if you can have
> both together.
> Said my request
> then added my surrender.[13]

196

My puzzle was… is it a sign of not trusting, if we ask God to do things for us? Then Mel explained, gently, that prayer is a time when we can "admit our needs to God". This helped me tremendously.

We can trust, we can do our best to surrender, and we can also be honestly human – admit when we feel weak and afraid. We can say "I want this so much" and "I ask this for this person whom I love and who is suffering". Or "I pray for this person who I do not know but whose plight I care about". We can pray for our struggling earth. We are then communicating with the divine, and God *wants* us to do this. God even gives us a way of personal communication, through Jesus. God is our parent and wants to listen. And we are only children. It's OK!

*

I have learned so much from what I believe Jesus showed us in the Garden of Gethsemane, and from when he was nailed to the cross. He teaches me that we can be human; we can be willing and asking and hoping for our needs to be answered and we can use our determination, while at the same time we can surrender ourselves to an ultimate trust in God's knowing love. We can say and feel "Thy will be done". To me, this lesson is at the centre of the cross, and is such an important one for us to realize. In Mark 14:35–36, when Jesus is in Gethsemane, we see how he is predicting, dreading, and then surrendering to his Father for his coming death (KJV):

> And he went forward a little, and fell on the ground,
> and prayed that, if it were possible, the hour might
> pass from him. And he said, "Abba, Father, all things
> are possible unto thee; take away this cup from me:
> nevertheless not what I will but what thou wilt."

A prayer sent to me by Margaret, which helps me further understand what prayer can be for us. It is an adaptation by Margaret of a William Barclay prayer, for a time of worry and anxiety:

> Dear Lord, you know how worried and anxious I am
> just now. Calm me down, Lord, and help me to see
> that, although I cannot help worrying, you are always
> there to strengthen and console. Help me, Lord, to
> trust in you and to know that nothing can happen to me
> through which you cannot bring me, and that nothing
> can separate me from your love. Help me to lose my

anxiety in the certainty that your everlasting arms are
underneath me and about me and give me something
of the peace that the world cannot give and cannot
ever take away.
This I ask through Jesus Christ our Lord,
Amen.[14]

And here are some words I found stitched onto a small cushion:

Life is fragile,
Handle with prayer.

So, what now? What for the future?

This is an important question for me to answer, but first I need to answer
another vital one...

CHAPTER THIRTEEN

Am I a Christian?...Are you?

The light shineth in darkness; and the darkness
comprehended it not.
John 1:5 KJV

Here is this same verse with a slightly different translated meaning, in the
NRSV Bible:

The light shines in the darkness, and the darkness did
not overcome it.

I am hopeful for the future and enthused by the sparks of light for greater
clarity, comprehension, and positive change within the church, which are
happening all over the world. I do want to become a part of all this, but first
need to be sure... am I really a Christian?

Christianity is a "journey of faith". Very much. But we do not call
the religion being a "Jesusian". We name the religion after Christ. This
must mean something important? I now understand that it does. To be a
Christian means to follow Christ.

Christianity is defined in my dictionary as (simply) "a religion based on
the person and teachings of Jesus Christ, or its beliefs and practices". Many
Christians believe in the Holy Trinity, many believe that Jesus rose from
the dead, many believe in us "gaining" eternal life in heaven by believing
in and following his teachings, which are recorded in the New Testament.
But *how* we see the Truth of Christ is not pre-set, or exactly defined, for
Christians (which is a wonderful thing!). All Jesus asks is for us to follow the
light, his way of Love, as best we can comprehend this. To move along on
the mountain with him, on the clearest path we can trust.

This, for me, was the song of Jesus: *to know our belonging to the divine, and to live out that which we truly are – unconditional inclusive Love*. This is what it means, for me, and I believe now for many people, to be a Christian.

Jesus Christ lived, and lives on, and the Holy Spirit comes to help us comprehend the sacred Truth of the Light within us, which needs some guidance, and courage, for us to see.

*

I believe and trust that I am a Christian. I can say that now. And later in this chapter I will suggest you clarify your own answer(s) to this foremost question of the book, by going through the "interview" for yourself. But first, before you best describe and voice your own beliefs, we could look at a background question which I laid out in the introductory chapter: what is our preferred spiritual "language for God"? This way of speaking and thinking, describing the "indescribable" was done differently (even if to subtle degrees) by every person I interviewed. Fascinatingly so.

Exploration of faith for this adventure has taught me that language is what can seem to divide us, even when deep down we are not divided. Jesus also brought a new kind of "language for God" – for inclusion, for compassion, for service. He reminded his fellows of the old ideals but with a new energy. New parables. Words and symbols that motivated people. He did not conform to tradition when he knew that change was needed. In the years of his active preaching and healing he lived and worked passionately "on the edge" of his Jewish religion. His is a great example to follow – with constant humility.

For me it is the ways in which we interpret the three important concepts of "Oneness", of God's "presence", and of "justice", which make me seek change.

But can I still call myself a Christian? Yes! I very much believe so. Why should people with fresh "language" and hope for change be excluded or keep walking away from the church? This is causing stagnation. Some people might say that my faith is outside of the "criteria" for being a Christian. That, because I do not believe in certain things which they understand from the Bible (particularly in Jesus being crucified as a sacrifice to "pay for our sins", or in God sending anyone to hell as a "punishment") then I am not fitting in with the "biblical truth" of their religion. But I believe in Christ, and I know this makes me, as it makes many people now (and may also make you), a Christian. Christianity is and needs to be the faith for people who seek and follow the Love of Christ.

As a Christian I need to describe and understand our God and our Christ in a "new" language – which has strong connecting threads to the "old". So, what are the three ways I hope we can (as Christians or otherwise), refresh our "language for God"?

1) Oneness – God is not a he or a she, God is One divine Love, containing both masculinity and femininity, because in truth the great paradox is that God is "non-dualistic" and has no opposition. God is all that truly exists. **God is all of us.**

2) Presence – we can "awaken", "invite", and "welcome" Christ and the Holy Spirit into us, but we do not in truth need to ask for any part of God to "join us" or "come to us today". Because God is *always* here. We need only to become conscious, to "reconcile" to this great Truth, of Christ being always within us. Jesus is the living Christ, who never died. Jesus showed us that as humans we physically die but our soul, our divine belonging with God, is eternal. **God is ever-present, ever in us.**

3) Justice – God does not judge or condemn us as sinners or non-believers, in the way we humans comprehend judgment. God's justice is ever-loving grace, ever caring as the "parent" of our souls, helping us to "come home to heaven". This is when we can at last fully long for our re-connection to God's Love. God decides our "justice" in whatever way God knows is best, in this life or thereafter, because God knows us, knows our fears and struggles, and **God's justice comes from eternal love for us.**

These are my three big passions for "new language" and change within "the church"… but they are not just mine! Many people now believe and are Christian, or are followers of Jesus, in forward-moving and *inclusive* ways, with all three aspects of knowing God described above – that is in God's **being, presence, and grace.**

*

The answers from people in this "anthology of faith" have helped both form and alter my own beliefs, when I could genuinely meet, be still, and listen to them, with a willingness to change. And I *keep* learning from them. John shows me the meaning of active devotion to God – only yesterday he emailed me to say that he had just returned from taking fifty young students to Rome! This was, he said, to help them gain a sense of the "universal church" to which they belong. When they brought home rosary beads for their grandparents, he wanted this to help them to sense the long and continuing "family" of their Catholic faith.

All the "pilgrims" in this book help me to answer, "where am I?" with regards to my faith. To become clearer (not cloudier) by being daring enough to "mingle" and cross pathways with others. I hope the same for you. I hope you can now make space and time to ask yourself the "fourteen questions" (perhaps in the order which I followed on Iona, or whichever way you choose) and find your own answers.

Write them down or speak them as spontaneously as you can, listening to your genuine responses in heart and mind. And use the "language for God" which is your own. Your statements will not be mine or anyone else's – I do hope! They could contain inspiration from what you have read and listened to here in this book. They could strongly contest or firmly agree with some of these beliefs. They could be fresh and radical! There could be some questions which make you realize you have doubts about God. But you can remember then the words of Tennyson: "There lives more faith in honest doubt, / Believe me, than in half the creeds."[1]

And trust yourself to keep moving along with your answers. Some will come to you easily, others you may struggle with and need to really dig deep or ask about, listen more, think and read, and pray... and be silent.

Listen not just to other people or words in books but also to God within you. God often speaks quietly, so we need to be quiet to hear. It is also true, I believe, that the more we are open and want to listen, the more things come to us – signs are shown, non-coincidences fall our way, or we meet the person who says just the thing to inspire us and move us along... or we hear it in the line of a song, or a prayer, in a poem, film, or in a river...

I hope you find this exciting, thrilling even, as you ask yourself to listen and let things come to you. Then you can also ask yourself, "Am I a Christian?" and understand that this word describes many kinds of people, all with different "languages for God", but all with a devotion to Christ. Christianity as a religion has a big umbrella, which you may or may not choose to come under and belong to. Or to remain under. There are of course many other denominations of Christianity, which you could explore. I hope that from reading this book you have heard enough to develop an idea of what Christianity is and can become. Also, what devotion to Jesus as a great teacher (keeping outside the edges of religion) is and can be. What *you* believe. What your honest faith is. And so begin to know what you can do, here and now, to live it.

*

Some powerful words now, from 1 Corinthians 13:2 (KJV).

> And though I have the gift of prophecy, and understand
> all mysteries and all knowledge; and though I have all
> faith, so that I could remove mountains, but have not
> charity, I am nothing.

More modern versions of this verse, such as the NRSV, use the word "love" for charity. Both words hold such answers and motivation for us.

CHAPTER FOURTEEN

What Next?

Back on North End beach, my favourite place on this island. I listen to the waves and when I return home, the sound of these "deep running waves" will be my link to peace. Another sunny day.

So, where do we go from here? It is time to gather the energy that drives us forward and consider how we have changed, before we take clear new steps, even a new direction.

Do we want to join a church? At the beginning of this adventure, I was like so many people and simply called myself "spiritual" – loved to go into empty churches and light a candle, pray quietly to God, but did not enjoy or connect to a lot of what was said or sung in church services. Often felt troubled by the words used. Yesterday I went to a talk in the Iona Community shop. It was by an art historian called Debbie who said she was Christian "by faith but not by religion". Association with the very word "religion" was not comfortable for her. How many people feel like that – wanting to connect to Christ but not to Christianity?

But I also wonder now how much the individualism of our Western culture has encouraged many of us to "go it alone" with our spirituality, or be antagonistic toward any structured groups? And how much does our inward-looking, separated-out society lead us to mental and physical unhappiness, even illness? Do we perhaps as humans *need* a way of coming together with shared beliefs, even rituals, liturgies? Do we long to hold a common sense of purpose and belonging – of being an "us" rather than always an "I"? And crucially, could the "us" not need to persistently exclude, oppose, and criticize the "them"?

The changes I believe in have all been said before. We do not need new ideas about Christianity so much as to revive with passion the true song of

Jesus. And, as people in these interviews have shown me, we need not only to say what we believe in, but to act upon it. I feel the need to step out of lazy hypocrisy and purposefully *be* the Love of God. To "justify" the Love. And perhaps justice is really this? The duty (and deep soul desire) within us all to honour what is at the core of us. To declare and bear good witness to this Love.

I believe that Christianity needs to acknowledge (as soon as possible) that "judgment" in terms of "punishment" – in a human sense of the term – for our sins or lack of faith, is an absolute antithesis to who God is. To state (and rejoice) that there is no one at the "gates of heaven", summing up whether we can come in or not. Seeing God with any kind of weighing scales for our pass or fail is not my God, or my Christ. And I believe this idea repels many people now, because they see through it. As Bob said, there can be no *ifs* to unconditional Love.

In this way of seeing, God judges us only in that God sees and decides upon what our soul needs next. In his song "Anthem", Leonard Cohen suggests that all our hearts will come back to love, like refugees.[1] Yes, I believe *every* human will come to God's love, eventually, even if we come from "exile". But to get there, do we need to go – where? Do we need to experience – what? Knowing that is beyond us. Maybe to experience healing or to appreciate peace. And if I am going to be honest here, experiencing healing could mean experiencing illness first, and appreciating peace could mean suffering trauma or conflict, and coming through. It could even mean "coming through" such things without physically surviving... but none of this do I *need* to ever fully understand, because I trust that God does. Whatever happens to us when we die, wherever we go, whatever we need to do or learn, it will be full of God's grace. I trust that, and it is a wonderful thing for us to have faith in. For Christianity to encourage us to believe.

If "the church" (or any Christian group or church denomination) can teach and "justify" as in explain and bear witness to this unconditional loving, rather than warning of "hell and damnation" for unbelievers and sinners, it will be a time for celebration. And I think this is beginning to happen. Of course, we still need very much to follow moral guidelines and act with real compassion, be more responsible, loving citizens of our planet, care for each other, not be cruel – but because we *want* to be the Love that we are, not because we are afraid of hell.

*

Some words in church services will never resonate with me, but I would feel lost without the ones that uplift. And some rituals, such as Holy

Communion, even bowing my head to God as I leave a church, these have within me increasingly significant value. It is a balance we each need to find, for what soothes our soul from the past as well as what ignites sparks in us for creating a new future. And as I read over these words, I think of a quote which inspires my poetry. Sister Barbara Hance (1928–93) once said, "Show me a day when the world wasn't new". How true this is. The future is born anew *every* day.

*

This book quest has taught me how, if we stay solo on our search for knowing God, we may lose the extra power given to our faith (the "umph" to our footsteps) which can come from worshiping as a "two or more" group. Jesus recommended this. Why? Because by *community* we can perhaps find our true humanity, and our true strength.

Wendell Berry talked of "community in the fullest sense" consisting of *a place and all its creatures*. How community is perhaps the "smallest unit of health" and that to speak of the health of an "isolated individual" is a contradiction in terms.[2] From my life so far, I can really understand this. It is when we feel alone that we can fall "into ourselves" and I have seen people I love become very ill because of this.

I hope and believe now that the church can help keep us in a community of faith. To do this, the church itself needs to be courageous enough to really listen, to *exchange* ideas, and be truly willing to change. This would mean that we could really step forwards in our communal movement toward God. Winston Churchill is believed – if only in our cultural memory – to have once said "It is the courage to continue that counts". This need not only be a good motto for times of horrid war – it can be the best way for moving together bravely toward God's peace.

*

It's also good to consider a new way of *sharing* our faith. For so long in our Western culture and education system, in our whole way of thinking and learning, we have held meetings, sermons, lectures of all kinds, where the "many listen to the few" – a leader or teacher or two basically giving everyone else the ideas and practices to follow. This is good but does not have to be the *only* way to communicate. We can also dare to meet with no leaders, no set speakers, but some good "principles for meeting" which help us do our best to exchange between ourselves the beliefs and ideas we each have.

(A pause as I read through this text and see the word "communicate", which I imagine has strong links to the word "communion". I look for the definition and yes, "communication" means to "share or exchange information, news or ideas". And "communion" can be defined as "the shared participation in a mental or spiritual experience". A *two-way* sharing process is the key, be it by words or experiences.)

To communicate well in an equal group with no leaders is often not easy, because we are so used to one-way speeches by "experts" or professionals. When there is an "open space" to speak, some of us have egos that want to grasp any attention possible, which prevents us from hearing the wisdom within us *all*. And some people are nervous to speak, even when they have a lot to offer. We may need someone who is a good "facilitator" to help us learn and practice this, but if we can listen and interact well together, we can then process a whole thriving network of ideas.

*

Can we dare to tread into such "new territory" as a faith? Can we remember it is not "heresy" or lack of commitment which causes any of us to ask for space to consider new questions or confusions? It is the opposite – enthusiasm! Like teenagers we are coming to new understandings, and this could be a great thing. It is difficult, full of growing pains, full of stumbles and realignment, but with the right support, guidance and love from our "family" of the church, just think – where could we reach?

Perhaps as a vibrant community we could be helped to understand what Jesus meant when he told his disciples about the power of true belief – how much they could do to "move mountains" of any problems on earth, if they only had faith:

> For truly I tell you, if you have faith the size of a
> mustard seed, you will say to this mountain, "Move
> from here to there," and it will move; and nothing will
> be impossible for you.
> *Matthew 17:20*

*

And what about the other religions of the world? What about Islam, Hinduism, Buddhism, Sikhism, Shamanism, New Age spirituality; what about the non-religious, the humanists, those choosing to follow a very individual spiritual path...?

Born in 1977, Malala Yousafzai is the youngest ever recipient of the Nobel Peace Prize (at age fourteen). Recently, when talking on the news about her brave mission to help Muslim women and girls in Pakistan and around the globe to receive the chance of an education, she commented, "My focus is only working for the good".[3] If we do this, then we are moving toward God, toward Allah, or whatever we choose to call that which creates us. We are coming home. I want myself to make this journey with Jesus, through conscious connection to what my religion calls the Christ, but if other people find other good ways up the mountain to divine Truth, then I want to listen and try my best to understand, to learn from them.

I would encourage anyone with no faith, no religion, to follow mine and become a Christian now. But I would never tell a practising Buddhist to give up his/her own faith, or a devout Muslim, or Hindu, or anyone. For I am not a believer in "only one way" in terms of the language and philosophy used to find our true Oneness. As Richard said, I believe everyone who does find Oneness with God (in heaven) will know Christ, because Christ is there in heaven. But the words used to understand this communication, this extension of God's Truth into humanity, are not the sole "property" of any one religion.

There need be no "higher righteousness" either between faiths or between different Christian denominations. We just need to remember not to see any people as below us but to see the Christ in them. When we can stop judging the souls of others, we can hopefully one day come to stop judging ourselves so harshly, and together find our common thread – our completeness.

*

Perhaps when our heart feels connected to God and pushes us along, when we resonate inside with Spirit (even only occasionally), do we lose our "exactness"? Do we reach a point of calling God, as Jyoti does, "the highest of whatever", and feel content with that? Do we stop looking for specifics? Love is not exact and perhaps, in many ways, neither is God? Love has a vast dictionary of possibilities...

God is *creative*, so when we enjoy and practise the arts, we can celebrate and connect with God's creative essence.

I was recently admiring a painting by the American modern artist, Georgia O'Keefe (1887–1986). By the side of the abstract painting (*Black Abstraction*, 1927) was a great quote by O'Keefe:

The abstraction is often the most definite form for the intangible thing in myself that I can only clarify in paint.[4]

How true this could be regarding our desire to clarify the "intangible" truth of divine Love... how often creative "abstract" art, poetry, literature, music, can be the most "definite form" for expressing and communicating this – releasing our awareness of God from our inner being.

And when we immerse ourselves in inventiveness, or (as people like Andy do) in scientific and philosophical *thinking* then we can strengthen our connection to divine purpose. Science can be reason, but it can also be wonder! The more we marvel, ponder, research life, and look for new evidence, guidance, theories, the more we can engage with the divine.

We can also engage more with God through *service*. Jesus served humanity. He gave to us so that we can receive. Whenever we help other life on the planet, then we act out God's love through ourselves – Mark 10:45 says, "For the Son of Man came not to be served but to serve".

However – how often there is a "however" – I spoke recently to Brigid about my belief in active service to God. And here is another example of how, by listening to other ways than our own, we can learn. Brigid explained to me that an important teaching in *A Course in Miracles* is to *rest in God*. The belief is that by resting deeply in God, we can be shown guidance toward what is best for us to do next with our lives. For some this may be to actively "build an ark", to serve God with demonstrable "in the world" acts. For others, it may be to work upon their own inner enlightenment, the transcendence of their own ego, perhaps by silent meditation... but why?

I must admit I did not fully comprehend this. How does the enlightenment of one soul serve God and all of God's creation? Because, she tells me, if we believe that the selfish human ego is the cause of disharmony on the planet, then any work toward losing our own ego, connecting back to God, will diminish the power of all human ego on earth, and will therefore be a service. So, whether we are moved to become a priest or to help run a youth club, to pray for others or, yes, I now begin to understand, if we choose to spend our life working toward our own enlightenment, in whatever way God guides us in our heart, then we serve God.

Our service can be in the passionately active form, such as encouraged by Christ in Matthew 16:24: "If any want to become my followers, let them deny themselves and take up their cross and follow me." Or it can be in the way described by Thomas Merton (a Catalan Trappist monk 1915–68, whose writings still influence many people's faith): "The monk is not defined by his task, his usefulness; in a certain sense he is supposed to be 'useless', because his mission is not to do this or that job but to be a man of God."[5]

Or, as with most of us, the way we serve God comes somewhere in between, with the commitment and courage that our lives give us the opportunity to carry out.

We can also connect to God by *communication*. Whenever we speak out for human or animal rights or for protecting the planet we live on, we practise the Word of God. And whenever we encourage people to hear God's message of all-inclusive loving grace, we speak out God's Word. Whenever we show care to hear people's troubles or try to help people know they are worthy of being loved, then we are messengers for God, even if we do not describe our actions in this way.

*

As I come to the end of my week on Iona now, sat by a roaring fire in the St Columba Hotel, I remind myself of the importance of one more thing needed for a strong "new life" for Christianity, and that is *humility*. A lovely lady called Amanda served me porridge at my Martyrs Bay guest house this morning. She is training to be a shamanic healer. She spoke to me about the "ego trap" which we can all fall into. This is when we begin to think, even sub-consciously, that as people following a "spiritual path", we are somehow more "soul-wise" than others who are not apparently focusing right now on this dimension of their life. This kind of "higher-up" assumption takes us nowhere but into frustrating corners. And it is all a game for our egos, not our souls.

The best remedy to this ego-risk, for me, is to remember that some of the most spiritually connected people I have ever known were the disabled children I met in the orphanage in Vietnam. Children who could not speak or read, and were not taught anything in a school, only left on their beds, cleaned occasionally and fed. But they knew so much about forgiveness, about kindness, about finding some joy in life. I do not know how, but they knew love, in its true simplicity.

Likewise, we may all know of times when we have met people who are very wise and experienced in their journey toward Truth, yet they almost vibrate with non-egotism. I think of the time I queued up to meet the Dalai Lama in Dharamshala, and when he got to me, his handshake was honest, unassuming, yet he looked at my head and seemed to know that I was in a struggle with disease, and he expressed such love in his hands.

Jesus was not vain or self-promoting. He came to lead us like a lantern – in a "sacred circle". Jesus can lead us along a path until we can find our own Light. And then we will be as bright as the stars! Jesus knew this; he knew who he absolutely was before God, and this was all that ever mattered to him. Our lives will be fulfilled not when we change from being naturally "sinful" but when we realize the goodness that we are. This is a fantastic message to hear, if we dare.

*

In a book entitled *Iona of my Heart*, a fundraising collection of writings for the Iona Community, I wrote a piece entitled "Dare to Ask".[6] It is about my finding the courage to begin asking people about their personal faith, as we sat around that fire at the MacLeod Centre here on the island. I now understand that we do need to dare to ask questions about our confusions, or for our spiritual needs to be recognized. But more, deeper than that, I hope we can dare to listen.

*

"A Celtic Blessing"

Deep peace of the running waves to you.
Deep peace of the flowing air to you.
Deep peace of the quiet earth to you.
Deep peace of the shining stars to you.
Deep peace of the Son of Peace to you.

Amen.

And then I sailed back to the mainland, after my wonderful stay on Iona.

*

Hopefully you have taken the time and chance to answer the fourteen questions from the interview for yourself now, to understand more clearly your own beliefs and how you choose your best *spiritual language* to describe them. Where the unique "you" is on the mountain. We can now move on to look at the other two questions in the background setting for this book: "What do we understand to be 'spiritual truth'?", and "Can we find 'unity in diversity'?" Then we can decisively ask – what next? We can choose our next steps.

Spiritual truth

To begin with *spiritual truth*, what can this mean to us?

Some people are prepared to die for their beliefs. To literally sacrifice themselves. The three sixteenth-century "Oxford Martyrs" – Bishops Ridley and Latimer and Archbishop Cranmer –represent such commitment. For much of history, including the religious suicides in the world right now, people have believed that teaching and encouraging or even failure to oppose the "wrong doctrine" is punishable by being sent to hell (or its equivalent). They choose to lose their short life as humans rather than have their souls put into hellfire (or its equivalent) for eternity.

Last time I was in Oxford, I went to light a prayer-candle for this book in the University Church, St Mary's. I read a note above the candles; it told me that it was at this very spot a space was cut into the stone pillar in order to erect a platform for Cranmer's trial in 1556. It was here that he was expected to read a pre-written sermon, fully supporting the ruling Catholic beliefs. But instead he reversed his previous submission and spoke out defiantly for his Protestant faith, then walked proudly into the wooden fire, lit ready for his burning. But for what? What religious "truth" mattered so much to Cranmer that he feared he would burn in hell if he supported the wrong teaching?

Cranmer had refused to accept the transubstantiation of Christ at the Eucharist as "real". He opposed this Catholic doctrine, as a "protesting" Protestant. But if we look again at the word "transubstantiate" it comes from medieval Latin and means "to change the form or substance of something into something different". *Substance*… what do, or can we mean by this, when we talk of Christ?

What if many religious problems and fighting, even terrorism, have for centuries been caused by people trying to make an "absolute truth" from something which is really a "poetic truth" (as Martyn has helped me to see), and is more genuine for being so?

Yes, politics and other cultural differences are also behind a lot of the continuous fighting in our world between people of different beliefs. But have we often lost track of the meaning of terms like "spiritually true"? To try to restrict this to a literal "absolute" is the realm where such greatness as the Christ, as our God, does not singularly dwell.

Christ is also in the symbol and the feeling. And Christ is more than *all* these words. Christ is to be found in our souls, and is *substantially* there, in a profound "poetic reality". A reality which some people throughout history could accept and not denigrate by arguing over definitions. And for the people of the past who could *not* do this, hopefully we can begin to do it now? We can "evolve".

The substance of Christ is including and beyond what any of us can understand as a physical dimension. Can we stop losing the glory of God by trying to pin God down into physical atoms? To "particularize" our God, who is beyond all particles – because even though we are each "parts" of God, there is no *actual* separation between us; no true "boundaries" within God (of "God"/"not God") because all that "separates" me from you the reader right now is air, land, water, bricks, bodies... which *all* belong to One God. By being almost neurotically determined to be "precise" and "containing", both in our binary thinking in/out labelling system, and in our definitions of spiritual truth, do we lose our way in a muddle of limitation? Like children trying to make dolls out of sunlight.

Perhaps we can find our clear way, find Light on the mountain, when we accept that the dimension of Love is never bound by any oppositions or natural laws of time and space as we understand them. And be awestruck.

All over our world, throughout time, people seem to argue over clumsy "truths", perhaps in frustration because we cannot ever encapsulate God's Divine Truth (which I have put into capitals here, because it is too sacred to define). We dispute our "absolutes" when we could find such empowering wisdom in our shared worship of the "beyond-all-human-absolutes".

As Christians, if we could accept our common reaching, how much could we achieve? If we could put the passion which those three Oxford Martyrs (and *so* many people before and since) have shown, being prepared to die for their faith, and the powerful dread people have of hell, into us *living* a vitalized, united Christianity, could we begin to find heaven on earth, together?

And how different this world could be, if all of us who believe or even have an inkling that there is a God could be united not in our chosen pathways to God, not in our languages and mind-sets for expressing our faith, not even in our religion; if we could *accept* all these differences (go *with* them, rather than try to nullify them) and carry on with something which can reconcile us all – our common trust in there being One Love – yes, that would be a new world, a "kingdom of heaven".

Imagine.

Here is a poem from my collection, *In the holding*:

Solved

I love you, she says.
I know, he replies.
She looks at his face,
the way his cheeks are creased

in a grin like a schoolboy
who came first at woodwork,
and all her study of meaning
is crystallised in a breath:
her heart knows what the brain
strives towards but may never touch –
love which is the physics of God.[7]

Perhaps you could take a moment now, before continuing with this text, to reflect upon what the idea of *spiritual truth* means to you? And of course, I mean *your* understanding of spiritual truth, not mine. We all have nothing to be afraid of and everything to hope for, when it comes to God's Truth.

United in diversity

Next can we look deeper into the idea of being "united in diversity"? As I ask at the beginning of the book, how can we find such common fellowship? I have been pushed to think very carefully about what these three words can signify...

"Unity in diversity" is an age-old hope and metaphysical concept, which can be traced back to Sufi philosophers but which probably reaches far back into our ancient past. It is rooted in the idea of "oneness of being" – that we are all what some call different "reflections" or "shadows" but I would simply call "parts" of God. The exciting challenge is to embrace our variety and be enriched by this, finding unity in our movement forwards, without ever needing to be "uniform". We are *Homo sapiens* but need not be homogenous, because there is no pleasure in humanity being drearily over-blended.

So we can take the phrase "united we stand, divided we fall" and see the potential as well as the caution in this teaching. We can unite on different "scales" (from small collectives to worldwide) while always retaining and honouring our human wealth of "differentiation". But what is the backbone of such a hope? What could hold such unity steady?

I think it is to be able to say to others "your way is not mine, but I respect it" – and mean this.

But what if the other person or pathway promotes practices or beliefs which we find to be an antithesis to God's love? Then, and I need to be clear and honest here, I now understand how important it is to debate or oppose such beliefs. We need to live by our human consciences – to work for loving *justice* in our commitment to God, as well as to show acceptance and avoid narrow-minded *judgment* by being blinkered in a box. Yes, it is a crucial and often delicate human balance.

We need to use the minds and hearts which God gave us, to truly listen and discern if a belief being promoted is simply another way of finding God's love, and respect this, or if that belief supports inequality or oppression or persecution of others, and then… we could choose to speak out for change. Working for unity need not imply a passive lack of our human senses.

Such unity will not be simple or easy. My words describing it here do not read as simple text, because they are not. But a just and loving unity is a great thing for us to aim toward – it is the meaning of the word "fellowship" and it is achievable, if we keep in the Light.

An example of what I am reaching to say, to prevent all these words from just being hollow, could be as follows. I could meet a person who tells me they believe that the biblical prophet Jonah really did spend three days inside the belly of a whale (or big fish – see the book of Jonah) before being spewed out on dry land again alive, all as commanded by God. I do not myself need to take this story literally, but we both could agree that the message of the story is about God being able to rescue those of us who are "lost at sea", and thus save us in "supernatural" ways, just as Jesus later showed us. So we could find unity in our beliefs. We could choose to focus on the deep hope we share, not our superficial conflictions.

However, if the person then told me that anyone who is homosexual is committing a sin before God, which will be punished in the afterlife, I would either walk away, or, if there is a chance I could non-aggressively oppose such beliefs being promoted, I would "speak my truth" of what I believe Christ teaches about God's all-encompassing love. Speak against choosing to concentrate on a few words written by humans long ago, for Israelites struggling for security, people of another time who also, in an attempt to keep order, ruled that both working on the sabbath and blasphemy be punishable by death (Exodus 31:15 and Leviticus 24:16). I would ask them to be honest about their own possible selective prejudice in the way they interpret the Bible. To consider human cultural and spiritual change as a constant, necessary process. Because to stay silent around darkness is not the way to kindle Light. But I would always show the other person my respect, do my very best not to judge them, as I ask them also not to judge. It is not that we need to "accept everything" but that we need to *respect everyone* as a child of God; we evolve best when we each live as an example of what we believe.

But then again…! I look back now over this last paragraph, which at first may seem liberal and progressive, but yet I note the words "oppose", "against", and "prejudice". And I realize (from experience) that such an approach, while attempting to bring light and change, is not quite the answer. Why? Because it encourages an atmosphere for the participants in this discussion to be one of conflict and disagreement... which raises hackles. Not only this, it pushes people to behave defensively and without their best sense of reason – without connection to their hearts. It encourages us to talk and act from a "lower" aspect of our humanity.

What if I were to provide an environment of genuinely listening to other ideas, giving the person speaking them a chance to relax and come out of their "opposition" stance? What if I were to take the conversation away from one particular topic in the Bible and instead talk with my fellow human being about the idea of the Bible being read with an awareness of Christ who is the *Living* Word of God and thus it becoming a living text, rather than one which is "set in stone" and which therefore cannot be changed in how it is read?

We could look at how our *discernment* of the Scriptures is (or is not) something which God asks us to actively and willingly take part in, with the guidance of the Holy Spirit, and our conscious awareness of Christ. To consider and question how much we are ourselves living, changing, integral factors in the way we perceive what we read. Because this is really the *crux* of how we decide to learn or take instruction from the Bible. Do we allow ourselves to see that texts such as those supporting slavery (see 1 Peter 2:18) can be understood and revalued afresh, as we evolve in our fullness of humanity, or do we insist that the words in the Bible can only ever be read in one way... except when it suits us, for example, when we do not wish to stone our children or keep slaves or commit mass slaughter...?

Such lively and fascinating conversation could take us away from the hostile approach of debating "Is it right or wrong, in God's eyes, to be gay?" and allow us to look together at how we read the Bible, why we read it, and with whose guidance. We may still disagree, but such conversation can enable us to look deeper at what we are really talking about, which is the degree to which we believe humanity is continuously *involved*, and *evolving*, in both how we input into human language and how we understand God's Word – that is, how we put the "Word" into human words.

It is really the *tone* of our conversation that counts – because "conversation" means to talk *with* someone, and, as Jesus did, ask them questions, rather than talking *at* them. Telling a person what to believe, or how they "need to change", trying to drag them down a new avenue of faith, no matter how much we believe this new thinking will be a good step forwards, still never really works or endures. We all only change, deep inside ourselves, by choice. That is the gift from God of our free will, given to each of us to use to find our way home, however long that takes.

*

In Job 11:7–18a in the Old Testament we can read these words:

> Can you find out the deep things of God?
> Can you find out the limit of the Almighty?
> It is higher than heaven – what can you do?
> Deeper than Sheol – what can you know?
> Its measure is longer than the earth,
> and broader than the sea...
> If you direct your heart rightly,
> you will stretch out your hands toward him...
> And your life will be brighter than the noonday;
> its darkness will be like the morning.
> And you will have confidence, because there is hope...

I have chosen here words I love and respect from within this text, and omitted words I do not follow, because I believe the Bible gives us the opportunity to do this, and by doing so, I can "cross paths" with other people from long ago – the writers of this great book on their way up the mountain of God – and from each other we can learn so much.

*

My human sciences degree involved, as I said in Andy's chapter, looking at human beings from different viewpoints (such as psychology, genetics, health, and disease) to try to gain a wider understanding of humankind. This was education by open listening. But the real benefit of this approach came when we tried harder to *integrate* two or more different subjects together. For example, in my dissertation I looked at child-birth control in West Africa from the integrated perspectives of cultural studies (anthropology) and population studies (demography). The aim was to use both ways of looking, to find how this could facilitate understanding of the topic by each giving new perspectives to the other.

It is helpful I think to consider what the word "integrate" means. My dictionary includes these definitions: "to make or be made into a whole; to amalgamate or mix with an existing community; desegregate". How useful and healthy all these concepts could be for Christianity! And what about "integrity"? This can mean: "adherence to moral principles; honesty; unity; wholeness". I think we have a great word here, as a quality to aim for, in every one of us.

*

The book so far has been about temporarily "crossing paths" with others who have different beliefs about God, as we all move toward a greater clarity. But we could also think of an image suggested by some people in these interviews, when they talk of the cross of Jesus Christ as if it were a "bridge". A real "crossway". Could we help each other by building strong "idea bridges", which can enrich us all? Bridges between different denominations, then longer bridges which connect Christians with other followers of Jesus, and then fully stretched bridges to interlink all different religions… how far we could reach! And perhaps it is on the bridges where we learn the most?

I read recently about a "swing time" feat which took place from a high bridge in Brazil, when 245 "rope jumpers" stood side by side holding hands, each attached to their own nylon rope, and then jumped to create a synchronized "human pendulum" of people all swinging together from the bridge in colourful waves. Just imagine if this was people creating a pendulum not of bodies but of spiritual ideas about God – if we could build, jump, and swing together from bridges of faith into new planes of comprehension… this could not just be exciting, it could be truly liberating.

*

We do need to recognize, however, that some people, even among those whose beliefs I have recorded here, do not agree that a lot of integration is a good thing. Some people hold that there is "only one truth", which they follow. And if some of us believe there is only a single way home, how can that conviction also be respected? Perhaps we need to find how we can be open to all understandings of God, even those which state there is only one understanding! The more we can find the real capacity to listen and not judge, I think the more "integrity" we can own.

It's also important to acknowledge that some people who have spiritual faith will *never* want to become labelled as belonging to the Christian or *any* one religion. They find it too "containing". Such people are often brimming with ideas which we can still learn from by interaction, even if they remain outside the "edges" of Christianity. Brigid reminded me recently that strong spiritual communities can also be found in non-religious groups, where people work together to develop their knowing of God with intense enthusiasm, often with a sense of "evolution" in the moving forward of their faith.

I thought about all this as I was transferring water recently from one small new pond, which is vibrant and constantly refreshed with inflowing water, into an older, bigger quite stagnant pond nearby. The old pond was drying up in the summer heat. It needed help to keep life flowing within it. This taught me to value renewal.

I hope these reflections have helped you to further develop your ideas and choices regarding "unity in diversity" and actions for fellowship. Can you be your unique self, speak your truth, and still hold onto what connects every one of us?

*

Now for us to choose our next steps. From our "pause" on the mountain, can we choose our new direction? Can we feel well-prepared and equipped with the "gear" of ideas/beliefs/language that suit us best, to now get going?

We could engage with the ethics which I heard a preacher called Irene talk about recently, when she was recalling the dynamic energy of the churches which she visited in rural areas of Argentina. The focus there, she told us, is always on giving and receiving a true "*welcome*". And the word "welcome" can be defined by its seven letters:

Warmth
Embrace
Leadership
Community
Openness
Machines of movement and
Engagement.

The machines needed for movement in the church there are motorcars, to get priests and preachers across huge distances between churches, but we also need "machines for movement" in our own culture, be that by media or digital technology or by new organizations set up to help us discuss our faith and enable outreach.

We need to be on a "mission for movement", as the early apostles were and Jesus himself still is – to give the word "mission" some new credibility and rid it of links to an image of people imposing one set of beliefs upon others. We also could improve the image of being a Christian. Often, when people ask me what I am writing about now, the moment I mention the word "Jesus", they look at me with the supposition I will be a bit "odd". Either a "Bible-basher" or someone with fixed, judgmental ideas. This presumption is itself boxed in... but we can join those who are working to break down old stereotypes. We can make "Christians" a kind of person who others want to connect to, with an image of being engaging and inclusive.

*

Of course, it may be that you have read this book and answered the questions yourself and come to know that Christianity is not for you. The whole theme of this quest is about finding our personal way to God, and I have only asked you to "try on my walking shoes" here, just as we have tried those of eleven others in Part One... but in the end we must choose our own. It may be that you choose to follow Jesus as well as other great spiritual teachers. To become or remain "spiritual-non-religious". Or perhaps another faith such as Buddhism resonates better with your soul. But if, like me, Christianity can actively help you on your journey toward knowing God's love, I hope we can take our part in this with boldness, passion, and integrity.

*

In a great sermon Tim gave recently, he gave us the words reputedly spoken by Gandhi to a Christian: "I like your Christ... but your Christians are so unlike your Christ."

How much we need to make this not true! But to be good representatives of Christ, thereby encouraging others to want to join us, we do need to be strongly rooted to Jesus. In John 15:5 Jesus says, "I am the vine, you are the branches. Those who abide in me and I in them bear much fruit, because apart from me you can do nothing." We need to show ourselves as being very much changed by Christ, so now "bearing good fruit" – which means we want to and do give strong compassion out into the world, by actions and by prayer. We work for justice and peace, as Jesus did and can now do through us.

Because we can only *represent* being followers of Christ by being Love, to the best of our capacity. And by forgiving ourselves when we fail in this.

*

I've now come "full circle" in a physical sense, as I began this book's adventure sitting among the supporters at a Huddersfield Town football match, wishing a faith in God could excite us this much (!) and now (without any planning) I have arrived at the Scapegoat Hill Baptist Church in Golcar, near Huddersfield, to listen to my brother sing with the Colne Valley Voices choir, as part of the annual village fete.

Before the singing a lady called Nicky gives me some coffee in the church basement. She and I talk about the Churches Together movement – how perhaps the people who resist this do need to understand that it could be essential for the healthy survival of especially rural churches. Combined, bigger congregations could become more buoyant, and then attract "more to the more of us", as we humans often prefer to be where the atmosphere seems vibrant, rather than forlorn. As Nicky tells me, the many divided denominations of the Christian church are very much a "man-made thing". Not done by God.

We agree and part, and I go to sit on a pew in the Baptist church, ready for the singing. As I wait, I open the Bible in front of me at a "random" page, after asking God for guidance. I come upon 1 Corinthians 1:10–18, which is all about "Divisions within the Church" (!). Paul appeals to his fellows of the early church in verse 10:

> Now I appeal to you, brothers and sisters, by the
> name of our Lord Jesus Christ, that all of you should
> be in agreement and that there should be no divisions
> among you, but that you should be united in the same
> mind and the same purpose.

I feel quite shaken by such a perfect verse to read just now. Then I read further and find the section in 1 Corinthians 2 on "The True Wisdom of God" verses 9–10. It reads as poetry –

> But, as it is written,
> "What no eye has seen, nor ear heard,
> nor the human heart conceived,
> what God has prepared for those who love him" –
> these things God has revealed to us through the Spirit;
> for the Spirit searches everything, even the depths of
> God.

Most important to me here, is the belief that "what God has prepared for those who love him" is for every one of us, as we ultimately come to know the Love of God within us. And we *will* all come to knowing this, eventually, no matter how long this takes. The wonder of heaven is not a reward, it is an *unconditional gift*. Such a difference.

But this is my truth, right now. As I move along, my comprehension of the Truth will change (and, hopefully, become simpler!). I sit appreciating all this as I listen to the choir sing and, as a finale, they offer us the incredibly moving "Hallelujah" by Leonard Cohen.[8] I feel like singing Hallelujah too! Because becoming aware of God's love for us can surely involve joy. Can lift us up. I am not fully arrived home with knowing God, or feeling like life on earth is a perpetual heaven, not even close yet – there are still plenty of times when I feel a heavy love-lack of insecure fear instead – but the trust in where I'm going is the best thing, and the journey is a gift. A circle (or spiral?) of being found. For me and for you.

*

I would like to tell you about a special gift I received recently from my cousin Hazel, together with a note. She and my godmother, Aunt Renee, had decided to give to me my grandad's own precious Bible, which was presented to him in recognition of his being accredited as a Methodist Local Preacher... and she brought it me on the very day the first draft of this book was finished! I can't tell you how much I felt held and watched over.

The Bible had inside it a letter from the Local Preachers' Department in Westminster, London. This encouraged my grandad Frank, with the words,

> You will be standing in our pulpits in a time of difficulty
> but of immense opportunity. It may not be true that
> there is a revival of religion in our country, but there is
> a revival of interest in religion. Men and women who
> are bewildered and confused, are really seeking a
> way of life... I would remind you that the criticism of
> preaching which one hears all over the world is that
> it fails because it is not relevant to the life men and
> women are leading, and to the difficulties they have to
> face. You have a great opportunity to meet their need
> if you offer them the essence of Christ's Gospel, and
> best of all if you offer them Christ Himself.

The fascinating thing is that this letter and Bible were given to my grandad in 1956! Perhaps we imagine our "modern time" to be the only one when people are feeling honestly disillusioned by the church, actively seeking a clearer light. It is not. We have always needed good community in the church, good preachers, good listening skills, and courage to follow the true teachings of Christ.

In the note from my cousin, she told me that the following lines:

> Show me the truth concealed within thy word
> And in thy book revealed
> I see the Lord

are written inside a Bible which our grandad gave to her when she was a child. Under these words, he had added "May this always be true for you"... I hope very much that this can be true for all of us who have read and been involved in the quest of this book. We can each make our own pilgrimage toward knowing God's love for us. Plus, we can each find our own way to comprehend and uphold some other words, which follow on from these lines above, and which I have discovered are all part of a hymn.

The hymn is called "Break Thou the Bread of Life" by Mary Artemesia Lathbury (1841–1913) and the words continue:

> Bless thou the truth dear Lord, to me, to me,
> as thou didst bless the bread by Galilee... [9]

May our truth be blessed.

*

Here are some profound and beautiful words from Psalm 139, verses 1–18, written long ago by someone with a deep awareness of God. I enjoy reading this psalm very much, but choose to stop at verse 18, because, for me, the words after this do not justify God's love. Then and now, we are each empowered to make such choices.

The Inescapable God

> O Lord, you have searched me and known me.
> You know when I sit down and when I rise up;
> you discern my thoughts from far away.
> You search out my path and my lying down,
> and are acquainted with all my ways.
> Even before a word is on my tongue,
> O Lord, you know it completely.
> You hem me in, behind and before,
> and lay your hand upon me.

Such knowledge is too wonderful for me;
it is so high that I cannot attain it.

Where can I go from your spirit?
Or where can I flee from your presence?
If I ascend to heaven, you are there;
if I make my bed in Sheol, you are there.
If I take the wings of the morning
and settle at the farthest limits of the sea,
even there your hand shall lead me,
and your right hand shall hold me fast.
If I say, "Surely the darkness shall cover me,
and the light around me become night,"
even the darkness is not dark to you;
the night is as bright as the day,
for the darkness is as light to you.

For it was you who formed my inward parts;
you knit me together in my mother's womb.
I praise you, for I am fearfully and wonderfully made.
Wonderful are your works;
that I know very well.
My frame has not hidden from you,
when I was being made in secret,
intricately woven in the depths of the earth.
Your eyes beheld my unformed substance.
In your book were written
all the days that were formed for me,
when none of them as yet existed.
How weighty to me are your thoughts, O God!
How vast is the sum of them!
I try to count them – they are more than the sand;
I come to the end – I am still with you.

Putting faith into practice

And now the vital question of how will we put our own (refreshed) faith into
practice? For me, this can be done by worship, study, and action. Following
my interview with Tim, and realizing how he inspired me, I have begun

to attend my local Methodist church in Penrith. I am not a Methodist, I am simply a Christian, but here I feel a sense of community and am encouraged that I can join people to together *walk with Christ...* not just talk, not just listen, not just ponder, but to actively, vibrantly, walk. I have become involved with a task group which works to help the Methodist Church as a whole to voice and develop its understanding and practices for marriage and relationships of all kinds. This teaches me a lot about group discussion. I also follow the way of spiritual contemplation with the Kentigern School in Cumbria and enjoy the daily meditations by Richard Rohr from the Center for Action and Contemplation in America. The courses and teachings offered from this centre inspire and excite me so much.

I am also training in facilitation skills for discussion groups with Place for Hope, an organization based in Glasgow which helps people to reach their potential to be peacemakers, in times of conflict and change for their faith. And, since the beginning of this book quest, I have now become a member of the Iona Community, which has its base on the island I so love, but which has a principle of very much reaching out, of working for your active faith in love, peace, and justice wherever you live in the world. Phew!

Gradually, I also learn to listen more to the need within me for some balance to all this activity, and so to spend time quietly connecting to the earth, to the stream near my house, the birdsong, and the trees... remembering that to "be still" is an important ingredient in a busy life because we cannot work to serve our faith if we neglect the peace of our minds and bodies.

And my faith has one passionate calling – to try to help people (through my writing, meditations, and workshops) return into the embrace of God. Translations of the Qur'an of Islam say that "we are all returning to God" ("we belong to Allah, and to Him we will return" Ayah al-Baqarah 2:156). Christianity can also say this. The Sufi mystic poet Rumi described us as drunks returning home from a tavern. We may fall down, get lost, go in the wrong direction, but we will eventually return home. And if we want to be held in the arms of God sooner rather than later, Rumi recommends "open[ing] your hands, if you want to be held";[10] that is, be loving, to help yourself be loved. Be open. Be graceful. Be not afraid of the other.

*

To work against violent anger and aggression in our world we need to believe, and encourage others to believe, that God does not hold these emotions. A (possibly) Buddhist saying I respect says "beneath anger is hurt, beneath hurt is love".

If God is what is beneath everything, then God is this Love. God is beneath anger. God is so much more. To believe less is an insult. By encouraging people to believe that there is no need for vengeance in God, we can reduce the power of all calls for vengeance in our world.

*

How does the climate crisis and the urgent need for us all to care more lovingly for our earth, affect the way we can choose to serve our faith?

I was recently at a gathering in Glasgow (organized by Place for Hope) which brought together a network of bridge-building and faith-reconciliation organizations. I attended a workshop on "Deep adaptation: Peace-making in a context of climate breakdown" led by Dr Justine Huxley, CEO of St Ethelburga's Centre for Reconciliation and Peace in London. She asked us to imagine the worst-case scenarios for our planet, then to feel and discuss how we could help reconcile people through such potentially violent and hostile challenges we might face. Through such disease and poverty. This really pushed my buttons and I became disgruntled.

Why? Because I was adamant that I have complete trust "everything will be OK" – because "God's love will save us". It was as if I were trying to show that if we encourage people to have strong faith, and live by this faith, then we need not set about desperately trying to prevent or prepare for such catastrophes. "Helping people connect to Love" would be our route to salvation. But I see now how such a statement is a blind-folded, weak half-answer. By refusing to see God's world, our world, as it is, while being caught up in the fresh enthusiasm of my Christianity, I was not serving my faith at all.

It was like being inside a house, blankly ignoring the floodwater coming in through the front door, while I busily opened the curtains and enjoyed the sunlight upstairs!

I am now finally waking up to the truth that our earth, which we are the guardians of, urgently needs us to activate our faith and react more, realize more, question more, *do* more to challenge the crisis which global climate change could bring.

At an infant-school nativity play which I attended this Christmas, when the children sang of "dreams for our future", it hit me in my heart just how much we risk taking this dream away from our children, and their children, which we must not. And, as much as we need to honour the future for our planet and its inhabitants, we need to safeguard the treasures of our past – the giant chest of jewels of discoveries and creativity of the human race. From aboriginal art to the genius of astrophysics to the music of Beethoven, all such gems need our care for the earth which *holds* them, if they are not to be forever lost. Such words do not of course include the wonders of nature, which we now hold in our hands, and we do need to choose what God's creation means to us.

To serve God I realize I need to prevaricate less, pretend less, and try to be there "on the ground" as a representative of Christ's teaching. To come out of any "loftiness" and act out Christ's call for peace, justice, and unselfish compassion right now, for all of our earth. Even sacrificing some of my own "wants" for what matters and is needed more. It is not that I don't trust in God's love, but I remember that God wants to act out this love, through a relationship with us.

Since I began writing this book the impact on our world of the global coronavirus (Covid-19) pandemic of 2020 has clearly shown us how we need to act now, for the love and care of our earth, and for all of humankind, as we struggle to respond to this crisis as a planet of connected people, rather than as selfish individuals or separate countries. We are hopefully learning, and can help each other to learn, that to think of the whole is to think and care for all our futures, and to care for the "stranger" is to care for our family, in God.

What if we feel we cannot possibly make a difference now? Does it seem too late? Are we too small? In response we could take the teaching of an ideal person for this challenge – St Francis of Assisi, who so loved all of God's creation: "Start by doing what is necessary, then what is possible, and suddenly you are doing the impossible."

There has never been a more apt time to start. And we can all have faith for that.

Over to you

But of course, these are my beliefs and actions. It is crucial that, just as I write these words now, you see that your own words are what count. What do you discover from others in this book and within your soul? What challenges have you come upon? How do you feel most comfortable in reaching toward what God offers us? Can you begin to take the "hand held out" of Jesus, in your own personal way? And where do you feel guided to walk? To act?

Perhaps it would be good to draw a little sketch on some paper, with yourself as a figure in the middle, wearing some good strong walking shoes, and some arrows pointing out from yourself showing (in writing or pictures) where you are going now, what new steps you will take. And, as ever, I am reminded that such steps can be in prayer and meditation, as well as in the outside world, because this inner loving is still a way of actively being with God, of walking with Christ.

I joked with my friend that if all religions and spiritual belief groups are like football teams, and God is the "game of football" in its purest sense (the old metaphor of football coming up again!), then we humans may all believe our spiritual team is the "best", but no team ever does play "perfect football". However, we all "*are*" football" when we play, because we are all a part of the game, just as we are all a part of God, as we live our human lives.

We took this debate further and I saw how, just as the "football" metaphor falls apart after a while, so all spiritual texts are limited and cannot ultimately describe the Truth of God. But we can try. And, unlike the game of football, which has "boundaries", the joy of God's love, to me and to many people now, is that no boundaries exist in God. We all belong and, as Tracey Emin states in her wonderful installed sculpture in Liverpool Cathedral, we can feel God and know we are loved.

*

We can let go of fear right this second now and choose to take a brave step – to turn around the title of this book and be "Daring to Listen" to the "Talking God" within us; to the deep longing of our souls. We can let go of resisting and reducing ourselves, and begin to realize how great we are, because we are a part of God. I say "great" not in an egotistical singular way, but in the sense of being not alone, not separated from God. We all belong to the great power, potential, and bravery of God. Realizing this is how we can let go of fear, a step at a time… and find heaven.

A heaven when we know in our souls that God is both "transcendent" (beyond us) and, with celebration and relief, we dare to know that God is "immanent" (within us). That God enjoys loving through us and we love inside God. *We* abide in God. Every one of us. How wonderful is that!

This truth has been glimpsed for centuries, in the days when the Bible was written and throughout history, among brave people who dare to listen and find the joy, of our Oneness:

> Greatly ought we to rejoice that God dwells in our soul;
> and more greatly ought we to rejoice that our soul
> dwells in God. Our soul is created to be God's dwelling
> place, and the dwelling of our soul is God, who is
> uncreated.
> *Julian of Norwich (1342–1413)*

I find these words of Mother Julian so powerful, and explore the truth of this concept in a new book I am now writing called *Talking Unity: Because God is the Love That We Are.*

*

Earlier I wrote about how personal faith moves in circles, even spirals. Now I see how a spiral is much more accurate as the "shape" of how our beliefs can grow and develop. All of us, if we have even an inkling of faith, have a *living* faith – and this faith changes through time. We question, we ponder, we discard, we feel, and we know. Since the beginning of this book journey, and from now onwards, the people involved in the book, including myself, all have an active spiritual awareness. Our beliefs and ideas, our service and practices, have never stood still. That is real faith. And I hope the same for you. Faith can change and move forward (even upward!) in spirals of understanding, and that is something for us all to celebrate.

*

Just one more step now, before this quest together comes to a pause, where I would like to focus on one adjective that struck my heart when I attended evensong at Christ Church Cathedral in Oxford. It was the night before I would witness Andy becoming ordained to be a deacon. The Archdeacon, Martin, prayed for those who would soon be taking this special promise to serve God, just as John Wesley had promised many years ago, in this place where people have prayed for over a thousand years.

After his prayer for the new deacons, Martin offered a prayer for "General Thanksgiving". He thanked God, and we all joined in this prayer with such feeling, for God's Immeasurable Love.

Indeed, the prayer, which Archdeacon Martin advised us is best said slowly… says it all.

A Prayer for General Thanksgiving, from the Book of Common Prayer
(1979 edition)

Almighty God, Father of all mercies, we your unworthy
servants give you humble thanks for all your goodness
and loving-kindness to us and to all whom you have
made. We bless you for our creation, preservation,
and all the blessings of this life, but above all for your

immeasurable love in the redemption of the world
by our Lord Jesus Christ; for the means of grace,
and for the hope of glory. And we pray, give us such
awareness of your mercies, that with truly thankful
hearts we may show forth your praise, not only with
our lips, but in our lives, by giving up ourselves to
your service, and walking before you in holiness and
righteousness all our days; through Jesus Christ our
Lord, to whom, with you and the Holy Spirit, be honour
and glory throughout all ages.

Amen.

God is Love – it is that simple.

Thank you. God Bless.

Endnotes

Part One

1. Simone Weil, letter to the poet Joë Bousquet, 13 April 1942, *Correspondance* (Lausanne: Editions l'Age d'Homme, 1982), p. 18.

Chapter One: Margaret

1. For the "Q" Gospel, see *The Lost Gospel* by Burton L Mack (New York: Harper Collins, 1993).
2. See John 14:2.
3. See 1 Corinthians 1:23.
4. Margaret herself has written a book with the title *Women of the Passion*, which I found a most enjoyable way to help me get to know some of the great women of the Bible. See Margaret Ives, *Women of the Passion* (London: Canterbury Press, 1998).
5. See Mark 14:36 and Luke 22:42.
6. Dietrich Bonhoeffer, *Letters and Papers from Prison* (edited originally by Eberhard Bethge; first English translation 1953 by SCM Press). This edition translated by Reginald H. Fuller and Frank Clark (New York: Touchstone, 1995).

Chapter Two: Bob

1. See John 14:12.
2. See Matthew 15:11.
3. Neil Douglas-Klotz, *Prayers of the Cosmos* (New York: HarperOne, 1990). See also his Abwoon Network website: www.abwoon.org.
4. See Matthew 7:12.
5. John 14:6.
6. From Bob Morley's poem "Identity and Images" in his self-published booklet *The Golden Thread* (Printworks, 2020).
7. "but by loving" is from my poetry collection *In the holding* (Beaworthy: Indigo Dreams, 2019).
8. John Betjeman, "Before the Anaesthetic" in *Collected Poems* (London: Hodder and Stoughton Limited, 2006), p. 106.

Chapter Three: Carol

1. Romans 7:19 (KJV).
2. Luke 23:43.
3. See John 3:1–21.
4. Exodus 20:5 and 20:3.
5. The famous quote "only connect" by E. M. Forster is the epigraph in his novel *Howard's End*, first published in 1910.

Chapter Four: John

1. John 14:6.
2. Luke 22:42.
3. John 8:12.
4. See John 14:2.

Chapter Five: Martyn

1. It was being the first Poet in Residence at Carlisle Cathedral that led Martyn to publish his poetry collection *Sanctuary* (London: Canterbury Press, 2014).
2. Martyn's own 2008 thesis is called *Rembrandt's Sandwich: Poetic Truth in Times of Exile* and is held by the University of Lancaster.
3. "Prayer" by Carol Ann Duffy appears in her collection *Mean Time* (London: Anvil Press Poetry, 1993).
4. *What is the Truth?: A Farmyard Fable for the Young*, by Ted Hughes (London: Faber and Faber, 1984).

Chapter Six: Helen

1. See Romans 13:14.
2. See Matthew 22:37–39.

Interval

1. Ideas on "the truth cannot all be relative" from Ravi Zacharias in his 2015 YouTube talks on "The Leadership Collective".

Chapter Seven: Jyoti

1. "Track through" is from my poetry collection *In the holding* (Beaworthy: Indigo Dreams, 2019).
2. Wendell Berry, ideas about particularizing language in *Life is a Miracle* (Berkeley: Counterpoint Press, 2000), p. 41.

Chapter Eight: Richard

1. See 1 Timothy 5:18.
2. See John 19:30.

Chapter Nine: Brigid

1. Foundation for Inner Peace, *A Course in Miracles* (London: Viking, 1996; first published 1975).
2. Jayem, *The Way of the Heart* (Heartfelt Publishing, 1995); *The Way of Transformation* (Heartfelt Publishing, 1996); *The Way of Knowing* (Heartfelt Publishing, 1997).
3. The quote reference to Eckhart Tolle saying Jesus (and Buddha) were one of humanity's "early blooming flowers" is on p. 6 of Tolle's *A New Earth* (London: Penguin, 2005).
4. *The City of Lists* is a novel by Brigid Rose which encapsulates her philosophical outlook (Manchester: Crocus Books, 2009).

Chapter Ten: Andy

1. Richard Dawkins, *The Selfish Gene* (Oxford: Oxford University Press, 1976).
2. See John 16:12.
3. See John 13:27.

Chapter Eleven: Tim

1. See John 15:4.
2. See John 15:5.
3. See John 15:12.
4. Psalm 21:10.
5. "In Christ Alone", by Stuart Townend & Keith Getty Copyright © 2001, Thankyou Music (Adm. by CapitolCMGPublishing.com excl. UK & Europe, adm. by Integrity Music, part of the David C Cook family, songs@integritymusic.com).
6. See for example Luke 22:19.
7. See Genesis 1:2.
8. Tim read the recording by Betsy Ritchie of John Wesley's final words, in the nineteenth-century *The Story of John Wesley*, by Frances Bevan (published by Alfred Holness). The more recent edition was published by Bible Truth in 1975.

Part Two

1. "For You" – an installation of pink neon lights in writing by Tracey Emin at Liverpool Anglican cathedral, installed in 2008.

Chapter Twelve: Jacci

1. *Grapes of Wrath*, 1940, based on the 1939 realist Pulitzer prize-winning novel by John Steinbeck, directed by John Ford (20th Century Fox).
2. Deuteronomy 24:19.
3. Hughie O'Donoghue's words are from a book about his art published by the Irish Museum of Modern Art: Maeve Butler and Sean Kissane (eds), *Hughie O'Donoghue*, 2009.
4. "It's not the same" is taken from my poetry collection *In the holding* (Beaworthy: Indigo Dreams, 2019).
5. Luke 23:28.
6. Richard Rohr, "Feminine Incarnation", 9–14 June 2019 (https://cac.org/feminine-incarnation-weekly-summary-2019-06-15/, accessed 30 July 2020).
7. 1 Colossians 1:16.
8. 1 Colossians 1:17.
9. 1 Colossians 1:19.
10. 1 Colossians 1:20.
11. John 14:6.
12. "Dear Lord and Father of Mankind" is taken from a longer poem "The Brewing of Soma" by American Quaker poet John Greenleaf Whittier and was adapted into a Congregational hymn by Garrett Holder in 1884.
13. "Cumberland Infirmary" is taken my poetry collection *A Whole Day Through From Waking* (Cardiff: Cinnamon Press, 2016).
14. William Barclay's prayer, which Margaret adapted, was taken from *The Plain Man's Book of Prayers*, now sadly out of print, but there are several other collections of his prayers to look out for, including *A Book of Everyday Prayers* (New York: Harper & Brothers, 1959).

Chapter Thirteen: Am I a Christian... Are You?

1. Lord Alfred Tennyson, "In Memoriam A.H.H" which was originally titled "The Way of the Soul", 96, II. 11–12. First published in 1850.

Chapter Fourteen: What Next?

1. Leonard Cohen's song "Anthem" is from the 1992 album *The Future* and also in *Stranger Music, Selected Poems and Songs* (London: Jonathan Cape Random House, 1993).
2. Wendell Berry's ideas on the "community" as the smallest unit for health can be found in *The Art of the Commonplace: The Agrarian Essays of Wendell Berry*, edited and introduced by Norman Wirzba (Berkeley: Counterpoint, 2002).
3. Malala Yousafzai, 30 March 2018 (https://www.bbc.co.uk/news/av/world-asia-43599446/malala-yousafzai-my-focus-is-only-working-for-the-good, accessed 30 July 2020).
4. Words by Georgia O'Keeffe, *Georgia O'Keeffe* (London: Tate Publishing, 2016), p. 192.
5. Thomas Merton, *Contemplation in a World of Action* (New York: Image Books, 1973), p. 27.
6. *Iona of My Heart* anthology edited by Neil Paynter (Glasgow: Wild Goose Publications, 2018).
7. "Solved" is taken from my poetry collection *In the holding* (Beaworthy: Indigo Dreams, 2019).
8. Leonard Cohen's "Hallelujah" is from the 1984 album *Various Positions* and is also in *Stranger Music: Selected Poems and Songs* (London: Jonathon Cape Random House, 1993).
9. "Break Thou the Bread of Life" was written by Mary A. Lathbury in 1880, and is in Horder's (Eng) *Congregational Hymns* (1884).
10. From the poem "A Community of the Spirit", taken from the set of poems "On the Tavern", in *The Essential Rumi*, translated by Coleman Barks (London: Penguin, 1995).

Appendix

Poems

Below are two poems mentioned in this book: Bob's (created from a range of Aramaic translation line choices by Neil Douglas-Klotz), as a new version of The Lord's Prayer, and my own about Khanh, who inspired us to name The Kianh Foundation in his honour – a charity for children with disabilities in Vietnam (www.kianh.org.uk).

The Lord's Prayer

The possible Aramaic words of Jesus

Abwoon d'bwashmaya
Nethquadash shmakh
Teytey malkuthakh
Nehwey tzevyanach aykanna d'bwashmaya aph b'arha.
Hawvlan lachma d'sunquanan yaomana.
Washboqlan khaubayn aykana daph khnan shbwoqan l'khayyabayn.
Wela tahlan l'nesyuna
Ela patsan min bisha.
Metol dilakhie malkutha wahayla wateshbukhta
L'ahlam almin.

Ameyn.

---

*The Aramaic version of the Lord's Prayer can be found in *Prayers of the Cosmos* by Neil Douglas-Klotz (New York: HarperOne, 1990).

The Lord's Prayer

As a chosen version from various translations of the possible Aramaic words of Jesus

Creator God, your name is One, the Universe.
In stillness you are all embracing.
Create your reign of unity, now.
Help us love beyond our ideals,
And sprout acts of compassion for all creatures.
Help us fulfil what lies within the circle of our lives,
Each moment we ask no more, no less.
Loose the cords of mistakes binding us,
As we release the strands we hold of others' guilt;
By this we let go and embrace emptiness.
Don't let surface things delude us,
But free us from what holds us back from our true
purpose
All of ourselves come together once more,
Instantly, in the moment.
The healing – or making whole – is always here and
now.

Amen.

* Bob's version of these Aramaic translations can be found in his booklet *Contemplative Love* (The Cumberland and Westmorland Herald, 2016). The words appear here by permission of Bob Morley.

Khanh

He points to who hasn't had a biscuit yet;
squats in the yard to watch other kids playing football;
watches us all.

He can't walk or talk,
sing or dance,
but somehow looks like he could do all of these
and more,
or none of it and still laugh.

What I see in him,
like the big answer on a rice grain,
is forgiveness.

He has somehow forgiven
God, the world, his country, his family,
the workers who treat him
like cheap meat,
tourists like me
who try to make him their souvenir,
forgiven us all,
and for that

he has gained something
I can't get into focus,
but it is grace.

"Khanh" features in my poetry collection *A Whole Day Through From Waking* (Cinnamon Press, 2016) and in the anthology *Write to be Counted* (The Book Mill, 2017), a collection of poems in support of human rights, which I co-edited together with Kathleen Jones and Nicola Jackson.

Select bibliography

Here is a list, firstly of books highly recommended for you to read by each of the eleven people in the interviews. Then I list my own six (now seven!) best recommended and loved titles which have taught me so much. As Brigid said in her chapter, we need to remember that we all keep changing as we learn, and so "definitely maybe" or "ultimately maybe" are good phrases to keep in our heads!

Chapter One: Margaret

Tietz, C., *Theologian of Resistance: The Life and Thoughts of Dietrich Bonhoeffer* (Victoria J. Barnett, trans.), (Fortress Press, 2016)

Wright, T., *Simply Christian* (SPCK, 2006)

Chapter Two: Bob

Bourgeault, C., *Centering Prayer and Inner Awakening* (Cowley Publications, 2004)

Nataraja, K. (ed.), *Journey to the Heart: Christian Contemplation Through the Centuries* (Canterbury Press, 2011)

Sahajananda, J. M., *You are the Light: Rediscovering the Eastern Jesus* (O Books, 2003)

Chapter Three: Carol

The Holy Bible

Chapter Four: John

Heaney, S., *Seeing Things* (Faber & Faber, 1991)

Lee, H., *To Kill a Mockingbird* (J. B. Lippincott & Co., 1960)

Ricciardi, A., *Saint Maximilian Kolbe: Apostle of Our Difficult Age* (Daughters of St. Paul, 1982)

Chapter Five: Martyn

Bruggemann, W., *The Prophetic Imagination* (Minneapolis: Fortress Press, 2001, 2nd edition)

Morgan, A., *The Wild Gospel* (Oxford: Monarch Books, 2004)

Taylor, J. V., *A Matter of Life and Death* (London: SCM Press, 1986)

Chapter Six: Helen
The Holy Bible

Chapter Seven: Jyoti
Chidananda, Swami, *An Instrument of Thy Peace* (The Divine Life Society, 2007)

Pausch, R., *The Last Lecture* (Hachette Livre, 2008)

Watts, N., *The Way of Love* (Thorsons, 1999); a fictional account of the life of Sufi mystic, Jalal-Uddin Rumi, based in what is now Afghanistan

During a phone call to Jyoti to check on how to spell her book choices, she offered me the gift of an oak tree sapling, which she grew from an acorn and has tended for twenty years, taking it with her wherever she has moved, transferring it to increasing sizes of pot. I am going to plant this small oak tree in the field here, protect it, water it and pray that as it grows strong roots and spreads wide over the years, so shall our faith. It will grow for everyone who reads this book.

The growing tree will also be a way to remember Jyoti, who has now passed away to the next life. And in honour of her, here are three more book recommendations from beloved Jyoti:

Estes, Clarissa Pinkola, *The Faithful Gardener* (Rider, 1996)

Way, Robert, *The Garden of the Beloved* (London: Darley Anderson, 1986)

Whitworth, E. E., *The First Christmas Tree* (San Francisco, Great Western University Press, 1977 and 1995), about the mystery of the seventh wise man, based in Persia.

Chapter Eight: Richard
McCabe OP, Herbert, *Faith Within Reason* (London: Continuum, 2007)

Radcliffe OP, Timothy, *What's the Point of Being a Christian?* (London: Burnst and Oates, 2005)

Chesterton, G. K., *Orthodoxy* (first published 1909; most recent edition Cavalier Books, 2015)

Chapter Nine: Brigid
Gangaji, *The Diamond in Your Pocket* (Sounds True, 2007)

Renard, G. R., *The Disappearance of the Universe* (Hay House, 2004)

Tolle, Eckhart, *The Power of Now* (Hodder Mobius 2005)

Chapter Ten: Andy

Gosler, A. G., Bhagwat, S., Harrop, S., Bonta, M. & Tidemann, S., "Leadership and listening: inspiration for conservation mission and advocacy", in Macdonald, D. & Willis, K. J. (eds) *Key Topics in Conservation Biology 2* (Oxford: J. Wiley & Sons, Ltd., 2013), pp.92–109.

Gosler, Andrew "Surprise and the Value of Life", in Berry R. J. (ed.) *True Scientists, True Faith* (Oxford: Monarch, 2014), pp. 176–95.

Jablonka, E. & Lamb, M. J., "Evolution in Four Dimensions: Genetic, Epigenetic, Behavioral and Symbolic Variation in the History of Life" (Life & Mind: Philosophical Issues in Biology and Psychology series) (MIT, 2006).

Noble, D., *The Music of Life: Biology Beyond the Genome* (Oxford: Oxford University Press, 2006)

Shapiro, J., *Evolution: A View From the 21ˢᵗ Century* (FT Press, 2013)

Tallis, R., *Aping Mankind: Neuromania, Darwinitis and the Misrepresentation of Humanity,* (Acumen, 2011)

Ward, K., God, *Chance and Necessity* (Oxford: Oneworld, 1996)

Chapter Eleven: Tim

Webb, C., *God-Soaked Life: Discovering a Kingdom Spirituality* (Hodder and Stoughton, 2017)

McLaren, B. D., *The Great Spiritual Migration* (Hodder and Stoughton, 2016)

Chapter Twelve: Jacci

Borg, Marcus J., *The Heart of Christianity* (Harper Collins, 2003)

Chopra, Deepak, *The Third Jesus* (Rider, 2008)

Forster, E. M., *A Passage to India* (Edward Arnold, 1924). This was the novel which first taught me about unity in diversity, when we "only connect".

Linn, Dennis, Sheila and Matthew, *Good Goats: Healing Our Image of God* (Paulist Press, 1994)

Morris, Father Jonathan, *The Way of Serenity* (HarperCollins, 2014)

Siegel, Bernie, S., *Peace, Love and Healing* (Arrow Books, 1990). This was the first book to set me on my way to learn about love and so about God. It also helped me to survive.

In addition, I am in full agreement with Helen and Carol who recommend that we should read, enjoy, and learn from the Holy Bible. There are a great number of versions available today but there are also ancient Bibles sitting in antiquarian bookshops, full of spots of mildew and beautiful artwork, which can be a dream to find.

A recent discovery for me has been Richard Rohr's *A Spring Within Us: A Year of Daily Meditations* (SPCK, 2018). I highly recommend it.

Organizations mentioned in this book

Center for Action and Contemplation (**www.cac.org**)
Iona Community (**www.iona.org.uk**)
Place for Hope (**www.placeforhope.org.uk**)
St Ethelburga's (**www.stethelburgas.org**)
The Kentigern School (**www.facebook.com/Kentigernschool**)

Workshop for Listening and Connection Skills

Here is a workshop which you may enjoy practising in a study/discussion group, or with friends and family.

Guidelines for Good Listening

With thanks to Place for Hope (**www.placeforhope.org.uk**) and their 'ways for working'. Place for Hope equips people and faith communities to reach their potential to be peace-makers who navigate conflict well.

Whenever we meet and talk with others, in person or even "virtually", the following guidelines of "Respect" will help us all to be effective, compassionate, understanding, and gracious in our connection.

1. **Respectful listening** – listen to understand, intending to be influenced rather than to necessarily agree or disagree
2. **Respectful talking** – allow one voice to be heard at a time; "still the voice" in our own heads
3. **Respectful tone** – take care with the words and tone we use in our conversation
4. **Respectful sharing** – beyond the space we are in, agree to share only non-attributable wisdom or information
5. **Respectful air-space** – monitor how much or how little we speak.

During the following activities we hope to use these guidelines for good, effective listening.

Activity One
Aim: *To truly **hear** each other* – Pairs each tell the other about themselves, to practise listening rather than preparing to speak.

1. Divide into pairs.
2. Each tell the other something that you are passionate about for about three minutes.
3. Feedback to the whole group on what the person you heard was passionate about.
4. Talk about listening carefully to each other. Very often we spend time thinking of our own words to say next, rather than hearing the person speaking. This exercise will give us the opportunity to see how much we each really listened to our partner, with quiet open minds.
5. If there is time, we could repeat this exercise in different pairs, to see if we are learning to listen well.

Activity Two
Aim: *Understanding* – Look at two opposing beliefs to enable us to explore different beliefs to our own. This exercise will help us to try to see things from a totally different perspective to that which we think is "correct" or "true".

For example, discuss Brussels sprouts – those who are in favour of eating Brussels sprouts* and those who are against. Or discuss going on rollercoaster rides at the funfair. Or wearing T-shirts with slogans printed on them. Or think up a similar, light-hearted difference of your own within the group. Divide into "for" and "against" as two "sides" for the discussion.

Introduce the Quaker practice of speaking followed by silence for reflection, then another person speaking. Consider how this can help us to better consider and understand the ideas and beliefs of others.

Encourage people to use this Quaker practice of speaking during their discussion.

After the discussion, reflect as a group on how listening to the "other side" and considering the other point of view has perhaps changed your own way of seeing things. Can you understand a different perspective, even if it is not your own? Can humour and light-heartedness help us to appreciate our differences?

*Brussels sprouts or rice pudding or Marmite!

Activity Three
Aim: *"Unity in Diversity"*
Find a full-page colour picture in a magazine or a similar poster or print.

Cut this up into small irregular-shaped pieces, enough for each person in the group to have one piece of the "jigsaw". Everyone shares out the pieces. Now try to "fit together" again to make the whole picture.

Discuss how this can be understood as everyone being different parts, but together creating the whole. How does this relate to sometimes feeling "different" from others around you? Can you be "different" but also belong? What would it be like if we were all the same? How do the different jigsaw pieces connect to each other? How do people?

To **conclude**, everyone can discuss the topic or feeling which was most important to them in this workshop... while remembering to intentionally practise the listening and connection skills which we have learned.

Finally, say together this adaptation of the Prayer of Teresa de Avila below,* and then consider silently in your hearts how we can all be different parts of the body of Christ, working together for God's love in the world. If it feels comfortable to do so, join hands to say the whole prayer, or to say the "Amen".

Prayer of Teresa of Avila

Christ has no body now but ours. No hands, no feet on earth but ours. Ours are the eyes through which he looks compassion on this world. Ours are the feet with which he walks to do good. Ours are the hands through which he blesses all the world. Ours are the hands, ours are the feet, ours are the eyes, we are his body. Christ has no body now on earth but ours. Amen.

* The original prayer says "yours" where we say "ours".

Activity Four
(this optional activity can be included in the workshop *if* it is suitable for the group taking part).

Aim: *Understanding and connection at a deeper level.*
Now the group will be given a 'topic' within Christian faith which has a wide variety of ways of understanding. For example, the idea of God's love being completely unconditional, or that the Bible is quite literally the Word of God. In groups of up to six people, everyone follows the

guidelines for good listening which they have been practicing in the workshop so far, and gives each other the space to be listened to with open respect. The aim is not to convince each other of our own ideas being 'right' and theirs 'wrong' but simply to listen to the different ways by which we can all see and practice our faith.

We can spend some time sharing our beliefs and learning from each other's perspective on truth. Throughout this activity the focus is more on practicing good understanding and connection to each other, rather than on influencing each other's comprehension of God.

Also by Jacci Bulman

Jacci has published two collections of poetry:
A Whole Day Through From Waking (Cinnamon Press, 2016)
In the holding (Indigo Dreams, 2019)

Both collections contain her poems featured in this book.

New non-fiction books currently being written by Jacci are:
Talking Survivor: How to say "yes" to your life
Talking Unity: Because God is the Love That We Are

Jacci's writing, prayers, visualizations, and active outreach work can be found on her website: **www.thelovethatweare.org** and on her You Tube channel: **the love that we are**

What do you do when life falls apart,
and it feels as if God has left you?

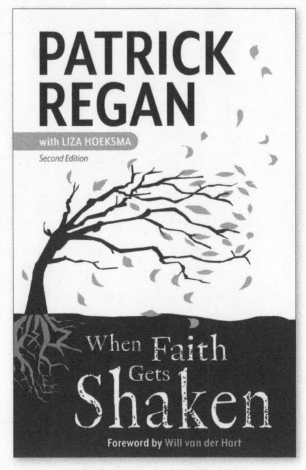

ISBN: 978 1 8003 0005 7

e-ISBN: 978 1 8003 0006 4

'A moving story of courage and faith in the fire.'
Bear Grylls, adventurer, writer and TV presenter

Frank yet approachable, *Stuck in the Mud?* is an ideal guide for those wanting to engage in the ups and downs of discipleship.

STUCK
IN THE MUD?
Stories of Hope for When You're Stuck

JOHN PROCKTER

ISBN: 978 0 8572 1992 3

e-ISBN: 978 0 8572 1997 8

'What an amazing book.'

Grace Wheeler, Head of Evangelism, Youth For Christ

By bringing together all of the available evidence on the life of Jesus Christ, this book offers a compelling biography of His time on Earth.

ISBN: 978 0 7459 8094 2

e-ISBN: 978 0 7459 8095 9